PÁIDÍ

A BIG LIFE

PÁIDÍ
A BIG LIFE

DONAL KEENAN

HERO BOOKS

HEROBOOKS

Published by Hero Books
1 Woodville Green
Lucan, Co. Dublin
Ireland
www.herobooks.ie
Hero Books is an imprint of Umbrella Publishing

First published, 2013

A CIP record for this book is available from the British Library

ISBN 978-0-9526260-7-7

Printed in Ireland with Print Procedure Ltd
Cover design and typesetting: Jessica Maile
Cover photographs: Sportsfile
Inside photographs: The Ó Sé family collection and Sportsfile

To The Man Himself

ACKNOWLEDGMENTS

Páidí was many things – a footballer, manager, character, seanchai, entertainer, friend to many and a rogue. Above all he was a husband and father.

When Maire Ó Sé was first approached about this account of Páidí's life being written she was immensely courteous and generous. Her encouragement at all times and her counsel at such a difficult time for her family will be forever appreciated.

Neasa, Siún and Padraig display all the determination, drive, ambition and humour that were such a part of their father's personality. I am indebted to them for sharing their memories and for the sense of fun they brought to this project.

There were many others who graciously gave of their time, none more so than Páidí's great friend, Mícheál Ó Sé whose eloquence and lyricism in portraying Páidí and the environment in which they live was an inspiration. He also provided me with the unique experience of driving around Slea Head in reverse!

Imagine the craic Páidí would have had when he heard about that!

Sean and Patricia Walsh were cordial hosts in Moyvane; my thanks to Sean Walsh in Tralee, to Darragh and Marc Ó Sé, and to Dara O Cinneide for all their help.

I am extremely grateful to Brian Cowen for his hospitality and contribution. Also sincere thanks to Kevin Kimmage for providing such a detailed account of the events surrounding that famous interview with Páidí carried out at the end of 2002.

In Westmeath, Seamus O Faolain, Denis Coyne and Dessie Dolan gave generously of their time. Páidí's great friend, Tomas O Flatharta provided encouragement, enthusiasm and valuable insights.

During my research once again the Mick Dunne Collection in the GAA Museum, cared for by Mark Reynolds, proved invaluable. It is a source of information to treasure and a fitting testament to a great journalist.

Thanks again to my own family – Abbie, Dara and Aoife – for their encouragement, understanding and patience.

– Donal Keenan,
October 2013

66 No matter
how bad it
was, we got away
with everything.

– Padraig Og Ó Sé

CONTENTS

" A part of
him was shy,
a lot of people
didn't see that.
He was most
comfortable in his
own environment
but he also loved
Dublin.

— Maire Ó Sé

CHAPTER 1

Páidí Ó Sé was not the sort of man who embraced domesticity with great enthusiasm.

That is not an idle observation. It is the considered view of his wife, Maire and their children, Neasa, Siún and Padraig.

Indeed, as Maire might gloomily attest, it was a side of their father that the children – the girls, especially – were delighted to exploit whenever the opportunity presented itself.

Those opportunities naturally coincided with Maire's absence from the homeplace, rare as though those absences were. With friends she would escape, from time to time, the responsibilities of home, school and the family business by heading to Spain or some other European destination for a little deserved time out.

Within minutes of her departure the normal, genteel, orderly routine of family life would descend into chaos.

'She wouldn't have gone through Dingle and the house would be turned upside down,' reveals Neasa. The house became a playpen and the older they got the worse the mayhem that was created.

When Páidí was added to the mix the situation got worse rather than better. Anything that could be dislodged from its orderly place was left in a pile.

'All we would eat while Mam was gone was takeaways,' reveals Siún, 'and everything would be left in a pile in the kitchen, including the plates.'

On the eve of Maire's return Páidí would rally the troops. 'Tidy, wash dishes … make beds … hoover.'

'There would be a huge clean-up,' recalls Neasa, 'and of course when it came to that he was useless. He would disappear and leave us at it, magically re-appearing when it was all done.'

Until the one time came when no one cleaned up.

Maire arrived home one day after a short break in Barcelona anticipating a warm welcome back. The sight she faced when she opened the front door of the family home erased all the memories of the beauty she had encountered during her visit to the enchanting Catalan capital.

Cushions were casually strewn across the living room. Football gear was dumped erratically. And the kitchen? Words failed her. She didn't even wish to imagine what the bedrooms would be like.

She summoned her family. Padraig was spared the full extent of her wrath because of his youth. He stood in a corner of the living room.

Neasa and Siún arrived together.

Their mother pointed to the couch.

They waited in silence for a few moments.

The front door opened.

Páidí slid in, shoulders hunched, head down. He sat between the two girls. 'He was just like a little bold schoolboy,' they say with a laugh.

Maire vented her fury. The tirade lasted just a few minutes. And throughout it all Páidí was mumbling quietly. 'Jesus Christ is she ever going to stop. She can't keep this up.' The girls spent the time trying not to laugh. They were in pain with the effort.

And when Maire had finished and left them to consider her words of warning, Páidí jumped up declaring excitedly … 'we got away with that one lads.'

As Padraig Og says, 'no matter how bad it was, we got away with everything.'

—m—

Neither did Páidí embrace orthodoxy.

Siún Ó Sé was just 15 years old when her father one day inveigled her to accompany him on a trip to Dublin. He always liked to have one, if not all three, of his children with him when he made the long journey by road to conduct whatever business had to be done.

Naturally, Siún needed an incentive. It came in the form of a cheque, made out to cash. A few hundred euro. The cheque could be cashed in The Merchant bar when they arrived in the capital. The deal was done.

Throughout the journey, while her father made a succession of phone calls or chatted about abstract things, such as football, Siún was planning her shopping expedition. Grafton Street and the St. Stephen's Green Centre would be the focus of the trip. She didn't expect to be bringing home any change.

They parted on the quays in the middle of the morning. 'Tell the O'Shea's I said hello,' said Páidí in reference to the owners of The Merchant. 'I'll give you a call around five. We'll head for home then.' Siún had a full day to buy, buy, buy.

She took her time in the first couple of hours and was just hitting full stride, finding little treasures here and there, when the phone rang. 'I'll meet you under Clery's clock at one,' said her father, and the line went dead.

They duly met.

'My meeting finished early … we'll head. Get out before the traffic.'

'No Dad, that's not fair,' protested a furious teenager with loads of unspent notes in her purse. You promised me a whole day shopping. You lied.'

'You'll be fine,' he said, not identifying the rage within. It was the pout that made him realise he was in a spot of bother.

'I was thick,' Siún recalls. 'I had a puss on me. He kept talking to me but I just ignored him.'

Páidí had one small task to complete. He needed a new suit. Páidí always seemed to need a new suit.

Best's Menswear was situated on the top floor of Clery's department store. He was greeted warmly by the staff when he arrived with a fuming daughter in tow. Siún sat on a window ledge scowling angrily while the manager fussed over Páidí. Her father looked over at her every 15 seconds or so, asking questions. All he received in reply was a monosyllable or silence.

He would pick out a suit. 'What do you think Siún?'

'Fine, whatever.'

'This cream one looks good, Siún.'

'Yeah.'

In his mind Páidí was thinking, *I'll get her to smile … get that puss off her.*

'I'll try this one on,' he declared.

The manager pointed to the dressing room.

'No … no,' said Páidí. 'I'll try it on here. There's much more room. I'd be smothered in there.'

Siún realised what was about to happen.

She jumped up.

'Don't you dare …

' … don't even try it.' The manager looked perplexed.

In the middle of the floor Páidí began a routine. He first removed his jacket, then his trousers. Then his shirt. The shop floor went silent.

In his briefs and socks Páidí began to do his own version of Riverdance across the floor.

'Jaysus, Páidí Ó Sé is gone nuts,' said a voice in a thick Dublin accent.

Siún did not know where to look.

So she looked at her father. 'He stood there in the middle of the menswear department, wearing nothing but his underpants and socks. And he winked at me.'

She burst out laughing.

Suit purchased, they headed for home. Happy.

—⁓—

He was typical of many Irish fathers of a generation. Attending the birth of a child was not in his nature. One can only imagine what he thought of fathers who would film births to store in the family archive and watch in the years ahead as the unfortunate child grew older.

Nappies were a complex web that did not need to be explored. In fact, his knowledge of the functions of the nappy was confined to the obvious. The changing of said item was not a skill he wished to acquire.

Truth be told, leaving a baby in his care was something best avoided. He was willing and the older the kids got the better care he took, and the more fun was had by all.

It was handy that his mother Beatrice was around to help. Sisters-in-law could also be called upon in times of need. That was a modicum of consolation for Maire if she needed to be away for any extended period of time – a few hours, for example.

If there was no one around it was likely that a crisis would occur.

It happened on one of those rare occasions in the early summer of 1994 when Páidí was required to look after young Padraig, who had been born on December 16, 1993. The little boy slept soundly in the early part of the day. Páidí pottered around the house, looking contentedly in on the peaceful child every few minutes.

The idyll was shattered around midday.

Páidí came running to attend to his crying son. He cradled him, caressed his back, muttering soothing noises in Padraig's ear. And the cries persisted.

He suspected the baby might be hungry. An attempt to feed was made. That didn't work. The boy refused sustenance and the cries became louder, the little face a bit redder. Páidí began to panic. That didn't help.

They left the house. Páidí hoped that fresh air and a walk might prove soothing. It is likely he also hoped that he would meet someone who might know what to do. The only people around were a few teenage boys who were not inclined to help.

Eventually, after what appeared like hours to the addled mind but was probably much less, help arrived. 'Did you change his nappy?' Páidí was asked.

His answer was silent.

The nappy was removed. A dead wasp fell out. His final sting had left a large red welt on the baby's bum.

—꿈—

Maire Ó Sé looked after the academic side of life in the Ó Sé household. Her husband was indifferent, to say the least.

A dedicated educationalist who teaches at the local Coláiste Ide, Maire assisted with the homework through the school years and advised on what her children would do at third level.

Neasa tells a couple of stories to illustrate Páidí's attitude. On the day Padraig's Leaving Certificate results came out Páidí arrived in the kitchen. He made himself a cup of tea and then abstractedly asked, 'How did the small man get on ... I suppose he made a balls of it.'

Maire scolded him. 'You can't speak like that about the young fella.'

'Arrah, sure he's only a thick fucker like myself.'

Padraig headed to the University of Limerick; not too thick. He has since switched to the Institute of Technology in Tralee, closer to home.

Until now Maire is unaware of the content of the next story. It involves Neasa, a trainee accountant these days with Cusack Garvey in Dublin, and occurred during her student days when she studied law and accountancy. She had trouble one year passing Capital Taxation. Sat the exam twice. Needed a third try.

On the night before the exam her father visited. They headed for a local pub. One drink led to another. 'I've got to go ... exam in the morning,' Neasa would lamely protest. 'Have one more, we'll go then,' her father would reply.

It was a long, long night. Neasa did not make the exam hall the following morning.

At 11.0 am the phone rang. 'How did it go?'

'Dad, I didn't make it.'

He started to scold. 'You could at least have turned up.'

'You'll have to get me a doctor's note,' Neasa demanded.

'Can't do it,' said Páidí.

'If you don't, I'll tell Mam you kept me out until five in the morning.'

'I'll ring you back.'

A doctor's note was duly delivered. Neasa did take the exam the following August and passed.

—m—

There were times when the adoration the girls felt for their father was tested. Lots of times. And it was always to do with football.

Dads can be embarrassing. Páidí was no exception. And in the days before big games when his personality changed and he became engrossed in football the girls had to invent all sorts of distractions and ruses to protect them from mortification.

It was okay in the house where no one could see him, especially their friends. This was Páidí in Championship mode. Walking from room to room talking to himself, sometimes shouting, issuing instructions to invisible men, exhorting them to mighty deeds of gargantuan proportions.

Siún paints the picture. 'His eyes would be narrowed to slits, the hands would be going, waving wildly. He would be talking to himself ... psyching himself up.

'The problems arose away from the house when he was collecting us from school to bring us up to Gallarus for training. Mam would be working so it would be Dad who would bring us. I would sit in the front and there'd be three or four girls in the back. And I wouldn't dare stop talking all the way; I wouldn't catch a breath in case he started.

'Because he would be lost in his own world.

'If there was a bit of silence in the car at all he would start practicing the speech he planned to make in the dressing room before the game the following Sunday. Or if he had something to say to a particular player, he would be practicing what way he would do it, banging his hand off the steering wheel to emphasise a point.

'The girls in the back would be cracking up if he got going. I'd be so embarrassed.'

It was always football.

Siún remembers when she was a child asking a friend of hers what her father talked about on the telephone. 'Because all Dad talked about on the phone was football.'

The girls and their mother were, however, enthusiastic supporters. And they were just as superstitious as the man himself when it came to their routine for the big match days. They always took the 7.0 am train to Dublin. They would wear the same jumpers, jerseys, socks and shoes, even hair bobbins.

They ate in the Bad Ass café in Temple Bar and ordered the same meal every time. While everyone else was mingling and 'having the craic' they would go the Mass in the same church each Sunday. Mother and daughters would head to Croke Park. Maire would wait until Amhran na bhFiann was played and she would leave again to go to pray.

In one of those years they met a woman at the top of O'Connell Street who offered to spray their hair. Green and gold naturally. The girls were delighted. Kerry won. So that became part of the ritual.

Then, one year, there was a ban on the use of aerosols. The girls were distraught. It was a Saturday evening game and they walked disconsolately up O'Connell Street. 'The further we went the more we began to panic,' says Neasa. 'We just knew we had to get it done.'

The lady was on her usual corner, selling headbands. She spotted the girls and recognised their trauma. 'Come on,' she beckoned. They went down a side street where the spray was surreptitiously produced. Two happy girls headed off to Croke Park, new hairstyle unique in the prohibition era.

They arrived back in West Kerry very late that night. Siún was the altar girl at mass the following morning in Ard an Bhothair. Maire had trouble waking her but eventually got her ready for the quick run across the road to carry out her duties.

'I forgot completely about my hair. When I arrived on the altar with my green and gold tresses everyone started clapping.'

He was an affectionate father.

He liked to be close to the kids. 'He would nearly sit on top of you on the couch,' says Neasa. 'I would give out to him … "Give me a bit of space, move over." And he'd give you that hurt look and say "sure I just want to be beside my babies." We were fairly big babies by that stage.'

—∞—

He always had a new story to tell.

'And he always put legs on a story,' remembers Padraig.

'If he could make a good story even better by adding something into it that might not have happened, he would do it.'

It wasn't hard to find material when you had Hollywood stars availing of your hospitality. Tom Cruise and Páidí shared drinks in Ard an Bhothair. Dolly Parton famously visited. Martin Sheen briefly enjoyed anonymity when he called. Páidí didn't know who he was. Once informed, Páidí ensured Sheen would never forget the visit.

Darragh Ó Sé tells the best story of all about Páidí and Hollywood. It was the day Gregory Peck met Páidí! Now that truly was a meeting of legends.

The Kerry squad was enjoying the fruits of its labours and success on a tour of America in the late 1990s. Naturally, the West Kerry boys spent a fair bit of time together, seeing the sights, visiting a few bars. Lots of bars, actually.

In Los Angeles, Darragh, Páidí and Fintan Ashe from Dingle hooked up with Fr James Kavanagh, a native of Ventry who was working as a curate in a Los Angeles parish that included Beverly Hills, where Peck lived in his mansion alongside the most famous names in Hollywood.

Kavanagh gave them the grand tour of the sprawling city. He had lots of contacts in the city and all doors were open to the Irish tourists. It was in mid-afternoon as they relaxed in a hostelry downtown that Fr Kavanagh began to talk about Peck. The famous actor was a parishioner, was a practicing Catholic all of his life and the priest had been a guest in his house.

Peck's maternal grandmother, who raised him from about the age of six, was a native of Lispole. Her name was Catherine Ashe. Fintan was aware of the connection. They were distantly related.

Kavanagh asked, 'Would you like to meet him?'

Darragh and Fintan were very keen.

Páidí shrugged his shoulders.

'Grand ... grand,' was all he said.

A phone call was made. The actor was at home and would be delighted to meet these fine men from the home of his beloved grandmother. Peck was in the process of organising a visit to West Kerry to meet his relatives. He had filmed parts of *Moby Dick* in Youghal and always had a soft spot for Ireland. He had befriended the legendary Dublin actor, Noel Purcell and he valued his Irish blood.

Darragh and Fintan were suitably impressed when they reached the gates of the mansion. Buzzed through by a servant, they were open-mouthed as the mansion appeared before them. It was grander than they would have imagined. Awaiting them inside was indeed the legendary Gregory Peck, older than they remembered him from his later films but still an arresting figure.

He proved to be a gracious host. His advancing years disguised an enthusiasm for showing these people around, talking about his films and his life story including the very strong connection with West Kerry. The two young footballers were fascinated; a more than willing audience. They fired question after question and Peck answered each and every one of them.

Peck brought them into the room where his Oscars were displayed. There were mementoes of his great films – *Moby Dick*, *The Guns of Navarone*, *The Big Country*, *To Kill a Mockingbird*, *The Boys from Brazil* – and paraphernalia that the actor had picked up in his many travels all over the world.

Encouraged by Darragh and Fintan, Peck began to recite lines as Captain Ahab in *Moby Dick*. They were a small and deeply privileged audience. *'Speak not to me of blasphemy, man; I'd strike the sun if it insulted me....'*

The performance was interrupted.

'Gregory, would you have a bottle of Miller or something handy there. I'm parched.'

Páidí was thirsty. And no Hollywood legend spouting lines from some 'fillum' would slake that thirst.

Gregory certainly had a bottle of Miller. Lots of them. The servants brought them out on silver trays, with tankards. Darragh, Fintan and Fr Kavanagh tried to swallow their mortification.

Páidí drank without a care in the world.

They took photos. The actor posed politely. He then excused himself; time for a nap. His staff would look after the visitors while they finished their bottles of Miller.

'Would you like a photo with one of the Oscars,' Darragh asked his uncle.

'I'm grand,' says Páidí, ' ... sure haven't I the AllStars at home.'

It was time to go.

Just another day in an extraordinary life.

CHAPTER 2

On any day, bar those black with rain and cloud, there isn't a grander sight in Ireland than that before you when standing atop Mount Eagle on the western tip of Kerry and gazing out over the Atlantic Ocean.

The sea, in various shades of blue and green ornamented by white waves, shimmers and oftentimes roars. Look down upon Dun Chaoin and beyond. The Blasket Islands rise majestically.

To the right is Inis Tuaisceart, christened back in time An Fear Marbh (the dead man). A quick glance and you can make out the shape of an entombed man in the rolling landscape of an island that is more a big rock.

In front of you little Beginish is dwarfed by An Blascaod Mor, where Peig Sayers - unable to read or write - dictated her laments to her son and from which generations of Irish schoolchildren were expected to learn their native tongue.

A little distant is Inis na Bro and on the clearest days you can see Inishvickillane, the island once owned by Charlie Haughey. Beyond them, not always visible, is the smallest island of them all, An Tiaracht.

Behind you, about 500 metres below, lies the crossroads of Ard an Bothair and beyond that Ventry beach and Dingle Bay.

It is wild and rugged country. Most days, when you take the time to stop and take it all in, it is breathtakingly beautiful. It is the sort of place where those of us who need assistance to construct a straight line would love to have been gifted the ability to draw and paint.

Like most natives Páidí Ó Sé was aware of the mesmerising effect this land had on visitors. The natives and Páidí – or simply plain P or PO - knew there was magic in the hills, the heather and the ocean, but they haven't always appreciated it the way a new set of eyes would.

Familiarity acts as a blindfold. So too does the harsh reality. For the tourist all that matters is the aesthetic. A fleeting visit is a tonic for the soul; a chance to re-group and to replenish the spirit before returning to the harsh real world.

To those who work the hills and hollows for a living it can be, however, an unforgiving place. Demanding, back-breaking. Even heart breaking. In the past many of those who did not have land turned to the sea to feed their families. And that could be equally and often more brutal.

It is a landscape best viewed from a road that rises from Ard an Bothair and snakes through Speicin Mharthain, with Mount Eagle to the left, and drops back down sharply to Dun Chaoin. This is the Clasach, where the young Páidí was sculpted and where the legend of one man of this soil was created.

On cold, dark and dank January evenings as he strove for the summit, his leg muscles aching and his lungs almost bursting as they craved oxygen, he didn't take stock of his surroundings. Not even on bright, sunny days in June or July did he allow his eyes to stray anywhere beyond the terrain in front of him.

The Clasach was where strength and endurance were found; where he became as rugged as his surroundings.

It was also the place where excesses were dealt with and the poundage accumulated in the less disciplined months was shed.

Sometimes accompanied but most often alone, he ran the Clasach not just to shape the body but to sort out the jumble of thoughts and moods that drove his ambition, his determination and his passion.

It is just five kilometres of a 21 kilometre run which Páidí regularly undertook when he became a Kerry footballer, but it was the stretch that defined the man and his destiny. The Clasach was the most demanding section of that run; the undulations were unforgiving, especially in the weather beaten months of the year that enveloped Christmas, and the steep climb which took him to the top of Mount Eagle always caused pain even when the body was as hard as stone.

There was further punishment when he strayed 'off piste', climbing the fences at the side of the road and chasing over the rough ground, avoiding briars and leaping over little streams, further stretching the limits of pain and endurance.

He would pause only briefly to take sustenance from the waters. He filled his cupped hands with the rushing water and swallowed thirstily, lips pursed to capture every drop. Nature had a natural formula for its water, and Páidí wanted to ingest all of the magic. Later in life he would bring his children to the streams and urge them to indulge.

They would laugh.

It was the only time he didn't join in.

The road starts at the family shop just across the road from the church. For the first kilometre and a half it is flat and kind; then it gradually becomes steeper as it weaves left and then right into the mountain, the colours of the land changing from green to brown the higher you go.

He passed derelict buildings from times never forgotten, captured by the story-tellers that fascinated him with their tales.

If he took time to look around and to his right he could see Ballyferriter where he would find his partner in life, and Smerwick Harbour in the distance. But the challenge of the run took all his attention.

After a small descent that brought mild relief he faced the steep climb that brought him to the summit where the Atlantic in all its glory and fury is exposed.

It is a short but brutal stretch that would break the spirit of the weak.

The final steps were always agonizing.

But to reach the top was ecstasy.

He would relax his body then as the mountain sloped down towards the sea, free-wheeling down towards Dun Chaoin, with Krugers public house visible on the right. The famous hostelry would play its part in shaping the future of this determined young man.

At the bottom of the mountain he would swing left and canter around the narrow and winding road that traverses Slea Head. Here, at the furthest point west on the island of Ireland there is no protection when the elements are unfavourable.

He loved the roar of the wild sea below.

Huge waves crashing onto beaches made famous by Hollywood directors enchanted by their surroundings. And, on sunny days, he would glance to his right and think … *next stop America*.

Páidí ran on back towards Ard an Bhothair.

Past the small but pretty national school at Chill Mhic an Domhnaigh where good teachers had cajoled and encouraged a less than enthusiastic pupil.

Just before the sanctity of home he would turn to the right.

Down past the cemetery.

Onto Ventry Beach.

An expanse of coastline that continues to delight visitors. He ran its length before turning back for the homestead where his mother Beatrice would have a glass of sherry and a hot bath ready.

After a long soak to ease the aches from the muscles, he would dress and head for the kitchen where Beatrice had prepared his regular meal.

A 'dry' steak. Well done. No adornments.

There was no science to this preparation. It was the invention of the man alone. Years later he would laugh at the incredulity of a sportsman putting himself through such torture in the middle of competition. In the modern world where science seems to play as much a part in sport as natural talent this kind of preparation would be mocked. But it was a ritual that created the state of mind required to compete at the level he demanded of himself.

'There were days," he would say years later, 'when I sweated black stuff on that mountain. There were other days when I swear I sweated blood.

'There were days when I hated it.

'I wanted to stop … so tempted. But then I thought about why I was doing it. And I kept going.'

He was doing it for Kerry.

In his mind he would find an image of himself in the green and gold jersey. Then he would recall the names of those West Kerry footballers who had gone before him – men like Paddy 'Bawn' Brosnan ... Tom Long ... Batt Garvey. He was in unique company as a Kerry footballer from 'back west'.

It made him pick up the pace.

'And when I got home and had it conquered I knew I was ready.'

Ready for Cork; ready for Dublin; ready for whatever torture Mick O'Dwyer had planned when the Kerry team got together to prepare for Championship football.

Man and his environment in perfect harmony creating the legend that is Páidí Ó Sé.

—\/\/\—

Tommy Ó Sé was still a teenager when he left behind the hills and valleys of West Kerry in the early 1930s to seek a future for himself.

Neither the land nor the sea of his birthplace held any prospects for him. His fate was shared by many thousands of young Irish boys and girls in the early part of the Twentieth Century. So they maintained that old Irish tradition of emigration; many taking the first tentative steps already thinking of coming home.

Tommy might have chosen the boat to the United States. There were natives of West Kerry living all over the eastern seaboard of America and it is likely there were employment opportunities there. London was the other natural choice. It was more accessible, closer to home and there were contacts there too. Family as well. Tommy chose the English capital.

There was work and lodgings. Tommy settled well. He enjoyed his life in the bustling city, the company of fellow travellers at work and at social events in the evening allowing him to embrace the new life.

Beatrice Lavin had arrived in London in search of employment in 1935. She was 16. Born and raised outside the small town of Ballymote in Sligo, Beatrice was one of 15 children and knew from her early teens that one day, soon, she would take the boat. She met Tommy Ó Sé in London and fell in love.

They married in 1938.

Tommy and Beatrice were a good team. They worked at all sorts of jobs, rising early and retiring late. At one time Beatrice started a milk round at four o'clock in the morning before heading off to her regular job in a local hospital.

Later they ran a boarding house which could have up to 30 residents at a time, many of them Irishmen working on the building sites. It was hard work but they were a determined couple who wanted to make the best of the opportunities available.

She gave birth to two sons, Michael and Tom, and they were a strong, happy family unit. That happiness and sense of unity, however, was threatened when Tommy was involved in an accident while cycling one day. The injuries would have a profound effect on his life. In recovery he began talking about home.

He yearned for Ventry – the peace, the air and the sea.

Beatrice listened and began to plan. They made contact with Tommy's family at home. It cannot have been easy for Beatrice. She would have known nothing at all about her husband's place of birth apart from what he would tell her. To a young girl from Sligo a place like West Kerry and Ventry would be as foreign as London itself. But she heeded her husband's yearning and made plans.

Tommy received compensation for his accident. With assistance from his family back in Kerry they invested in a shop across the road from the church at the crossroads known as Ard an Bhothair, a mile or so from the village of Ventry and five miles from Dingle. Young Michael and Tom set off with them on a great adventure to a new land.

On May 16, 1955 the family was completed when Beatrice gave birth to her third son in Tralee General Hospital.

They named him Páidí.

—␣ᔕ—

Stephen Fahy chose a different route in life to Tommy Ó Sé.

Growing up in Castlegar, just outside Galway city, he did not prepare for the emigrant's trail. He opted for life as a member of An Garda Siochana and was posted to the village of Camp, the gateway to the Dingle peninsula, 10 miles west of Tralee.

Castlegar was hurling country and Stephen had a deep passion for the game. It was a passion he hoped he could instil in the young men of the Dingle Peninsula. He endeavoured to set up a hurling club and soon learned the most important lesson for life as a Garda in that part of the world – nothing was allowed to interfere with football.

During his early days in West Kerry Stephen met the young Siobhan Ferriter from Tiorabhainn, just outside Ballyferriter and nestling along the Atlantic coast. Over the years he would hear plenty of football stories from the Ferriter family, their proud boast being that cousin Sean was starring for Donegal and Ulster, where he played with some of the great stars of the early 1960s, including Dan and Jim McCartan, Sean O'Neill, Joe Lennon and Paddy Doherty from Down, Jim McDonnell from Cavan, and Jimmy Whan from Armagh.

That was the sort of company that gained respect, even in the Kingdom.

Stephen and Siobhan had a daughter they named Maire. On the day before Maire's third birthday Stephen passed away. Siobhan was pregnant with her son, Steve. They moved back to Ballyferriter.

Years later, towards the end of the 1970s, Maire caught the eye of a young footballer who was acquiring considerable fame and a little notoriety. That was Páidí Ó Sé. They would form their own considerable team; another central part of the legend.

CHAPTER 3

Trepidation is the polite word to describe Mícheál Ó Sé's mood as he steered his car through the gates of St Brendan's College in Killarney. It was Springtime, either 1971 or '72, he's not sure today. But he is clear about the exchanges that followed and the events that led up to his arrival.

Mícheál had been despatched on a mission.

The local GAA club, An Gaeltacht from the environs of Ventry in the west of Kerry, were preparing to play a football game against one of their great rivals, Ballyvourney or Baile Bhuirne, another Gaeltacht area in south west Cork. Their battles through history were epic; it was a classic rivalry between two Irish language speaking communities that could never be understood from the outside; where pride in the home place demanded displays of passion and courage.

An Gaeltacht were a little fearful prior to this engagement. Baile Bhuirne, it was reported over the gossipy winds from the south, were 'going well'. In the vernacular that meant that the West Cork boys had put together a decent team and were showing impressive form in domestic competition.

The Ventry lads needed to plot, and central to the plot was securing the services of 'young Se', the schoolboy from the crossroads of Ard an Bhothair who was boarding at St Brendan's, the famed football nursery in Killarney where providing young men with a sound and proper education to prepare them to take on the world was also a priority.

Permission to seek the boy's release for the day was granted by his mother, Beatrice, who responded to the request with a sigh of mock-exasperation. 'Sure he might as well be playing football because it seems he's not doing much else in that place.'

The wise clubmen then chose Mícheál Ó Sé as the man to make the approach to the school. He was the one amongst them with the gravitas to impress the diocesan priests who ran the educational establishment that had through its history produced some of the most eminent men of the cloth who ruled the Catholic Church in Ireland at the time, with reputations that suggested they should not be trifled with.

The release of a boy from the boundaries of the school to play a football match of a prestige questionable to anyone not directly involved could indeed be described as a trifling matter. That the boy in question was just 16 years old and might well be in mortal danger playing against grown men, with some malice bubbling in their veins, merely added to the delicacy of the situation.

Mícheál, a two time All-Ireland winner with Kerry and at the time one of the county's most respected players, had dressed conservatively for his approach. He was polite and courteous as he explained to a secretary the reason for his arrival. She passed on the request to a priest who went off in search of the boy.

Minutes passed before Mícheál heard two sets of footsteps coming down a corridor; one set sure-footed, the other more of a pitter patter. Young Páidí Ó Sé was attempting to keep a straight face, staying out of the direct line of vision of his custodian as he turned a corner and spotted Mícheál. He had his football boots in one hand, a sports bag in the other, clearly elated at his impending release, however temporary.

'Thank you Father,' said Mícheál quietly. 'I know this is irregular but he has become an important player for us and everyone back home will be very grateful to you for allowing him to play today. I give you my personal assurance that he will return to the school immediately after the game.

'I will bring him myself.'

The priest looked at Mícheál, then at the pupil, for what seemed like minutes while he contemplated a response. Briefly the would-be teammates wondered if there was to be a change of mind. Then the priest spoke.

'My good man,' he said directing his words at Mícheál, 'If you decide to take him away from here altogether and not bring him back at all you would be doing St Brendan's and everyone within these walls a great service.'

—⟋⟋⟍—

Páidí Ó Sé was not born for education of the formal kind.

He was born lucky.

In later life he would argue that in sport you made your own luck. He would then accept that it helped to be born with it.

He was lucky to be born in Kerry, in West Kerry especially.

From his earliest days he was enchanted by the history of football in that part of the county and especially by the personalities from the Dingle peninsula who triumphed in the great stadiums of Kerry, Cork and especially Croke Park.

He was lucky to be born to a mother who doted on him, spoiled him and then indulged him. She also provided the moral and practical support a son needed when chasing his dreams, on and eventually off the football field.

He was also lucky that when he found his partner in life, Maire, he also found a woman who would provide the support and solidity at home that allowed him to pursue his dreams.

And he was lucky that throughout his life he was surrounded by circumstances and people that provided an environment in which his natural talents, for football especially, were allowed to flourish.

Because, for Páidí, life as a boy and a young man in West Kerry was all about football. Schooling didn't register as a priority. Preparing for life as an adult who could support himself financially and the possibility of rearing a family and taking responsibility were goals for others.

History would fascinate him later in life but the only history he absorbed as a child and as a teenager was the history of Kerry football. A child so active that all around him were exhausted simply keeping an eye on him, he would quieten only when visitors called and tales were being told of great feats on the football field.

He loved to hear about the skills of his blood relative, Tom Long, a nephew of his father. Long had won two All-Ireland s with Kerry and was feted for playing in all the central positions, from centre half-back to full-forward, in the service of Kerry. When visitors would regale the young audience about Long's prowess and bravery Páidí could not contain his pride. It fed his dreams and his dreams always involved a football and a green and gold jersey.

One regular visitor to the shop in Ard an Bhothair during the holiday period of Christmas and Summer was Batt Garvey, who won an All-Ireland medal in 1946. Garvey, a school principal in Dublin where he spent his working life, looked forward to meeting the youngster on his regular visits home and would regale him with stories of his contemporaries who had contributed to the proud history of West Kerry football.

Out in the field the youngster became all of the great heroes – Bill Dillon, Bill Casey, Sean Brosnan, Paddy 'Bawn' Brosnan were most prominent amongst the local men who had conquered the world in his eyes. He marvelled at the mere mention of Paddy Kennedy from Annascaul, widely remembered as 'the prince of midfielders'.

Often passing Bawn's pub on Strand Street in Dingle he would think that one day that might be the life for him. Sitting outside the counter, the door open to the street to welcome visitors, walls covered with football pictures – he loved to sneak in to look at the photo of the Kerry and Roscommon teams parading around Croke Park before the All-Ireland final of 1946, and imagining himself in the shoes of the Bawn – talking football.

Sometimes dreams do come true.

Going to the doctor was a pleasure because the doctor was himself one of the heroes. Jim Brosnan, a native of Moyvane in North Kerry, set up his medical practice in Dingle in 1959 when Páidí was just four years-old. He had been a successful player, coach and was about to become an influential administrator. Dr Brosnan was a stately man, kind hearted and kind faced who recognised the talent and the passion that lurked within the wiry frame of the young patient whose scrapes and cuts were all the result of mishaps in pursuit of a ball.

Páidí's appetite for stories was insatiable.

A kid didn't notice the waiting room filling up with other patients seeking the magic of the medic's hands. 'One day,' Dr Jim would tell him, 'you'll have your own stories to tell.'

All of his dreams were of wearing the green and gold of Kerry. He didn't think of club, An Gaeltacht, or the divisional teams, Na hAhasaigh or West Kerry. Neither were particularly successful at the time anyway. The seeds for the obsession with Kerry that would become so apparent later in his life were already sown.

That obsession did cause some confusion for the youngster from time to time. One afternoon his father, Tommy called him to the front of the shop. They had a visitor.

'You're always talking about great Kerry footballers and winning All-Irelands. Well here's a West Kerry man who captained a team to win the All-Ireland,' said Tommy.

'Hello young fella, my name is Joe Fitzgerald,' the visitor introduced himself.

The youngster looked perplexed.

He had heard all the stories of great West Kerry footballers; he thought his knowledge was almost encyclopaedic, yet there was no man named Fitzgerald in the folklore he could think of.

Recognising his confusion and the dilemma facing the kid, the two men laughed. 'Joe won his All-Ireland with Dublin,' his father explained with a laugh.

The explanation was expanded.

While living and playing football in Kerry Joe Fitzgerald had never attracted the interests of the county's selectors. Had he lived in Tralee or Killarney it might have been different but it was harder to attract attention the farther west you went.

He left the family farm towards the end of the 1930s to join the Gardai and was stationed in Dublin. The Geraldine P Moran's club in the south of the county (their pitch is still situated beside the Dunnes Stores complex in Cornelscourt) was a welcoming place for young footballers from the country and had a strong Kerry membership. Joe enjoyed his football there and was soon spotted by the Dublin selectors.

He was delighted to accept the invitation to join a team of cosmopolitan make-up. There were natives of Dublin included but also a sprinkling of Joe's countymen, as well as players originally from Galway and Longford. Dublin beat Galway in the All-Ireland final of 1942 and Fitzgerald, from Ballydavid, was partnered in midfield by a native of Dingle, Mick Flavin.

Opposing them in the Galway colours that day was Dan Kavanagh from Dunquin.

Páidí absorbed all this strange news, then asked quietly, 'But why did you not play for Kerry?'

'They never picked me,' was the honest reply.

After a pause the youngster commented, 'If I couldn't play for Kerry I don't know that I would want to play football at all.'

It was a love of Kerry that would remain with him for the rest of his life. Tomas O Flatharta, a lifelong friend and P Sé's wingman in Westmeath at the dawn of the 21st century, remarked one Sunday morning at the start of the new millennium that his pal was far chirpier than normal.

Usually full of superstitions and edgy before a big game, Páidí was cool and relaxed. Asked for an explanation, he replied, 'I've got my lucky mascot with me today. Everything will be alright.'

He dipped his hand into his bag and introduced the mascot – a well worn teddy bear clothed in green and gold.

—⁂—

It is a fact that the only examination Páidí Ó Sé ever successfully completed was the entrance exam for An Garda Siochana. And when later in life he would tell that to his audience there would always be a conspiratorial glint in his eyes that suggested some outside influences of an unspecified kind might have played a significant part in that success.

School days for Páidí provided the opportunity to play football. It is why, after one year in secondary school in Dingle, he badgered his parents to send him to St Brendan's. It wasn't to better himself at history, geography or French. He was attracted to St Brendan's because they had won the All-

Ireland Senior Colleges football title, the Hogan Cup, in 1969.

His father and mother were already aware that their youngest son was resilient when it came to avoiding schoolwork. If there was a chance that the opportunity to play football at a level suited to his ambition might encourage him to study, then it was best to allow him switch schools. And it was his growing reputation as a footballer that earned him a place amongst the boarders at the school.

He revelled in the atmosphere on the sports field. His strength and stamina were evident immediately. He was fiercely determined and showed no fear.

After just one year in the school he was allowed to train with the senior team, a promotion unique for one so young. He had an insatiable appetite for work on the football field. 'If only he would apply himself with the same enthusiasm to his studies,' was the consistent mantra in reports to his parents.

He won two Munster Colleges medals with St Brendan's and played in the All-Ireland final in 1972, his first game in Croke Park. They lost to St Patrick's of Cavan by 2-11 to 1-5. Ollie Brady, who would go on to become one of the finest footballers of the 1970s with Cavan, was one of the stars of that St Patrick's team.

In the *Irish Independent* the following day, Tom O'Riordan reported, *For Killarney Sean Falvey played well throughout at left full back. O'Shea, O'Hare and O'Donoghue between them did best.*

The *Irish Press* report did not contain any mention of the same O'Shea.

Off the field the pattern remained the same. If there was mischief in the making he was certainly at the centre of it all. He mixed well. There were regular scrapes with authority. The teachers enjoyed his humour but they could not convince him to give his subjects the time necessary to absorb sufficient knowledge to pass exams.

To infer from his aversion to completing the formalities of an examination paper that he lacked intelligence would be a mistake.

'The man who took Páidí Ó Sé for a fool was the only fool in the room,' is how his friend and teammate with Kerry, Sean Walsh puts it. 'He was a very bright guy. You saw that in his business life. And we certainly saw it in his contributions to team talks … the way he analysed our own team and the opposition.'

Páidí often talked to Maire about his attitude to education when he was a youngster. 'It was only much later that he had a few regrets,' she says. As a teacher Maire also identifies some of the reasons for his diffidence. He had a very short concentration span and lacked the patience to study.

'If he had a writer when taking on an essay, for example, someone to take over after five minutes, he would have done a lot better. He always wanted to move on to a different assignment or task.

'Throughout his life he was great for writing little notes to people; two, three maybe four sentences. He managed to convey whatever message he wanted in those brief notes.'

There are many people around Ireland and abroad who will have received notes such as those. He would congratulate people on achievements in their careers, on the sports field. On holidays he would often be found in a corner of the hotel foyer, with a table full of postcards which he would send to friends and acquaintances.

When he started contributing a column for the *Irish Independent* and later to *The Star on Sunday* and then the *Sunday Independent* he found comfort in having a ghost-writer. Páidí could provide his opinion in the spoken word and leave the time consuming chore of putting his thoughts on paper to his 'ghost'. It worked well.

Mícheál Ó Sé laughs when Páidí's schooling is aired. 'He loved playing that role, the man who failed all his exams. It portrayed a certain type of image. But he was a very intelligent man. He had a photographic memory … never forgot a face. And when it came to studying football he didn't have a problem with concentration.

'He was studying football videos before it became fashionable. He had all the videos of the Galway team that won three All-Irelands in-a-row in the 1960s – videos of great Kerry teams and he would watch them over and over, analysing them and learning from them."

The former Taoiseach, Brian Cowen, who became a close friend, felt this portrayal of himself was part of Páidí's character, his honesty. 'He was authentic,' says Cowen. 'The big problem with being authentic is that you can reinforce a stereotype. You are showing your pluses and minuses, you are who you are. That comes with downside risks.

'The people down there (Kerry) have distinctive characteristics and he was very proud of them and anxious to show them off. Sometimes that can project itself so much, be portrayed so one dimensionally that you become a victim of stereotype even though you are trying to show that you're not that stereotypical person at all.

'It's a balance that's hard to find,' concludes Cowen.

His life in St Brendan's came to an abrupt end in the late spring of 1973. Various reasons are recalled for his enforced departure.

Truancy could have been a factor. He himself admitted to storing some illicit material, acquired from the top shelf of a magazine rack in London, which was discovered in a search of lockers. Whatever the truth, expulsion did not come as a surprise. If football was a subject he would have gained straight A's. And if he had applied himself his other grades would have been a notch or two above what they were.

For his final year in school a place was found in St Michael's College in Listowel. His oldest brother, Michael was working and living in Listowel. He and his wife, Joan became Páidí's guardians for a year. It would be an eventful time for them.

There was still a lot of football to be played.

—⟶⟵—

Páidí, of course, was not the first member of his immediate family to line out in Croke Park. That honour went to his brother, Tom who won an All-Ireland minor medal with Kerry on September 22, 1963 on a team trained by Dr Jim Brosnan.

They beat Westmeath in the final, 1-10 to 0-2, and despite the one-sided nature of the result the entire occasion was a major source of inspiration for the youngest member of the family. Newspaper reports were read with pride and *The Kerryman* had kind words for the display of Tom.

A young John Barry reported, *'Tom O'Shea and Con Riordan will also have happy memories of this game. O'Shea held Kevin Kelly well, which was all that was required of him.'*

Barry's report also gave a great sense of attitudes towards football at the time. *Here were fifteen players dedicated to the cause of victory. They knew Westmeath were able to hit. The answer was to hit harder. Kerry did. And how! The Leinster Champions got the wind up in the first quarter and weren't too anxious to take shoulder to shoulder after that.*

Clearly in those days there were no concerns about black cards, or indeed yellow or red ones!

Ten years later Páidí received his first call up to the Kerry colours when he played for the minors in the Munster semi-final against Tipperary. He kicked four points but the game ended in a draw, Kerry 0-13, Tipperary 2-7. They did win the replay comfortably and played Cork in the final. In the team were players of the calibre of Denis 'Ogie' Moran, Sean Walsh and Pat Spillane who would spend many more years sharing rooms with the lad from the west. But in 1973 they could not prevent Cork from winning a seventh provincial minor title in eight years.

The youngsters were allocated seats in the old Athletics Ground stand in Cork and watched with considerable dismay as the senior team was dismantled by Cork, 5-12 to 1-15. Cork led by 5-3 to 0-2 after 25 minutes. Páidí and a group of the minors made an early exit. They did not wish to see more and had more enjoyable pursuits in mind.

In the *Irish Independent* the following day John D. Hickey reported on the state of the Kerry team. *Coming out of the ground I heard a Kerry supporter attempt to salve his wounds with a comment, "it was a wonderful comeback." My retort is – I suppose people are as gullible as they want to be. The Kerry of yesterday was so lacking in inspiration that I would have doubted it was a side from the county we were looking at were I not so familiar with all the players. I am unshakeable in the conviction that they were allowed back into the game by the carefree attitude of opposition which understandably lost its resolution in its apparent safety.*

Included in that Kerry team were the likes of Jimmy Deenihan, Ger and John O'Keeffe, Mickey O'Sullivan and John Egan. At full-forward was Mick O'Dwyer. It was his last game for Kerry as a player.

Out of the gloom rose the Kerry Under-21 team.

Paud O'Shea, as he was known at the time, was called into the squad for the Munster final. He came on as a substitute and impressed enough to be selected at midfield for the All-Ireland semi-final against Offaly. His partner, wearing No.8, that day was John Long. *Paudie Shea was good without ever being spectacular and played a lot of ball,* reported Eamon Horan in *The Kerryman.*

Kerry 3-11, Offaly 1-10.

He was selected for the final against Mayo at wing forward. Paudie O'Mahony was in goal; Jimmy Deenihan, Ger O'Keeffe, Ger Power, Paudie Lynch, Mickey O'Sullivan, John Egan and Mikey Sheehy were also on the team. Paidi scored one point in a 2-13 to 0-13 win but did not feel fulfilled by his own performance. Still, he was gaining notice in important places. Though still a schoolboy – he would sit his Leaving Cert in June of 1974 – he was already on a shortlist of players who would be promoted to the senior squad during the following National League campaign.

The number of teams he was playing for at the time is worth listing – An Gaeltacht minor, Under-21 and senior; Kerry minor and Under-21, St Brendan's and later St Michael's, and then the divisional team Na hAghasaigh, which represented parts of West Kerry in the Kerry senior . He loved it, though his promotion to the Kerry senior team for the first time – he played against Galway in the National League in Tralee on March 3, 1974 – was not greeted with any great fanfare.

The game ended in a draw, Kerry 1-8, Galway 0-11, and Hickey in the *Independent* was impressed.

He wrote: *It would not surprise me, however, if Kerry supporters' greatest comfort of the game was furnished by Paul (sic) O'Shea and sub. Pat Spillane. Both players were Kerry minors last year and if they, and Spillane in particular, have developed to the extent that the game suggested, they will 'roast' many a senior defence in the years ahead.*

The reviews were increasingly gracious though the youngster was oblivious. Although his dream of wearing the green and gold at senior level was being realised he had other distractions. He was playing well for St Michael's in Listowel and they qualified for the Kerry Colleges final where the opponents would be St Brendan's. It went to a replay. So too did the National Football League final with Roscommon.

In the mind of the youngster, heroics with St Michael's were just as important as playing for Kerry. It was not just that the opposition was the school from which he had been expelled; his new school had never won the O'Sullivan Cup before. The match, played on the Thursday before the League final replay, went to extra time.

He scored 2-2. A local hero.

On the following Sunday in Croke Park he also played well as Kerry won the League title. In *The Kerryman* John Barry was glowing. *In the Kerry defence, the player who undoubtedly created the biggest impression was Paudie O'Shea. Listed at right half back, he played practically the entire first half at midfield and he proved himself a very capable and dashing player, winning quite an amount of possession. He certainly wasn't afraid to have a bash at scoring himself and he almost did get one point in the second half with a great drop-kick. Unquestionably, a great prospect.*

John D. Hickey singled him out for praise. *So too did the Kingdom reap reward from promoting Paud O'Shea, a minor of last year, who gave an eminently sound performance at right half-back in a line against which Roscommon made scant worthwhile progress.*

The youngster had to readjust to a world without football for a few weeks. The Leaving Certificate loomed. He knew he was doomed. He hadn't done the work.

The result was inevitable.

Football, typically, was a distraction. Kerry entered the with an air of desperation around the team. Páidí made his senior debut against Waterford on June 16, 1974.

Kerry won by 7-16 to 0-8, John Egan scoring 2-3.

The selectors, Johnny Culloty in particular, coaxed the legendary Mick O'Connell out of retirement. The youngsters stood in awe when he entered the dressing room in Killarney for his first training session.

O'Connell was well past his prime but there was an aura about him. 'I played with Mick O'Connell,' remained a proud boast for the rest of his life.

O'Connell's magic could not save Kerry. A record attendance of 49,822 watched the Munster final on July 14 in Killarney. The GAA was experimenting with 80-minute games but that did not have any bearing on preparation. Páidí was already running the Clasach.

He was ready.

The Kerry team was not. On a day of driving wind and rain Cork retained their title with a degree of comfort, 1-11 to 0-7.

Paud O'Shea received favourable mention for his performance. In *The Irish Times* the correspondent Paddy Downey, later to become a firm friend, captured the scene. *The mists which came down from the reeks during the minor final had turned into vicious rain before the start of the big game and a strong cold wind multiplied the drenched spectators' miseries and added to the hazards of the playing conditions for the Cork and Kerry teams.*

Within minutes the pitch was as slippery as glass and to control the ball on the ground or in the air the players needed the art of a juggler. And to control it properly they required luck as much as the grip of gloves which covered 30 hands.

School days completed, the youngster from Ard an Bhothair was ready for a new beginning. No one could have foretold where it would bring him.

CHAPTER 4

In the creation of the Páidí Ó Sé legend there is no doubt that July 13, 1975 was a hugely significant date. It marked the birth of the team that would earn the moniker as 'the greatest football team of all time'.

It was also the date when Páidí threw the most famous punch in GAA history, a punch that is a YouTube sensation more than three decades later, a source of much amusement that Páidí certainly exploited and in some ways traded upon.

What it created at the time, however, was the image of a tough, maybe even wild, youngster who could inflict damage of almost epic proportions to anyone who stood in his way.

In some circles he was regarded as reckless, possibly even lawless within the confines of the whitewash. That created an element of fear amongst some opponents, though certainly not all, which Páidí would endeavour to use to his advantage.

An eloquent description of the young footballer was penned by Kerry native, Owen McCrohan in his biography of Mick O'Dwyer. He wrote: *In football terms he had about as much refinement as a broken bottle and whenever he pulled on a jersey he looked as endearing as a bulldog.*

As is many parts of his life, however, the image was not entirely accurate.

His disciplinary record in a playing career at the highest level that spanned 14 years is better than average. The only significant dismissal was in the All-Ireland final of 1979 and that was for two bookable offences.

At the end of his career there was also a serious incident in a club game, detailed elsewhere, about which Páidí felt enormous regret. Otherwise, however, he had a good relationship with referees and his only county manager, Mick O'Dwyer, was never concerned about Páidí's discipline.

The impact of 'the punch' on Páidí's reputation in the early years of his career did have a negative side. He won four All-Ireland medals and had played in eight Championships before he won his first AllStar in 1981. That was a wait that angered him and frustrated him in equal measure. He felt he was being judged harshly by the AllStar selectors - the mostly Dublin-based journalists who had founded the scheme in 1971, were responsible for the administration of the scheme and for the annual selections.

It was somewhat ironic that it was one of Páidí's closest friends in the media, Tom O'Riordan of the *Irish Independent*, who first pointed out that Páidí's 'reputation' might count against him in the AllStar scheme.

O'Riordan is from Ardfert in North Kerry and was one of the first Irish athletes to be offered a scholarship to university in the United States when he left home in 1957. He won many collegiate titles in the US, represented Ireland in the 1964 Olympic Games in Tokyo in the 5,000 metres and enjoyed a hugely successful career.

He joined the *Irish Independent* in the late 1960s and covered athletics and Gaelic Games. Colleges football and hurling was one of O'Riordan's beats and he was one of the first journalists to spot the talent of the schoolboy lining out with St Brendan's College at the start of the 1970s.

O'Riordan and Páidí, along with Paudie Lynch, quickly became friends when the Kerry team began to rise to prominence in 1975. They socialised together in Dublin and O'Riordan's wise counsel was often sought on training methods and any other subjects on which the two footballers needed advice

Later in their lives O'Riordan would become a valuable advisor when Páidí became the Kerry manager; helping to devise training regimes and strategies to improve the physical well-being of the players.

In a speculative piece about the 1975 AllStars O'Riordan had written that Ó Sé might miss out on selection because of his disciplinary record. There was a rule in the scheme that a player sent off in the year under review could not be considered for an AllStar, no matter how trivial the incident was regarded. It was known as the 'sportmanship rule' and was fiercely guarded by the founders of the scheme as well as the GAA hierarchy.

History shows, however, that a player did not have to be sent off to earn exclusion. The simple fact of a dodgy reputation, guilt by association with a suspicion of inner malice, was enough to scupper a player's chances of selection,

Had O'Riordan been a member of the selection committee he would almost certainly have supported Páidí's candidature. He had no intention of damaging the player's chance of an award but felt obliged to point out the potential problem.

Although Páidí had not been sent off in 1975 and had played exceptionally well in the All-Ireland final, also receiving accolades for his display against Cork, he failed to get an AllStar. The honour at right half-back went to Peter Stevenson from Derry. For the record the next five awards at No.5 went to Johnny Hughes from Galway, three in-a-row to Tommy Drumm of Dublin, and Kevin McCabe from Tyrone picked up the award in 1980.

Páidí would have been the first to acknowledge that those men were extremely talented footballers and there was no shame in losing out to them. But it is odd that he was overlooked so often in the years in which he played what many people believe was his best football.

The 'sportsmanship' rule did count against Páidí in 1978 because he was sent off in an exhibition game in New York between Kerry and Dublin, harshly it was agreed by the journalists who reported on the game and who would sit in judgment around the AllStar selection table later in the year. It also ruled him out of contention in 1979.

Almost annually when they would meet up, generally in the snug of the Palace Bar on Dublin's Westmoreland Street, Páidí would confront Tom.

'You cost me the All Star,' he would accuse.

Tom could have pointed out that one article written in 1975 could not have contributed to decisions made in other years, but knew silence was the best response.

Naturally, any cooling of friendship lasted until the next round.

'The Punch' did, however, make Páidí a household name. The television footage, grainy as it was, featured in the match highlights on television. Although no disciplinary action was taken against him, he was a marked man.

The incident occurred during the first half of the Munster final in Fitzgerald Stadium. Páidí was marking Dinny Allen and the early exchanges were eventful. What happened between the two is now the subject of folklore. Páidí loved to embellish the story, and Dinny rarely demurred though it was thought he did not agree precisely with Páidí's version.

Allen was a gifted sportsman, as proficient in hurling and soccer as he was in Gaelic football. He won an FAI Cup winners medal with Cork Hibernians in 1973 and his involvement with the soccer team cost him his place on the Cork football team that won the All-Ireland Championship later that year.

He had been capturing the headlines because of a rumoured move to the English First Division. Nottingham Forest were one of the dominant teams as the time and their charismatic manager, Brian Clough, was said to have been an admirer of Allen's range of skills.

Allen was back in favour with the GAA community in 1975 and made a very good start to the Munster final, scoring an excellent point from a difficult angle. It was one of the brightest moments in a game that was not going well for Cork. Their full-back, Martin O'Doherty had fumbled the ball into his own net to give Kerry the perfect start.

It was, however, an eventful game that involved two missed penalties. The Cork goalkeeper, Billy Morgan saved a first half penalty from Mikey Sheehy, and Kerry's Paud O'Mahony would later save one from Jimmy Barry Murphy.

Páidí's story is that after Allen scored a point he turned and said, 'I guess they'll be taking you off soon.'

'If they are,' retorted Páidí, ' … you'll be coming with me.'

The film does not shed light on the conversation. What we see is Allen gaining possession with his back to the Kerry goal and Páidí's right hand making contact with Allen's ribs. Allen swung back his right elbow and caught Páidí flush on the jaw.

Páidí immediately adopted the pugilist stance; he raised the right fist but then delivered a smashing left hook that floored Allen.

The referee, an experienced official named Brendan Crosse from Limerick, ran across the slippery surface to intervene but both his feet lost traction and he ended up on his backside. By the time he regained his composure the situation had cooled. The two players accepted his admonishment and were last seen shaking hands and running away, arms over each other's shoulders.

The incident hardly merited a mention in the following day's newspapers.

If the analysis of today was in vogue the incident would have been treated as a national scandal. One can only imagine how *The Sunday Game's* video enthusiasts would have dealt with it.

Páidí would have been slaughtered.

At the time only Jim O'Sullivan, the GAA correspondent of *The Cork Examiner*, wrote that *both players were lucky not to be sent off.*

In the *Irish Independent* John D Hickey said, *Paud O'Shea had a dream game.*

Hickey had other concerns that day. *Such was Cork's disarray,'* he wrote, *'that their ineptness bordered on the incredible. The causes of their inefficiency were not obvious but they may have in part stemmed from the confusion they themselves created - only seconds after the start Jimmy Barry Murphy was the only forward in the position in which he started!*

We can only imagine what Hickey and his contemporaries would have made of the modern game.

Those were different times. At Fitzgerald Stadium that afternoon the ball was thrown in at the start of the game by the Bishop of Kerry, Eamon Casey, who then scampered away as the four midfielders, Kerry's Paudie Lynch and Pat McCarthy, and the Cork duo of Denis Long and Dave McCarthy fought for possession.

No one realised it at the time but Gaelic football was about to undergo a monumental change.

—⟋⟍—

Mick O'Dwyer would one day break Páidí Ó Sé's heart but he always knew that he could rely on Páidí's spirit.

From the first time he laid eyes on the youngster from Ventry as an under-age player with Kerry, Micko felt a sense of familiarity. It was not an easily definable thing because in some ways they were utterly opposite characters.

Dwyer was supremely disciplined. He was a non-drinker who did not approve of the excesses of men of his own generation and the generation of footballers who followed them. He did not voice that disapproval but over the years he found ways on the training field to punish those who transgressed.

Páidí was fond of a drink from his mid-teens and was a social animal. It would always be that way.

But they shared a passion.

Football.

It was more than that, according to those who knew both men well. It was an obsession. Dwyer sensed that immediately when he got to know Páidí a little better. And the better he got to know Páidí the more he liked him, so the more he worked him because he knew he could get the best out of him.

'The difference between Páidí and the rest of us,' says Seanie Walsh, 'is that football was number one with him. We all had other priorities but nothing was more important to Páidí than football. There was no one else in the team who had that passion. The only one who matched his passion was Dwyer.'

The harder Dwyer worked Páidí the more the kid grew to like the master. They were never best friends during those years but they developed a special bond. Later in life they did become much closer. Dwyer relied heavily on Páidí's unbridled passion and belief; Páidí learned something from every outing with Dwyer and would apply so many of those lessons in his life and his football for the next 35 years.

The relationship between the two would take a new twist when the pupil himself became a master and they met as opponents on the sideline.

That is a story for later.

Their first close involvement was with the Kerry Under-21 team in 1974. O'Dwyer had retired from playing with Kerry prior to the senior Championship and had been asked to look after the Under-21s who were defending the All-Ireland title. Páidí and Mikey Sheehy were the only survivors from the 1973 team that had also included Paudie O'Mahony, Jimmy Deenihan, Ger O'Keeffe, Ger Power, John Long, Paudie Lynch, Mickey O'Sullivan and John Egan.

Amongst the new crop were Ogie Moran, Tim Kennelly, Pat Spillane, Sean Walsh and Ger O'Driscoll. Dwyer sensed there was a decent crop of footballers becoming available to step up to senior level. If he had a good year with the Under-21s who knew what the future would hold.

They played Cork in the Munster final in Cahirciveen. They led by 1-1 to no score after five minutes. Kerry were awarded a penalty. Páidí lined it up. The adrenalin was pumping. He lifted his kick too high. A point was not enough. Jimmy Barry Murphy inspired Cork to victory.

Páidí was quickly forgiven. *The Kerryman* simply reported that the young midfielder at one stage *was badly wide, as with previous attempts.* O'Dwyer knew enough by then. Once his appointment as Kerry senior manager was secured by the County Chairman, Ger McKenna, in January of 1975, Páidí Ó Sé's future path was decided.

Over the coming years no player would test O'Dwyer's patience to such limits. At times Páidí flirted with disaster, his casual way sometimes when socialising at the height of the season bringing into question his preparedness for Championship football. Yet, on the training field, especially in the early days, it was Páidí who responded best to Dwyer's demands.

The new Garda recruit was becoming accustomed to life travelling from the Training Centre in Templemore. He welcomed the demands of training in Austin Stack Park or Fitzgerald Stadium. At the weekend he would run the Clasach. It felt good to be in shape. He needed to be in shape. In a tough Championship encounter against Tipperary he took a heavy blow to the ribs. A man of lesser physique would have required a spell on the sidelines. There was too much competition for places to take that sort of chance.

It is important to quantify the significance of that victory over Tipperary. The final score of 3-13 to 0-9 suggests the usual casual affair as a prelude to the annual clash with Cork. It was far from that.

At half time the teams were level. Tipperary led briefly in the second half. Michael 'Babs' Keating, the hurling legend who lined out as often as he could with the county's footballers, was making a nuisance of himself. He had played with O'Dwyer for Munster and the Kerry manager was fully aware of his ability as a footballer and his physical power.

The new Kerry coach needed something special to happen. John Egan moved to centre-forward and scored two goals. He added two points. Kerry scampered away from Clonmel feeling relieved. The manager promised himself that he would never be so exposed again.

O'Dwyer had taken a massive risk in jettisoning many of the more experienced players from the Kerry squad of 1974, including some who were only in their late 20s and had won All-Ireland titles in 1969 and 1970. The oldest player in his new team, Brendan Lynch, was just 26. And he had strayed from the traditional catch and kick style of football preferred by traditionalists in Kerry, introducing widespread use of the handpass.

To beat Cork and Dublin O'Dwyer was convinced that he needed his team to be the fittest ever seen in football. Kerry trained for 27 consecutive nights leading up to the Munster final. Today it would be regarded as madness.

The manager knew no better.

The PE students and graduates in his squad were too afraid to shout stop. Dwyer was building fitness and stamina in the only way he knew. He hadn't studied any science but the science of life.

One man amongst them all loved it. Páidí

They certainly left Cork behind.

1-14 to 0-7.

And 'Paud O'Shea' was now a household name.

The *Irish Independent* summed up the performance. *Because of the overwhelming nature of Kerry's mastery it would be an entirely superfluous exercise to dwell at any length even briefly on the trend of the exchanges. It seems to be much more appropriate to individualise and to state that Kerry won so handsomely because their half-back trio, Paud O'Shea, who had a dream game, Kennelly and Ger Power, blotted out a variety of alignments in the Cork half forward line, plus the splendour of left half forward Mickey O'Sullivan.*

Brendan Lynch, Pat McCarthy, Pat Spillane, Jim Deenihan, John O'Keeffe, a brilliant John Egan and Paud O'Mahoney were other Kerrymen to stand out but all the others in the victorious side must have endeared themselves to new trainer Mick

O'Dwyer and the selectors.

In view of the emphasis on the superiority of Kerry one feels obliged to add that it was a very disappointing Munster final, the memory of which will not endure for long whether or not the winners carry all the way the torch they have ignited.

Back in his own household in Ard an Bhothair the banter had begun. Kerry would play Sligo, the original home of Beatrice, in the All-Ireland semi-final. There was a sense of romance about Sligo's success in Connacht, their first provincial title since 1928; a fitting reward for the talent of Mickey Kearins who was widely respected in Kerry.

But there is only so far you can go with respect.

The game is best portrayed in the words of Paddy Downey, of *The Irish Times* who hailed from West Cork and would develop a soft spot for this new Kerry team over the next 14 years, though you might not expect so from the following.

Paddy wrote, *The first of the All-Ireland football semi-finals at Croke Park yesterday could be summed up in a single sentence. Sligo were at least the length of the Shannon below Kerry's class, and Kerry's class on the day, was pathetic. But one is compelled to say some more, if only to acknowledge the occasion from which so many had expected so much and to commiserate with 32,215 spectators whose misfortune it was to witness the worst match in the All-Ireland series for many years.*

The most remarkable aspect of the scene was the patience of these spectators, only trickles of whom started to move to the exits six or seven minutes from the end. Perhaps they were rooted to their places by the crushing boredom of the event; or else, with Kerry unable to establish mastery when their rivals' unbelievable ineptitude flung open the door before and after half time the crowd hung on in the hope that, through some miraculous intervention, Sligo might yet perform a dramatic and memorable feat.

John D. Hickey was similarly unimpressed.

While conscious of the fact that the passage of time may have dimmed memories of previous disappointing games I have seen in a lifetime of reporting the national games I cannot recall an occasion on which so crushing a penance was exacted as in yesterday's torture.

The margin of Kerry's triumph might lead those who did not make the Croke Park pilgrimage yesterday to believe that the Kingdom were regal as they fashioned victory

by seventeen points. Nothing could be further from the truth. Their mediocrity was so
widespread that it was impossible to reconcile their performance with their splendour
against Cork in the Munster final.

Indeed so moderate were Kerry that only the most credulous of their supporters
are likely to find any joy in a win constructed on such shallow foundations. Had they
won by twice seventeen points on the day might have told little about their All Ireland
potential such was the innocence of a Sligo team that was clearly out of its depth in
an All-Ireland semi-final.

3-13 to 0-5.

Onwards.

To the Dubs.

—⚊—

'He loved the Dubs,' Maire Ó Sé says quietly. 'He could escape to the city,
lose himself there and be happy with the people. He just loved the fun and the
banter that he had with the Dublin people. It was a special place to him and
the people were special as well.'

It was a love affair that began in September of 1975.

He had not spent much time in the capital up to then and was indifferent
to its charms. In the years to come he would befriend many Dubliners or
country folk living in Dublin. In some ways he was seduced by the anonymity
he could find in Dublin when he needed a break from the constant attention
that would become an unexpected part of his life.

Dublin and its people would provide him with an escape. He could
socialise easily in places like the Palace Bar, Doheny and Nesbitt's, the Boar's
Head, The Merchant or the Burlington Hotel. He was looked after well;
protected and nurtured.

He had watched with interest as Dublin won the All-Ireland title in 1974.
It was the razzamatazz the Dubs brought to the game rather than their
actual talents that first attracted him. Even then Páidí knew the value of
entertainment, of putting on a show.

He wondered what it would be like to be on Hill 16 with the hordes
swaying dangerously, singing, waving banners like an English soccer crowd.

The city slickers against the culchies. That was his kind of gig even at that early stage of his career.

The Dubs presented themselves well.

For the 1974 Championship they had changed their playing gear. They wore navy shorts with the traditional light blue jersey. It was the innovation of a lady named Paula Lee who worked in the Dublin County Board offices. It wasn't a universally popular move with an older generation but it appealed to Dublin's new audience.

Only the Down teams of the 1960s had the temerity to break with the tradition of wearing white shorts. Again, this appealed to the young Kerryman.

His mother ensured that the young Kerry footballer would take care of his own appearance off the field in the days surrounding the All-Ireland final. While his teammates gathered at Killarney railway station on the day before the game in a variety of outfits, Páidí was kitted out in a new three-piece beige suit purchased by Beatrice especially for the occasion.

Beatrice started a trend.

Páidí loved his suits, loved the process of buying them, of kitting his teams out well off the field. There are men in many corners of Ireland and all corners of the world who might claim to have been tailors to Páidí Ó Sé!

The Dubs victory in 1974 brought other changes. The national newspapers, radio and television began to take a greater interest in the big GAA occasions. Though a far less populated area than today, the media descended on Kerry in unprecedented numbers in the two weeks before the final in 1975.

O'Dwyer welcomed them with open arms. He believed in an open door policy and knew the regular GAA writers well. The Kerry GAA officials were also welcoming. Men like Gerald McKenna, Frank King and Andy Molyneaux had befriended the likes of Hickey, Downey, RTE's Mick Dunne, Padraig Puirseal, Donal Carroll, Jim O'Sullivan and Peadar O'Brien.

There were no formal press conferences; no one bothered with formalised Public Relations. Good manners involving a handshake and a chat sufficed. Páidí was more reticent and it would take a few years before he became comfortable with the press.

On that train journey to Dublin for the 1975 final he was disconcerted by the presence of a photographer and a journalist in the team carriage. Both were representing the *Sunday Independent*, the newspaper with which Páidí would eventually form a very close attachment. On that Saturday he stayed well clear of the camera lens.

The article that appeared in the newspaper the following day caused great mirth around the breakfast table in the Grand Hotel in Malahide. For a few minutes Páidí forgot his nerves, the edginess he felt before big games, as he read aloud the words of the journalist, Jim Farrelly, a native of Meath who would later in his career spend time as Managing Director of *The Kerryman*.

Farrelly's piece was carried in the news pages of the newspaper the following day. He wrote, *Fifteen austere young men of Kerry watch the green hills flash by as their train rumbles up to Dublin.*

A monastery would be proud of them.

Bachelors all, they sit pensively – as if in meditation – now and then exchanging a nervous word or two. About football.

For these are "the men behind O'Dwyer" Kerry's youngest ever All-Ireland team, quietly confident of wresting the Sam Maguire Cup from the upstart Dubs at Croke Park today.

Wine, women and song have played no part in the lives of these magnificently fit titans for the past ten weeks.

They're all between 19 and 26 but not one of them is even engaged and cigarettes they spurn as the vice of softies.

Roaring with laughter Páidí passed the article around. 'Great footballers we are,' he laughed. 'And right eejits.'

The day of the game itself became grey and dank as a fleet of taxis brought the team and a large group of officials to Croke Park. There was some nervous banter along the way but all the serious talking had been done the previous night. In the years to come, as individuals and as a team they would develop habits, indulge in superstitions, but in '75 it was all new.

The game itself hardly matched the level of hype that preceded it. The conditions didn't help. Dublin did't play well; weren't allowed play well. The young Kerry team overwhelmed them with speed, skill and stamina. *The Day of the Kerry Dancers* was the headline in *The Irish Times* the following morning.

This was John Barry's reaction in *The Kerryman* the following weekend. *In the Kerry defence the performances of wing backs Ger Power and Paudie O'Shea had followers in raptures. They were simply unbeatable on the day. How could men playing with them not but be inspired.*

Paudie O'Shea seems to be getting better all the time. He certainly hit the high spots last Sunday, throwing Dublin back time and again with devastating power. When he goes to meet that ball he goes in with the throttle full out and he usually comes out best. Truly a five-star display.

It was the day when some of Gaelic football's biggest stars were born. And none would shine more brightly for the next three decades than the man they called Paudie O'Shea.

The players had put their heart, souls and bodies into the training regime laid out by their trainer. They did the same with the celebrations. They were young, strong and fit and could take it. They also had club commitments to fulfil. That brought a level of sanity back to their lives

For Páidí, Tim Kennelly, Ogie, Ger O'Driscoll, Sheehy and Spillane there was also the demands of an All-Ireland Under-21 final to be met. Again, Dublin provided the opposition with only Brian Mullins from the senior team in the starting line-up. The Kerry players were sufficiently focussed – and sober – and won comfortably, 1-15 to 0-10.

They were soon back in action with the senior team.

The National Football League resumed on the last Sunday in October. Kerry played Offaly in Tralee and won by three points, 1-9 to 0-9. Eleven of the team that started the All-Ireland final lined out. Amongst those missing was John O'Keeffe who was studying in England.

A significant introduction to the squad that day was an 18 year-old Seanie Walsh. He was the first member of the All-Ireland winning minor team of 1975 to be promoted and would play a central role in the future of the team.

Two weeks later, on November 9, the Kerry players returned to the scene of their September triumph, Croke Park, to play Dublin. Many observers believe it was this game more than the All-Ireland final that sparked the great rivalry that was just beginning. Dublin were still hurting from losing their All-Ireland title and over 25,000 spectators turned out to watch the re-match.

It was, by all accounts, a classic.

Dublin won, 2-11 to 0-13.

In the *Irish Independent* John D Hickey waxed lyrically. *Never have I seen a football test which excelled the first half of a game which, in its valleys as well as its peaks, was too good to last,* he wrote.

The fervour, the constancy of the exceptionally high standard of performance, the efficiency and speed with which Dublin fused and the gallantry of Kerry's resistance, a defiance that often gave them the initiative made that first half a football fantasy come true.

So enchanted, indeed so embroiled did I become in it all, that I confess to having neglected to make a note other than to record scores throughout the electrifying thirty minutes.

One could continue ad infinitive in extolling the glories of the spell and yet feel that this was football so great that its magnificence could not be translated to cold print.

Hickey also commented on the performances of the individual players and in the course of those added the following words, ….*in a Kerry side in which Paud O'Shea, Pat McCarthy and John Egan were uncharacteristically compliant to adversity.*

Off the field the young O'Shea was adapting to the changed circumstances in his life. His training in Templemore had been completed.

He was now Garda O'Shea, based in Limerick, and sworn to uphold the laws of the land. He would do so dutifully if somewhat unenthusiastically. Because, like everything else in his life at the time, the laws of the land simply were not as important as football.

CHAPTER 5

'Barbaric.'

Sean Walsh's voice is quiet.

He pauses in reflection and shakes his head from side to side, his forehead tightening as if battling an ache. Even now, three decades and more on, the memories of the 'special' training sessions Mick O'Dwyer conducted with a small group of his Kerry players make Walsh wince.

In his more tender moments O'Dwyer would refer to this group as 'the heavies'. When he was less pliant he derided them as 'the fatties.'

The group membership altered during the late 1970s and early 80s but the core was constant – Seanie Walsh, 'Bomber' Liston, John Egan, Tim Kennelly.

And, of course, Páidí.

They were the men who wintered well. That meant that they were generally unconcerned about physical exercise during the months that surrounded the Championship season. From time to time they filled in the leisure hours by socialising, often together, and gathered extra poundage.

Actually, in relative terms, these young men remained in fairly solid condition. They played club football and League games, and maintained a level of fitness that was greater than the average man on the street. But the average man on the street did not have to meet the demands made twice or three times weekly by Mick O'Dwyer, then into his 40s and fitter than men 20 years his junior.

O'Dwyer's early season training sessions were tough. They ran laps of the pitch in Killarney; then more laps. They ran sprints – to the 14 yard line, the 21 yard line.

Repeatedly.

And then the dreaded wire to wire across the pitch at full speed.

There was no place to hide. The trainer did it all with them. He goaded those who were slacking. If they could not keep up with their 40-plus year-old trainer how could they hope to cope in Croke Park against Dublin?

Dublin.

At times they kept O'Dwyer awake at night. In 1975 he had risked everything to beat the Dubs. He picked a team of kids. He got them fitter than any team had ever been. He changed Kerry's style of football and got away with it all because Kerry won the All-Ireland Championship.

But then came 1976.

Dublin wrestled the title back. Kerry sought redemption in 1977. They lost again to Dublin, this time in the All-Ireland semi-final. It was said to have been the greatest game of football ever played. It didn't feel like that for O'Dwyer and his team. It was a disaster, a calamity that threatened the future of the trainer and his team.

The players knew little of the politics of the GAA, especially local politics. O'Dwyer knew all about it. He watched as plots were hatched against him.

The chairman, Gerald McKenna, was challenged. If he had lost his post then O'Dwyer would have gone too. McKenna, typically, worked the hustings well. He went to North Kerry, his stronghold. The hurling club delegates were visited and charmed.

McKenna stayed as chairman.

O'Dwyer stayed as trainer.

And became more obsessed than ever.

On the beat in Limerick as Garda O'Shea or back west, climbing the Clasach, Páidí kept up to date with everything. He studied the manoeuvrings of GAA politicians, kept an eye on how O'Dwyer operated during this turbulent period and kept on learning. The lessons off the field were just as important as those learned on the field. It would serve him well later through good times and especially through bad times.

O'Dwyer discovered 'The Bomber' at the end of 1977, a six foot something bear of a man with a natural footballing instinct who needed to get fit. The trainer started working on that. Kerry had won the National Football League title in 1977 but O'Dwyer virtually ignored the competition in the 1977-78 season, not even attending the early matches. He thought of the Championship only. When Dublin won the League Kerry doubled their efforts.

The teams met in an exhibition match in New York in May 1978. They beat lumps out of each other in a monsoon. It was wild, a little reckless and often silly. The rivalry became inflamed.

Páidí, The Bomber and Pat O'Neill were sent to the line.

Páidí was regarded as unlucky. The *Irish Press* reported, *Five minutes from the end Paud O'Shea was unlucky to incur marching orders from referee Seamus Aldridge.* The sympathy didn't last sufficiently long for the player to be awarded an AllStar later that year. He failed to get a nomination under the infamous 'sportsmanship rule'.

Pat O'Neill had hit Jimmy Deenihan.

'Sorry,' Dr Pat said to Deenihan in a Manhattan bar later that evening. 'I thought you were Páidí.'

The Dubs.

It was all about the Dubs.

Cork were spooked by this stage. Good Cork teams that might have achieved greater things in another era were beaten before they left the dressing room. Kerry were careful before they played Cork but they were always confident. The 1976 Munster final had been the watershed. They re-opened Pairc Ui Chaoimh and the crowds spilled onto the playing area. They drew 0-10 each. Cork could have won it. The replay was described as 'brilliant'.

Kerry won after extra time, 3-20 to 2-19.

Páidí was majestic.

The journalist Gerry McCarthy was gushing on his praise for the football produced in the replay. He wrote in the *Irish Press*, *Words fail to describe the tension, excitement, thrills, misses, joy, despair and confusion of a game that will never be forgotten by the crowd that thronged Pairc Ui Chaoimh in ideal conditions.*

Fortunes fluctuated to such an extent during the 70 minutes of actual time that many spectators were limp with excitement. However, 30 minutes of extra time were dominated by Kerry who never looked like losing once they had pulled themselves up by the bootlaces after defeat had stared them in the face mid-way through the second half of normal time.

McCarthy was well acquainted with Kerry football. He was the goalkeeper on the Waterford team in 1959 that famously defeated Kerry in the Munster Championship.

Cork were broken by that defeat. It would be years before they provided another real challenge.

Dublin provoked a different mood.

—◊—

In the days leading up to the 1977 All-Ireland semi-final the Kerry players came together in Fitzgerald Stadium to chat about the forthcoming game. It was a discussion O'Dwyer actively encouraged. It contributed to the team ethic and it gave him a chance to assess the mentality of the players, experienced and not so.

Sean Walsh was 19 years-old. He had been with the squad since the winter of '75 but had spent the summer of '76 starting on the bench and making important appearances as a substitute.

In the replayed Munster final of 1976 he replaced Mickey Ned O'Sullivan and scored 1-3; in the All-Ireland semi-final he was sprung for Pat McCarthy against Derry and scored 1-1. He was dubbed 'Super Sub' in the newspapers. It was a moniker famously attached to the Liverpool soccer player, David Fairclough.

The two players hated it.

Walsh wanted to be a member of the starting fifteen. His wish was granted during the 1977 Championship. He was selected at full-forward to play Dublin. He also felt he should contribute something to the team meeting in Killarney.

He had prepared himself, watching videos of the Dublin team and focusing on their full-back line as well as their goalkeeper, Paddy Cullen. He hatched a plan.

'Lads,' said the kid, 'I've been looking at videos and it's got me thinking. I think I should rough Paddy Cullen up a bit. He gets a lot of easy ball, and I was thinking I should go in and give him a tumble into the net.

'It might cost us a free but so what, it would give him something to think about. We might get something out of it later in the game.'

The other players pondered the notion.

Some nodded approvingly.

The kid was showing cojones.

A good sign.

Páidí narrowed his eyes as he regarded his young friend. His innocent young friend.

'Seanie boy, that all sounds like a good idea.

'But I'd have one problem with it. You see I'd worry about coming back out. Because … first, you're going to have to pass (Gay) O'Driscoll.

'And if you get that far you have to meet (Sean) Doherty.

'And if you're lucky enough to be still going … you have to get by (Robbie) Kelleher. I'd watch myself if I was you passing those fellas.'

The plan was ditched.

—⚏—

Nothing would satisfy O'Dwyer during the summer of '78. He was on a mission and he drove the players hard. They beat Cork by seven points in the Munster final and that wasn't enough. The critics were still sniping in the wings, and as much as O'Dwyer tried to ignore them he did become irritated.

A week after the Munster final 'The Fatties' were summoned.

O'Dwyer was aware of the extent of the celebrations and was determined to deliver a message. It was a ritual that would be repeated over the next four years as O'Dwyer laid out exactly what he wanted from his team.

For the extra training in Killarney O'Dwyer would take the lead himself. He would start running laps and the small group of players would follow.

Lap after lap, O'Dwyer kept up a brutal pace. 'Come on … ye're in a terrible state. Not fit … not fit at all.'

Forty laps later he would stop.

Panting heavily, but not heaving like his players, O'Dwyer would keep up the mantra in between gulps of air. 'Not fit … terrible state.'

'It was boot camp stuff,' recalls Walsh. 'It was barbaric. You wouldn't dream of doing it now. But he was also mentally grinding us down, forcing us to realise what was at stake … how much it meant to him and how much it should mean to us.'

Walsh reckons that on that first night alone he must have shed eight pounds. It took minutes for the players to find the energy to just leave the field and return to the dressing room. Slowly trudging towards the exit he was joined by Páidí. 'Jesus Seanie … that was fucking torture,' Páidí said in a choked voice.

'We'll never stick another session like that.'

Jogging along behind them was O'Dwyer, still muttering, 'not fit at all.' He turned to the two players. 'Lads, it's not good enough. We going nowhere like this. Ye're not fit enough.'

'Well,' retorted Páidí in a booming voice that belied the pounding of his chest as he sought to replenish his reserves of oxygen, 'you'd better get us out here every night this week … and get us fit.

'Because, without us … you'll win fuck all.'

O'Dwyer, almost but not quite defeated, walked away clutching at clumps of his hair and still muttering in exasperation.

'The truth is,' says Walsh today, 'that only Páidí would have got away with saying something like that. I'd say he would have got rid of any of the rest of us if we had made that comment, but he would never even think of getting rid of Páidí.'

—m—

For months of the year Páidí lived in a caravan in the back garden of the family home in Ard an Bhothair. It was a matter of convenience for both the dweller and his parents. Beatrice supplemented the family income by keeping students during the summer months who came to An Gaeltacht to learn or improve their Irish.

Páidí's room could generate income so he moved out.

Amongst those who stayed with Beatrice during those summer months was a young girl named Emily O'Reilly. She would become one of Ireland's best known journalists, before becoming Ombudsman.

The new digs for her youngest son meant that Beatrice could ensure Páidí would not be disturbed when he required rest. Even then they understood the need for rest for the elite footballer, and the comings and goings in the house meant there was no guarantee that he would not be interrupted from his sleep.

Once her youngest son was installed in his temporary dwelling only God himself could have intervened to protect anyone from the wrath of Beatrice if Páidí's garden sanctuary was invaded. His nephews – Michael and Joan's sons, Fergal, Darragh, Tomas and Marc – learned it was wiser to tiptoe through the garden and to keep their own footballs far away; though there were days when they strayed over the boundaries that were deemed acceptable. Uncle Páidí was a mischief-maker himself so they learned from him and paid him back for some of the tricks he played on them.

Each year, in the week after the Munster final, the caravan itself became a hostel of sorts. The Championship schedule meant that they could have as much as a six-week wait for the All-Ireland semi-final. O'Dwyer had worked them hard for two months up to the provincial decider so he gave them the week off.

They made the best of it.

The Heavies – Páidí, Seanie, 'The Horse' Kennelly and The Bomber – were joined by Ogie, Paudie Lynch and sometimes the likes of Ger O'Keeffe. Seanie Walsh had been born and raised in Ballyferriter and was related to Páidí. Something like a fourth cousin. He knew the entire Ó'Sé family. 'I consider myself half a West Kerry man,' he says.

From Monday to Thursday they toured the Dingle Peninsula – Dingle, Ballydavid, Ballyferriter and Krugers. They drank plenty, told stories and listened. There was music too.

In the early hours of the morning they would return to the caravan. Beatrice would have prepared a feast of sandwiches which would be quickly devoured. They talked until they slept, finding whatever free space they could to stretch out.

The following day they would wake, not early, and feast on whatever Beatrice had prepared on the frying pan or in the oven.

There was laughter and camaraderie. It was part of the magic, the mix that made the unit special.

The nephews would often come around to sneak a look through the windows and see which of the legends was there. Toddlers would get lifted to have a look. Their whispers and giggles did not disturb the men within from their slumber. The big danger was that Beatrice might catch them.

Then there would be trouble.

'It wouldn't be tolerated today,' Seanie Walsh says of the week long escape. 'At the time it was thought that ourselves, the Dubs and one or two other teams had broken all barriers in relation to fitness. But we weren't anywhere close to the levels that have been reached today. We effectively trained for just three games, the Munster final, the All-Ireland semi-final and the final.

'We enjoyed ourselves after the Munster final. We let off a bit of steam, but Páidí would soon be out running again. Running the roads meant he built up great strength and stamina. He would get me out running too. I wasn't too fond of training but he would get me out.'

By the following weekend the fun was over.

O'Dwyer was boss again.

—⚬—

For all the tales of ribaldry and fun it is important to note the schedules kept by these footballers and Páidí especially during the years between 1975 and 1982 during which they reached seven All-Ireland finals.

They did not train much for the National League campaigns, which in those days was played between October and May, but they won it twice in 1977 and 1982, and reached the final in 1980.

Páidí also played regularly for Munster in that period. The Railway Cup competitions were fast losing their grip on the public consciousness but there was still a semblance of respectability about the competition when Páidí first played for the province in 1976.

Croke Park was the venue for the semi-final, played on February 16, with Ulster as their opponents. Páidí was part of a large Kerry contingent called on to wear the provincial blue jersey – Paudie O'Mahony, Deenihan, Ger Power, Ogie, Mikey, Mickey Ned, Egan and Spillane were all there as well.

There were a number of faces in the dressing room Páidí did not recognise as he took a place in the corner under the old Cusack Stand. There was the usual banter associated with these games, when the door opened.

In walked Dinny Allen.

The combatants were now teammates.

He played on successful Munster teams in 1978, 1981 and 1982. In 1980, for example, Páidí lined out for Kerry in an exhibition game against a Rest of Ireland selection in Newbridge on January 28. He played both games in the Railway Cup for Munster – they lost to Ulster in the final – and played right through the later rounds of the League, including the final in which they lost to Cork.

'Páidí might have enjoyed himself during the winter but he always kept up the running,' says Seanie Walsh. 'That's what made him different.'

Páidí's single-mindedness at the time meant that he took little interest in other sports. But in the autumn of 1977 he did play rugby for the Limerick club, Highfield. It was an experience he enjoyed and it gave him a greater appreciation of the game and an interest in rugby in Limerick, and the Munster team in later years.

It was also part of a regime that prepared him for the 1978 Championship and the tough schedule that O'Dwyer laid down. In the intensity of the Kerry camp there were moments when Páidí let his guard down. On the night before the All-Ireland semi-final against Roscommon he went drinking in a Dublin pub.

O'Dwyer, naturally, met him on his return to the Grand Hotel and was furious. Nothing could be allowed jeopardise his plans to win the All-Ireland title and prove his critics wrong. What should the trainer do?

He could have dropped Páidí and would have been justified in doing so. But how would that affect the team?

Páidí was lucky. He had built up enough credits to get away with it. Just once. And it probably helped that selectors like Liam Higgins and Joe Keohane were fond of their young defender, knew they could rely on him in a tight corner, and would have prompted O'Dwyer to let the breach of discipline pass.

It was an unnecessary distraction but it meant that the young player did focus properly when the semi-final was won, and another final meeting with Dublin loomed.

On the night before that final, on September 23, Páidí didn't stray far from the Grand Hotel. O'Dwyer introduced some new routines for that weekend that would be observed for years to come. The squad gathered on Malahide strand and walked while O'Dwyer talked. They would gather in a group and O'Dwyer would invite contributions from players.

That night the discussion was winding down. They had discussed everything, dissected Dublin and dissected themselves.

The mood was buoyant.

Training had been good. Jack O'Shea, the young midfielder, was in majestic form. The forwards, with the 'Bomber' in situ at full-forward, with Sheehy and Egan on his flanks, were flying. Ogie, as captain, said a few words.

Calm, reassuring words.

Then Micko asked, 'Páidí, what do you think?'

The last words.

No one recalls precisely what was said. But it was passionate Páidí-speak, the perfect send-off to four in-a-row.

—∞—

On a late October evening in 1981 the telephone behind the bar at Kruger Kavanagh's public house in Dunquin rang. The landlord answered and recognised the voice of a Dublin-based friend.

'You made it this time,' was the simple message.

Páidí left the bar, drove to his parent's house in Ard an Bhothair, and joined them in the kitchen. As his mother poured a cup of tea she waited for whatever news she knew her son had brought home. Though he was trying to keep a straight face, the curl of a smile was forming. It was good news anyway, Beatrice thought with relief.

'Out with it … whatever you have to tell us,' she commanded. 'You've kept us waiting long enough.'

'I'll be needing a tux,' was all he said.

Páidí O Sé an AllStar.

At last.

The official announcement was not due until the following morning when the selection would be the big news on the sports pages of the national newspapers and on the early morning radio bulletins. Beatrice and Tommy were concerned that he might still be disappointed and cautioned against such expectation.

'Don't worry, my source is impeccable,' he told them.

The following morning the news was confirmed. In the *Irish Independent* news of Páidí's selection led the page. *The long wait had finally ended for Paudie O'Shea with the announcement yesterday that the 26 year old wing half-back from Ventry, one of Kerry's most staunch defenders since the emergence of the current side in 1975 has been honoured with his first AllStar award,* was the opening paragraph.

He was not alone in requiring patience.

Also awarded All Stars for the first time in 1981 to showcase with five All-Ireland medals were Jimmy Deenihan and Ogie. A total of nine Kerry players were chosen – Paudie Lynch, Jack O'Shea, Sean Walsh, Pat Spillane, Mikey Sheehy and 'The Bomber' joining the newcomers.

It cannot be doubted that his reputation as a 'hard man' certainly militated against his selection pre-1981. He missed out twice because of the sportsmanship rule that did not allow any player sent off during the year under review to be considered, which included his dismissal in that exhibition game in New York in 1978.

Between 1981 and 1985, however, Páidí looked forward to the annual gathering of the nation's best footballers and hurlers in the Burlington Hotel just before Christmas. He won a total of five All Star awards, two at right half-back and three at right full-back.

Certainly he played some of his best football in 1980 and 1981 as Kerry completed four Championship successes in-a-row. By his own admission he had not enjoyed the 1979 Championship. His life was beginning to change off the field; a return to civilian life was looming as he began to find it almost impossible to juggle football and guardianship of the peace, and that was affecting his form.

Kerry were untouchable in 1979.

They won the four games necessary with ridiculous ease. Hapless Clare were the victims of the 'Milltown Massacre', 9-21 to 1-9, in the opening round. They had 10 points to spare over Cork in the Munster final in Killarney, 2-14 to 2-4 – and scored 2-12 from play. They annihilated Monaghan in the All-Ireland semi-final by 5-14 to 0-7 and met the old foe, Dublin, in the final.

Páidí reserved his best performance of the season for the final. He was masterful on the right wing, bouncing into and out of tackles, careering down the field on inspirational sallies. His hunger and enthusiasm would lead him towards trouble. He was booked by the referee, Hugh Duggan from Armagh, for a foul on Tommy Drumm in the first half.

It didn't slow him down.

Midway through the second half Anton O'Toole got possession for Dublin and headed for goal. Páidí tackled in a manner he might have seen in his days with Highfield, not dangerous but too high. The referee took out his black book again and Páidí made the lonely walk. Kerry still won by 3-13 to 1-8.

He had no complaints. The pressmen surrounded him in the dressing room. 'I can't say the sending off was a harsh decision,' he told them. 'The referee has a job to do and I think I can't complain. I think my sending off was the turning point in the game. There was no way we were going to lose then. I am very sorry about the sending off but Kerry's win was great.'

His teammates consoled him.

John Egan told reporters, 'The fact that he was put off inspired us much more than it did Dublin.'

'The Bomber' spoke in a similar vein. 'The adrenalin really began to flow when he was put off.'

Later that evening Páidí was struggling emotionally with the experience. Unusually, he went to his room early. Paudie Lynch found him. 'Come on, this is no way to celebrate an All-Ireland,' he insisted.

And they re-joined the throng in Malahide.

In the following morning's *Irish Press* Páidí's performance was hailed by their correspondent, Peadar O Brien. *Paudie O'Shea at right half-back had the game of his life and it was pure over-enthusiasm which caused him to be sent to the line.*

O'Brien also reported that *the great hearted Gaeltacht defender was sent off for his third personal foul.*

Pat O'Neill, the Dublin defender, was quoted in the same newspaper. *I thought the decision taken on Paud O'Shea was a harsh one. A backman must take action like this at times and both sides were guilty of similar offences.*

It meant another year without an All Star.

What happened in 1980 in the AllStars selection room remains a mystery. Páidí had an outstanding year at right half-back as Kerry won their third consecutive Championship, beating Roscommon in the final. Seven Kerry players were chosen – Charlie, 'The Horse', Jacko, Power, Spillane, 'Bomber' and Egan – but the right half-back berth went to Kevin McCabe from Tyrone.

The All Stars mattered to Páidí.

Years later as Kerry manager, he would delight in revealing details about AllStar selections when they were supposed to be veiled in secrecy. The personnel within the selection committee changed over the years but Páidí always had a source, the identity of whom was never revealed.

On the historic evening in December, 2007 when his three nephews, Marc, Tomas and Darragh were selected together, Páidí relayed the news to a packed bar in Ard an Bhothair just minutes after the meeting broke up in Dublin's Westbury Hotel.

He always had friends in the right places.

CHAPTER 6

Páidí Ó Sé was an unlikely and, as it turned out and he freely admitted, an inefficient policeman.

He respected the law and he admired many of the people who upheld it. He liked Limerick, where he was stationed, and he was extremely fond of the Costelloe family who cared for him during his years in the city, John and Anne.

Looking back now it is hard to imagine him handing out tickets for failing to have tax displayed on a car; ticking a lad off for doing 80 in a 60 mph zone. It is even less plausible to imagine him carrying out a raid on a pub serving alcohol after hours.

But, more significantly, he always felt the tug of home. It was almost an addiction and one that he would never shake off. No matter how much he came to love Dublin, even New York, he always hankered after a while to return to Ard an Bhothair. Other places provided him with a necessary escape from time to time. He was a great traveller and loved to explore other countries but it was always temporary.

He could not imagine spending his life anywhere else. Much later in life, when his children had grown up and were ready to make their own way in the world, Páidí found it very difficult to come to terms with the fact that they would spread their wings and establish a life away from West Kerry.

Not that he stood in their way.

But Neasa, Siún and Padraig always knew that he was happiest when they were at home close to his warm embrace. 'He always wanted us to be here … around him. When I said I was moving to Dublin to finish my accounting he didn't really want me to go. He wanted me to stay here,' Neasa explains.

From the earliest days in Limerick he was planning a return home. As early as 1977 he had enough savings to convince a bank to give him a loan to purchase some land across the road from the shop. He applied for planning permission to build a public house in 1978 but his application was refused *on grounds that there was a sufficiency of licensed premises in the district* according to *The Kerryman*.

In hindsight it was probably the best outcome, though he didn't think so at the time, because it led him to Krugers in Dunquin. He acquired the lease to the famous public house from the O'Neill family and over the next five years learned a lot of lessons about life and dealing with people that would help him become a successful businessman.

Páidí Ó Sé was a shy man.

Yes, he was full of devilment and was constantly up to mischief amongst family and friends, but he held a sense of insecurity about him that not even his outstanding success on the football field or the support of those around him could shake off.

'There was a part of him that most people did not see,' says Maire. 'That was the shy part. He wasn't always comfortable dealing with people, that was something that developed over the years and he learned much of it from his time in Krugers.'

Mícheál Ó Sé saw the changes occur in his personality. 'It is hard to visualise because of his public persona that he was such a shy … very shy man. And he learned an awful lot from Krugers. There he was dealing with the islanders, and there are no better men for telling yarns and putting you in your place.

'He learned so much about the language, about our culture from the people in Krugers. He learned how to tell a story. You didn't always have to stick to the facts if you could make it better. He discovered how to deal with people and he lost a lot of the fear that he had when he was younger amongst people he didn't know well.'

Taking over the lease at Krugers inevitably led to his departure from An Garda Siochana. It was a relief to Páidí and, despite their support over four years, almost certainly a relief to his superiors who found their rosters at the whim of a Kerry footballer whose charge sheet was never that bountiful.

Krugers was a busy place with a turnover that ensured the young publican was well rewarded for his efforts. With the support of his brothers he built up that trade. During the summer months the tourists flocked to West Kerry. Páidí's fame as a footballer continued to grow as Kerry added a third successive All-Ireland title in 1980, beating Roscommon in the final. The locals added their support to the district hero. Life was good.

It was in Krugers, Easter 1980, that Páidí met Charlie Haughey for the first time. The Taoiseach was visiting his island, Inisvikillane, with his family and had arrived at Dunquin pier by helicopter, anxious to meet the famous footballer. They chatted easily, found each other's company comforting. They became firm friends and Haughey never had a more loyal supporter, even when his fame turned to notoriety.

Páidí's brother, Tom was the closest he ever had to a business adviser. Haughey brought that to a new level. He introduced Páidí to people in the tourism industry, including the hotelier, PV Doyle. Páidí made valuable contacts, built up a font of knowledge about business and methods. And he often turned to Haughey who would, in turn, seek out answers from his own advisers.

Páidí still had his dream.

He wanted to turn the piece of land across the road from the shop into his place. He could see the name over the door – Páidí Ó Sé. It was a picture that came to him in his early teens when he passed by Paddy Bawns in Dingle. It had never left him. He thought about a small hotel. That fell into abeyance.

A new pub went back to the top of the agenda.

That brought its own problems. When Páidí applied for a license there were objections. Ventry publican, Paid Quinn felt, understandably, that his business would be adversely affected and fought to protect his interests. The community was split down the middle, pro and anti-Páidí. It was something he had not anticipated and would have avoided if he could. But he wanted a future at home and a pub in Ard an Bhothair was that future.

It was during 1980 that another important element of Páidí's future was put in place. He had been friendly with Maire Fahy from Ballyferriter for a number of years. The relationship took a romantic twist and Maire was a constant presence in Páidí's life. She encouraged him in his business pursuits, providing moral support and often practical advice. Maire was a stabilising factor in his life and on March 10, 1984, they became husband and wife.

His commitment to football remained but he now allowed other responsibilities to take a small hold. He had learned to take time for his customers, the regulars and the tourists, make them feel that the publican cared for them and wished to look after their needs. He would listen to their stories, trade banter. It was something he was slowly beginning to enjoy and to feel comfortable with.

Maire encouraged him as he chased the dream of building his own pub. The atmosphere that built up in the locality was upsetting. She too had grown up with the people who were now lining up against her husband. She would also play a big part in healing the wounds when the court cases all came to an end.

Páidí launched an appeal against a Circuit Court refusal to grant him a license. It was heard in the High Court sitting in Tralee on March 11, 1985. Paudie Lynch, his old teammate now practising as a solicitor, was at Páidí's side. Hugh O'Flaherty and Paul Gallagher were Counsel. O'Flaherty took the lead when the case began.

The Kerryman reported: *It would be contended on behalf of the applicant that this other licensed premises would be a great convenience to the area, where there is need for such a service. It would be said that the population (of the area) had gone down and while this would be accepted by the applicant it bore no relation to what happened in the Summer months. It is an area which people have discovered in increasing numbers and the film 'Ryan's Daughter' made the place famous.*

Mr O Flaherty said there would be evidence that about 250,000 visitors came to the area in 1983 and that the numbers were up further in 1984. Then again many people go to the area to 'brush up' on their Irish.

And many of them are thirsty,' jocosely interjected Mr Justice Egan."

That was a good sign.

Mr Justice Egan, after a lengthy hearing, allowed the appeal. Finally, Páidí Ó Sé could build his pub.

That decision launched the most frantic few months of their young lives. To this day when asked to reflect on their years together Maire automatically talks about 1985. Undoubtedly, it changed their lives.

—⟋⟍—

He always contended that if Kerry had won the five in-a-row All Ireland titles in 1982 that his inter-county football career could have ended.

It is easy to understand why. Kerry always celebrated well. Imagine if they had created history against Offaly. He thought Mick O'Dwyer would surely have stood down and that would have meant the end of some of the players. The celebrations would have taken care of a few more. Possibly Páidí.

Defeat in that final to Seamus Darby's goal, following by a last minute loss to Cork in 1983 to a Tadhg Murphy goal, probably saved some careers. He would argue that it is unlikely the famous five – Páidí, Mikey, Power, Spillane and Ogie – would have gone on to win a record eight All-Ireland medals.

That was the first summer in more than a decade when Páidí's life was not consumed by football. His father Tommy, also known locally as Tom Power, died suddenly. He had never enjoyed good health following his accident in England but his death came as a shock. The youngest son's teammates, along with their manager and Maire were his props during those days.

At the end of '83 the players met and vowed that they would return, give it one more shot. O'Dwyer asked for a full and complete commitment. Páidí was the first to respond. 'I'll give it everything Mick,' he declared. It was just what the boss wanted to hear.

P Se was the one man he could rely on going to war.

Of course, it would not be that simple. Páidí and Maire were planning their wedding. Páidí also had another surprise in store, especially for Micko.

By his own admission Páidí had never given priority to his club, An

Gaeltacht, or the divisional team that played in the Kerry senior Championship, West Kerry. The county team was everything to him. Anyway, West Kerry teams were difficult concoctions. They were made up of players from a variety of clubs. There were good players but it was difficult to make them a team.

There were intense local rivalries.

Young men who were willing to give and take belts when lining out for Lispole, Annascaul or the Gaeltacht could find common cause when wearing the green and gold. But down the decades they had not found the source of an identity that would convince them to compete as West Kerrymen. It was a mentality, a state of mind that was very difficult to alter.

With the GAA celebrating its centenary in 1984 there were a number of like minds in the western division who believed a special effort should be made to make West Kerry competitive. They hadn't won anything of significance since the 1940s and it would take a substantial effort and a great deal of guile and guidance to create a competitive team.

There was one man, they agreed, who might be able to weave the magical spell necessary to create a unit from the disparate parts. Convincing him to take on such a job would also require some form of sorcery.

Páidí was approached to become coach to West Kerry. It came as a complete surprise. His first thought was of O'Dwyer's reaction. He knew it would not be positive. He thought about his impending marriage, the business, Kerry.

'Jesus, have I not enough to be doing,' he thought.

Men like Paul Scanlon, Derry Murphy and John O'Sullivan were persistent. He consulted with friends like Mícheál Ó Sé. O'Se told him, 'Think of everything you've learned. If anyone can get the lads to gell you can. They know you ... respect you.'

He thought about it.

He became irritable. This sort of hassle he did not need. Then a whisper in his ear. 'You know if West Kerry win the Championship next year who will captain Kerry in 1985.'

'I'll take it,' he told his pursuers.

'But for fuck's sake ... don't tell Dwyer.'

It wasn't long until Dwyer's famous network brought him the news from the peninsula. He was, in fact, less concerned than Páidí would have anticipated. As long as Páidí trained well with Kerry and kept his form, Dwyer felt that the responsibility of coaching the divisional team would be good for the player. It would help his discipline. Coaching and marriage would curtail any temptation to stray during the year ahead.

The appointment proved to be inspired. Páidí approached the role with zeal. It was infectious. The players responded. The once unwieldy collection of individuals became a unit. Páidí himself prospered. His role with Kerry had changed. He was now playing right corner-back. He was iffy about it when it was first mentioned but his respect for the manager was such that he agreed to try it. It worked.

Páidí and Maire had returned from their honeymoon in New York in time for him to participate in the final stages of the National League in April '84. Kerry discarded any notion that they were 'past it' by winning the League. They beat Galway by three points in the final.

Paidi was right corner-back, Vincent O'Connor was at full-back.

O'Dwyer was still making changes. Tom Spillane started that day at full-forward and moved to centre-forward. Jack O'Shea was the star of the show at midfield.

When the two teams met in the All-Ireland semi-final less than four months later Sean Walsh was at full-back and the youngest Spillane was at centre half-back. Jacko was still capturing all the headlines. *'Mighty Jack O'Shea'* was the headline in the *Irish Independent* over the report on Kerry's 2-17 to 0-11 victory.

In the *Irish Press* Peadar O'Brien was unimpressed with Galway. *Sadly, the only conclusion we can reach after this boringly dull and sometimes farcical All Ireland senior football semi-final at Croke Park yesterday, is that the standard of Galway football is at an all-time low.*

Kerry had simply scampered through the Championship, unchallenged and reached the All-Ireland final. Dublin, the reigning champions, provided the opposition. It was a new team. Only Mick Holden, Tommy Drumm, Brian Mullins and Anton O'Toole from the old guard remained.

Kids like Joe McNally were walking the walk.

Brian Cowen was sitting in the Hogan Stand and he recounts a tale. 'Those were the days when the players all went to their positions after the parade. There were no huddles then. Páidí was marking Joe McNally.

'When McNally arrived in his position Páidí stuck out his hand. McNally ignored it … kept running and dumped Páidí on his backside.

'There was a huge cheer from the Hill.

'It was the one time during a National Anthem at an All-Ireland final that I never looked at the flag. I kept my eye on Páidí to see what he would do because I knew he would so something. He gave the anthem sufficient respect and then just before the end he gave Joe the best toe up the arse I have ever seen.

'Joe had a quiet game.'

There were moments of concern for Kerry before the game. They had no jerseys! As the players went through their normal rituals in the dressing room just minutes before being called onto the field it was discovered that the bag containing the shirts was missing. It had been left on the bus.

But the bus was locked and the driver had taken up his seat somewhere in the stands. A call was made over the public address system and the driver was eventually located.

By the time Páidí received his shirt he was not in the sort of mood to put up with a young kid trying to bury him into the ground.

Kerry won by 0-14 to 1-6.

When it was all over he heaped praise on his colleagues. 'It was a fantastic display from our backs. This unit is as good as any I have played with and compares well with the backs of 1975. Sean Walsh and Tom Spillane were brilliant today.

'I was never really worried during the game. Generally I am finicky before a game but even last night I knew we would win. Dublin had not been tried or exposed before.'

Two weeks later West Kerry won the Kerry Championship. It was their first victory since 1948 and it was earned the hard way. The final score read 1-7 to 1-6.

A South Kerry team that contained Jacko, John Egan, Ger Lynch and Ger O'Driscoll had put up a stubborn fight. Kevin Maunsell kicked the winning point from a free, his sixth of the game, one minute from the end.

Páidí Ó Sé had weaved his spell.

He would also be Kerry captain in 1985.

—⟋⟍—

In the third week of March in '85 the builders moved onto Páidí's patch of land across the road from his mother's shop.

The site was cleared and levelled. 'Ten weeks boys,' he would tell them a couple of times a day.

'I want to be pulling pints here in 10 weeks.'

Before the foundations had been properly laid he was planning the opening ceremony. It would be the height of the tourist season; the football Championship would be reaching its peak.

The Kerry captain and his new pub.

That would surely attract a few headlines, the kind P Se liked. He also had a few other ideas that would help announce his new venture. Páidí and Maire were young and ambitious. Their enthusiasm never waned, despite the pressure.

He would rise early and cross the road to meet the men as they arrived for work. After spending some time with the builders he would drive over to Krugers, where he would hold the lease until July. He would make that journey a few times a day, driving over the Clasach, avoiding the tourist traffic that was growing summer after summer.

In the evening it was football. Kerry trained in Tralee that spring and summer. On alternate nights he was coaching West Kerry. They were games almost every Sunday. The GAA had introduced an open draw competition to celebrate the centenary year in 1984 and continued the competition between the end of the League and the start of the Championship in '85.

Páidí could have done without the distraction of the extra games. Typically, Kerry reached the final. On the last Sunday in May they played Cork in Pairc Ui Choimh and won comfortably. The new Kerry captain made his first victory speech.

There was hardly anyone around to hear it.

They played Limerick in the Munster semi-final and won by fifteen points. On and off the field targets were being met. So far, so good for Páidí as he chased his dreams. With Páidí on the road most of the time it was left to Maire to keep a watching brief at home. Family friend, Diarmuid O'Suilleabhain began organising the official opening of the new public house, issuing invitations and organising the entertainment.

On the week before the Munster final the final touches were being put to the new bar. The opening date of July 25 was a deadline that had to me met. Charlie Haughey, leader of the Opposition, had happily agreed to the invitation to perform the official opening and would arrive by helicopter.

'Just make sure you beat Cork first,' warned Haughey when he spoke to Páidí.

Cork.

In the midst of everything football had, for the first time, become secondary. He wasn't worried. He had been around the block so often then that he was happy he would be tuned in. The captaincy mattered to him. He wanted to be a winning captain and he certainly did not want to be the captain of a team beaten by Cork.

He was always tense before big games; 'wired' is how his teammates describe it. The captaincy added to the buzz. Others were just as nervous but were better at hiding it, or else hid in the toilets until it was time to leave.

The dressing rooms in Pairc Ui Chaoimh were so small they were almost claustrophobic. Dressing rooms were not built to accommodate someone like the Kerry captain. He was always manic, whooping and hollering, moving all the time, seeking a release of the emotions that cascaded through him. He needed space.

On the day of the Munster final Páidí was bouncing, the ball in his hands was almost a weapon. Some players were waiting for his speech. Others, Tommy Doyle and Charlie Nelligan in particular, were chatting and laughing in one corner.

Páidí was preaching fire and brimstone, expletives colouring the atmosphere. He bounced the ball. It was a weapon. It flew up and smashed the fluorescent light in the roof. Glass sprinkled everywhere.

Doyle and Nelligan were doubled over with laughter.

Páidí never noticed.

He was shouting and swearing, calling his men to arms.

Cork provided some resistance but Kerry won with a degree of comfort.

There was time for a few celebratory pints but that was all. He was in the District Court on the following Tuesday finalising licensing details. A few days later Charlie arrived through the clouds to perform the official opening. Steve Cooney and Seamus Begley provided the entertainment.

Tigh Páidí Ó Sé was packed for days.

People came from all corners of Ireland.

'It was amazing,' recalls Maire. 'He had made so many friends from his days in Limerick and they all came. They kept coming over the years. We had great support. There was music all the time. It was exciting. We had hoped it would be a success but I don't think we ever dreamed it would become so big.'

It wasn't all down to Páidí's football and contacts.

'He worked very hard at it,' says Maire. 'He was always thinking of new ideas, events to attract people to the pub ... especially outside the tourist months. You could find him anywhere around West Kerry putting up posters advertising whatever was going on. It didn't matter what the weather was like he was out there doing his thing."

Mícheál Ó Sé adds, 'There were many sides to Páidí – there was Páidí the footballer, Páidí the entertainer, Páidí the politician and Páidí the promoter.

'The promoter in him worked very hard. There was always something going on here. He would bring Sean Nos singers down from Connemara; he had singers like Dolores Keane, Mary Black, Finbarr Furey ... they all came. And there was never a charge on the door.

'The winter was just as important as the summer.

'When the tourists were gone Páidí made sure that there was something going on to entertain the locals. It might have been a game of cards, a quiz ... but there was always something. He never stopped working and that is why it was a success.'

His new responsibilities did not interrupt his football schedule. On the Sunday after the opening he lined out, at centre half-forward, for West Kerry in the Kerry Championship. They beat Austin Stacks by a single point, 0-12 to 0-11, with Kevin Maunsell again scoring the winning point from a free.

Kerry played Monaghan in the All-Ireland semi-final and the game finished in a draw. Kerry had not played well, almost certainly taking the Monaghan challenge lightly. That would not be allowed happen in the replay. They re-focused.

Monaghan had a decent team but Kerry would not give them a second chance. Páidí was more motivated than most and had an outstanding game in the replay. The captaincy had its benefits.

There were, however, signs that the Kerry team was showing its age. The *Irish Independent* reported, *Some of the parts are getting rusty, the engine does not run as sweetly anymore, but the Kerry machine is still a better model than most others. Their triumph over Monaghan yesterday was built on craft and know-how, with a little help from a surprisingly generous opposition.*

Age is beginning to take its toll this Kerry team. The heavy bandages on the legs of at least four players are giveaway signs of fatigue.

Paidi was bandage free and 'in sparkling form' according to the report.

The new pub was besieged in the build-up to the All-Ireland final. People from all over Ireland journeyed for the first time to the Dingle Peninsula, drawn by the publicity that the pub opening had generated and the fact that the owner was the captain of the Kerry football team who was in search of a seventh All-Ireland medal.

Amongst the journalists visiting were many of the familiar men whom Páidí had known and whose company he enjoyed. They noticed how Páidí Ó Sé was spelt above the door. Until then his name was written in English in newspaper reports about his exploits on the football field, Paud (or Paudie) O'Shea.

A feature in the sports pages of the *Irish Independent* on the Wednesday before the final was the first time 'Páidí' was used. It was done with reluctance. The journalist had also used 'Ó Sé' but the sub-editor had anglicised it. It was in the match reports the following Monday that the full Irish version was first used.

By the time his managerial career began the English version of his name had been jettisoned.

The captain appeared in many newspaper photographs that week but one photograph became particularly newsworthy. The Kerry players were pictured in a full page advertisement in the Sunday newspapers standing around a washing machine.

The sponsorship deal with Bendix was controversial for a number of reasons. The photograph showed the players standing around in shorts, or with towels covering their modesty. This was considered in poor taste.

Also, there were questions about the amount of money involved and whether the deal breached the GAA's amateur status. The Kerry Board got a rap on the knuckles from the authorities while it was widely reported that the players were rewarded with a sum of £5,000 to be paid into their holiday fund.

Páidí, as team captain, had been involved in the negotiations. He was concerned about funds that summer. Kerry were planning another holiday. They had called in a lot of favours in 1981 to fund their world tour. They could not go back to the same people again. When the Bendix offer came up Páidí seized on the opportunity.

Rather than settle for the £5,000 sum reported, Paidi and his fellow negotiators received a far bigger sum of £30,000.

The GAA's top brass would have keeled over if they knew that at the time.

—w—

Seanie Walsh remembers that final well. It was, he laughs, one of the few times in his life he was afraid of Páidí Ó Sé.

Páidí was his usual self.

Full of superstition. Last thing to come off in the dressing room were his socks. He was full of nervous energy, bouncing on his feet, dispensing advice, muttering to himself in Irish, cursing, snapping at people.

Then the game was going well. Kerry led by nine points at half time. Jack O'Shea was in brilliant form at midfield. Páidí was keeping another forward scoreless, Kieran Duff this time.

A speech had been prepared for him by his friend, Diarmuid. Lines kept coming to him. He tried to banish the thoughts from his mind.

'Don't tempt fate,' he told himself.

Dublin fought back. Joe McNally was playing full-forward and was marked by Walsh. He scored one goal when latching on to a breaking ball. A bit of good fortune for the lad whom Páidí had taken to the cleaners a year earlier. The margin was slowly coming down.

With about seven minutes to go a high ball was driven towards the Kerry goal. Páidí stuck close to Duff, didn't let him near it.

Seanie would take care of McNally.

'People didn't realise just how big McNally was,' says Walsh. 'I jumped with him. He swung a fist at the ball and connected. I heard the roar of the crowd before I realised it was in the back of our net. It wasn't the crowd that I was worried about. Páidí was glaring at me … and I could imagine what he was thinking.'

'His old pal had messed up.'

Kerry recovered from the setback. They quickly kicked a few points. The last seven minutes trickled by. When the final whistle went there was mayhem. He didn't see Páidí until they reached the sanctity of the security cordon in front of the Hogan Stand.

'Seanie boy,' said a beaming Páidí, ' …you fairly tested me today.'

The victory speech, delivered in Irish, was short and to the point.

Behind him Charlie Haughey sat, applauding. The Sam Maguire Cup would visit the Haughey home in Kinsealy before being brought back to Kerry and pride of place behind the bar at Ard an Bhothair.

—⚍—

Páidí loved Leinster House from the first day he visited. It had grandeur, style, mystery and history.

Just inside the door from Kildare Street – the back door, he would correctly point out – he would stop to admire the high ceilings; the paintings of famous politicians including Michael Collins, Cathal Brugha and Eamon De Valera, and the framed Proclamation from 1916.

Climbing the carpeted stairs that lead to the Dail chamber, he imagined some of the great world leaders like John F. Kennedy, being impressed with the exquisite architecture of the place.

He felt the sense of power coming from the walls. There was always a bustle in the corridors, the feeling that exciting things were happening. The people, politicians and civil servants, were buzzing with energy.

In the Dail bar he would identify faces from television and the newspapers. He was fascinated. As the years went by he himself became the focus of fascination from the politicians as his status as a footballer and then as a businessman grew.

Friends say his interest in politics began in his early days in secondary school. His loyalties were never in question. His support of Fianna Fail was unstinting. He was just 14 years-old when he canvassed for Chubb O'Connor in the South Kerry constituency. He later provided similar support for Johnny O'Leary and John O'Donoghue.

It was, almost certainly, O'Leary who first invited the young footballer into Dail Eireann in the mid-1970s. Páidí would be a regular visitor thereafter, though he did not confine his contact to Fianna Fail members.

'He loved the cut and thrust of politics,' says Maire.

'It is what attracted him to Dublin in many ways. He enjoyed the people in politics ... he loved the political scene. It didn't matter what party. He voted Fianna Fail but he enjoyed the company of politicians from every party.'

It was during one of those early visits to Johnny O'Leary that Páidí first met a young law student from Clara in Co. Offaly.

Brian Cowen, studying in UCD, had called to Leinster House to meet his father, Ber the Fianna Fail TD for Laois/Offaly. They shared more than an interest in politics. Cowen was a football fanatic as well who represented his native county at under-age level.

It was the start of a friendship that would grow over the next three decades. They met more often when Cowen entered politics himself in 1985, following the sudden death of his father. 'Páidí had a curious mind. He had many different types of friends – people in the arts, people in journalism, in business, politics … and, of course sport. He was interested in what people think,' the former Taoiseach recalls.

'He was shaped by the environment he lived in. I think you always get a feeling from the people in that part of the country that they do have a genuine pride in where they're from; that they are very conscious of the heritage, the rich heritage, from which they spring, their commitment to the Irish language and Irish culture in its broadest sense.

'That's not a phony thing … that's very much part of what they are and they are very proud of that and present it in a very attractive way. It is not the zeal of a convert, just a natural part of who they are.

'I always felt comfortable with that and I found him an interesting person to be with. We could be serious or we could be having a laugh. He was one of those people that you felt good after having spent time with him.

'Sometimes maybe we would spend a bit too much time together.

'He was passionate about things, including politics. He was also loyal, especially to his friends. He was loyal to what his view of life was, he didn't expect everyone else to share it but he felt it was more representative than it was being portrayed.

'He wasn't afraid to put himself out there. There are a lot of people who decide not to put themselves out there and there is nothing wrong with that. His personality was such that he was never going to be a 'don't know'. He was either a 'yes' or a 'no' man and I admire that,' says Cowen.

Páidí had many friends in politics and not all of them were affiliated with Fianna Fail. He was very fond of Pat Rabbitte, the senior Labour party politician. Rabbitte's deep love for Mayo football helped form their bond. But they could also argue about social policies, about politics in general and their friendship was never in doubt.

He got to know the current Taoiseach, Enda Kenny extremely well. Again, football was a factor but their friendship was based on more. People like Rabbitte and Kenny accepted that Páidí was a Fianna Fail supporter and that they would never change him. They wouldn't insult his intelligence by trying to.

Sport and politics never caused a conflict for Páidí, except when it was manufactured. During the European Elections of 2009 he was asked if he would vote for Sean Kelly, the man who had first appointed him as Kerry manager.

Kelly was standing as a Fine Gael candidate. The question was meaningless. Páidí said he would not vote for Kelly. The headlines suggested a lack of loyalty to a man who had been loyal to him, despite the fact that Kelly never expected Ó Sé's support in a political battle. Their friendship was never in danger.

Brian Cowen goes on: 'In politics I have never had a problem with people disagreeing with me. We all know through the history of politics many of us are a certain affiliation because of the people before us. That's the one irrational part of our being in one sense but what you do is say that's where I'm coming from, that's my tradition and I'm going to work in that tradition to do whatever bit of good I'm intending to do anyway.

'You can do that and have mutual respect for people who come from another tradition. Páidí never had a problem developing friendships with people who in every other respect might like him but disagreed with his politics.

'I found that myself.

'He liked politics and respected the institutions of the state. He was a person who wanted to see his country go well … his community go well and he understood that politics was part of how we progress, whether we like it or not. It is the system we know and he was always anxious to be part of that democratic system.

'He valued citizenship and believed in being involved and participating; he didn't want to stand behind the counter or sit on the fence and prognosticate about everyone's limitations and not do anything at all himself. He had a positive outlook and he participated. He felt he had to be involved because he felt it was the way to know what was going on.

'You saw that in terms of some of the projects he was involved in. He liked contributing and bringing a point of view that was legitimate. He was well able to articulate it.

'He liked community life.

'It was one of the reasons his tournament meant so much to him. In a lean part of the year the B&B's would be full, the pubs were busy and his own business was busy as well and that's fine because you can have benign self interest allied to a wider community benefit.'

As 1985 came to a close Páidí was in the place he wanted to be – All-Ireland winning captain of Kerry and master of his own destiny.

CHAPTER 7

He never saw the end coming. Yes, there had been some alarms that had given him pause to ponder but only in hindsight did he recognise the signals.

On the night of June 25, 1988, he had arrived back from a game in Beaufort in time to help out behind the bar. The usual weekend crowd was swelled by locals and tourists anxious to watch boxer, Barry McGuigan's latest comeback fight which was being screened by RTE.

Normally, Páidí would have taken an interest himself. He admired McGuigan, the tough and wiry little guy from Clones who had lost his world title a couple of years earlier but was slowly re-building his career. But on this night Páidí was serving up pints with heads that he would have sent back himself.

'What's wrong with you tonight?' one offended punter enquired.

'Yes, what is wrong?' asked Maire.

'Dwyer.' The answer was abrupt. She knew she would eventually hear what the manager had done this time.

It was just eight days to the Munster final.

The Beaufort GAA club had opened their new clubhouse that evening. Mick O'Dwyer and his selectors had used the occasion to hold an unofficial trial. Probables versus Possibles.

Páidí was given a Possibles jersey!

Mick Spillane, Tom Spillane and a new kid from Tralee, Morgan Nix, formed the Probables full-back line.

'Is he messing with my head?' Páidí asked no one in particular.

'Who else was on your team?' asked his friend, Diarmuid.

He had to think. 'The Private (Tommy Doyle) was beside me. Powery … Jacko came on as a sub. Mick Galwey was full-forward. Jesus, what's going on? He's playing games. Dwyer's up to something.'

Despite the placatory noises from his friends Páidí remained unsettled. The game had been a mismatch. He was chasing the play. Young Gerard Murphy had given him the slip once or twice. Páidí had been caught watching Maurice Fitzgerald once, Spillane (Pat) another time. Trying to do too much instead of minding his own patch.

He heard the delighted roars of the crowd in the pub. McGuigan had delivered a knockout blow to Tomas Da Cruz in the fourth round. Páidí developed a sense of foreboding.

Another pint poured without due care and attention earned him a final rebuke. 'Go back across the road and don't wake the child,' he was warned. The thought of little Neasa, their first child born on May 11, softened his mood.

Over the next few days a sense of optimism began to return. He had assessed his situation and come to the conclusion that his selection on the Possibles team did not reflect a new status. He hadn't missed a Championship game for Kerry since 1974. He had played 52 Championship games in those 14 years, collected 12 Munster Championships and eight All-Ireland Championships.

Yes, the old team was breaking up and there were a growing number of new faces at each training session. Seanie Walsh and Mikey had quit after the 1987 Championship. 'The Bomber' and Jacko were carrying injuries.

They were all getting older. But he was enjoying the gaiety and enthusiasm the youngsters brought into the dressing room. Young Maurice Fitzgerald had been promoted a year before and it was no burden to train and play with the magical kid from Cahirciveen.

Páidí had wintered quietly, opting out of the National Football League. He returned to training in the spring, having prepared himself at home and on Ventry beach. The manager expressed some surprise at his condition when he arrived back in April. 'Being doing a bit of sneaky work to try and cod me,' joked O'Dwyer.

Waterford were travelling to Tralee for the first round of the Munster Championship on May 29. Páidí played a few challenge games.

O'Dwyer and the selectors were happy to pitch him in as usual at right full-back. Waterford had a couple of teenage forwards, guys with quick feet like Derek Wyse from the St Saviours club. That would test Sé.

It was a test he passed comfortably.

The teenage Decies player was never a match for his opponent, Paudie O' Shea. The Gaeltacht man was a real tour de force on Sunday and there was much to admire about his surging out of defence. But, no doubt, it's tougher the going will get, wrote Eamon Horan in *The Kerryman* the following week.

Kerry won by 3-19 to 1-7.

As training for the Munster final intensified, Páidí felt good about himself. He wasn't as quick as before and he was carrying more weight. But he still believed he was playing sufficiently well. Dwyer was pushing him hard all the time but that was always the way, so Páidí thought.

In fact, O'Dwyer was worried. In practice games he had played a number of the younger forwards on Páidí and they had given him the sort of trouble that Páidí would not have had a couple of years before. There was a big decision to be made. The 'trial' game in Beaufort suddenly became a more significant event.

It cannot have been a comfortable few weeks for O'Dwyer and his selectors. Liam Higgins was not just a great friend of Páidí's, he remained an ardent admirer. Tim 'The Horse' Kennelly had soldiered with him on and off the field. Eddie 'Tatler' O'Sullivan had befriended him a decade before in New York and their bond became greater when 'Tatler' came back to Ireland. Kevin Griffin was also well acquainted with Páidí .

Páidí trained as usual on the Tuesday evening before the Munster final and headed home as the selectors retired to make their final choices. He expected to be named in the line-up and smiled when he heard the news on the radio from Cork. Dinny Allen was back after four years out of favour.

'Jesus Christ, fair play to you, Billy Morgan,' Páidí chortled. His old pal

Morgan, now the Cork coach, had been trying to get Allen back into the Cork colours for three seasons despite fierce opposition from elements within the County Board.

'Would you believe it … Páidí versus Dinny … 15 years later!' he thought.

Reality struck with brutal effect the following morning.

The Kerry team was made public.

The full back line read M Spillane, T Spillane, M Nix.

Páidí was dropped. For the first time since 1973 Kerry would start a Championship game without him. He had played 52 Championship games, been taken off once and was sent off once. Now he would wear the No.16 jersey on a bench that included Ogie, 'Bomber' and Powery, as well as Donal McEvoy and Joe Shannon.

He was dumbstruck. There had been no warning. Rightly or wrongly in those days a player did not get a phone call when he was dropped. It had never occurred to him before because it had never happened.

He was a forlorn figure in Pairc Ui Chaoimh. Dinny Allen scored a goal and a point. Powery and 'Bomber' were brought on. So was Joe Shannon. Páidí remained rooted to the bench and was seething. A massive brawl broke out at the end.

Páidí sat on his hands in the dug out. Furious.

Cork 1-14, Kerry 0-16.

A one point defeat, and Dinny had scored 1-1.

'He wouldn't have scored all of that if I was out there,' he muttered angrily to O'Dwyer as he left the field. It was a line he repeated to Tom O'Riordan in the dressing room before making a quick departure.

The mood within the Kerry camp was becoming rancorous. Páidí kept his counsel. Others did not.

In an interview with Radio na Gaeltachta a few days later Liam Higgins vented his frustration. A former teammate of O'Dwyer – they had won two All-Ireland titles side by side in the Kerry full-forward line in 1969 and 1970 – Higgins revealed that he had felt isolated in his role as a selector that season. The interview was conducted by Mícheál Ó Sé, another member of that

1969-70 Kerry team.

'I think it is time that Mick O'Dwyer stepped down as manager, at least temporarily,' Higgins said.

'By temporarily do you mean six months ... or something like that?' questioned Ó Sé.

'I would have a longer period than that in mind,' Higgins replied.

Naturally, it created a storm nationally. Higgins intimated that O'Dwyer was no longer listening to his selectors, either at selection meetings or during games. He also said that O'Dwyer found it difficult to drop older players, that he showed a preference for those who were loyal to him.

'For Christ's sake," said Páidí when that remark was repeated to him. 'He didn't find it difficult to drop me.'

Adding to his wounds were the reports of the final. Under a heading *A triumphant return for Dinny Allen* in *The Kerryman* John Joe Brosnan wrote, *He looked very sharp from the start and quickly demonstrated that the old footballing brain was as keen as ever. He was able to make space for himself and his passes to other players and particularly across the field to Shea Fahy immediately after the start of the second half had real class about them.*

Páidí threw down the paper in disgust. 'And where was I while he was making those passes? On my arse on a plank of wood, that's where.'

When the *Sunday Independent* appeared, the dropping of Páidí featured prominently. Tom O'Riordan, who was closely associated with the Kerry camp, provided a fascinating account of what had happened in the days before the final.

He wrote, *It was against a background of disagreement and dissatisfaction that Kerry selector Liam Higgins called on Mick O'Dwyer to step down for a period following the county's defeat by Cork in last Sunday's Munster final.*

The tension began to build up among the selectors five days before the game, the night they met to pick the team. When it came to right corner-back Paudie O'Shea was proposed and seconded. It seemed to be a formality as O'Shea had played in that berth in every Championship since '83, winning three All-Ireland medals in the position.

A third selector also voiced an opinion in favour of O'Shea and that virtually assured him of the position. He was, at that time, officially selected. It was then that

Mick Spillane was proposed and seconded for the same position. Mick had played in the left corner throughout his career but it seemed unanimous among the selectors that Morgan Nix would now fill that vacancy.

It was the opinion of one selector that if Mick Spillane was not selected it might upset his two brothers, Tom and Pat, who captained the side. Eventually a second vote was taken and this time it favoured Spillane by 3-2. Effectively that vote also served to remove O'Shea from the team and that had every reason to upset Higgins, who represents the interests of West Kerry, for whom O'Shea has played all his life.

In light of developments that night it would not be surprising to some that Higgins should have come out as he did, asking for O'Dwyer to take a break. O'Shea was fuming after Sunday's defeat and pointed a critical finger at the Kerry defence prior to storming out of the ground.

Nevertheless, O'Dwyer, Higgins and their fellow selectors must take criticism for their lack of action during the final. Cork won on the field of play – but they also won the game on the sideline. The switching of Larry Tompkins to midfield with Teddy McCarthy taking over at centre-forward proved a master stroke.

The Kerry selectors might be excused for not instructing Ambrose O'Donovan to follow Tompkins but where they must carry total blame is their abysmal failure to repair the situation at midfield midway through the second half when Jack O'Shea and Dermoit Hanafin began to tire. That was visible for all to see but, while Hanafin was replaced, the move came far too late.

O'Riordan then posed the following, *It has been said all along that the placing of Tom Spillane at full back was a big loss to Kerry's outfield strength. Why then did the selectors not bring Spillane out to midfield? O'Shea would have benefitted from the less taxing position at full-back and Spillane, a player full of reserves, would have been just the man, with pace and energy, to diminish the effectiveness of Tompkins.*

—⁂—

Much later in life Páidí admitted that the final curtain had begun to fall shortly after Kerry had won the All-Ireland Championship under his captaincy in 1985. He had pledged his support for Tommy Doyle's captaincy in 1986 but the toll of so many long summer campaigns was showing, mentally as well as physically.

In his 20s Páidí had nothing to worry him except Kerry football. In his 30s, when the body is naturally slowing down, he had other onerous responsibilities. He was married, running a thriving business and making plans for the future. And he was managing the West Kerry team and they were winning Championships.

In his 20s he had sweated off the effects of celebrations with ease. By the mid-1980s that was getting more difficult. 'I think the celebrations began to get longer and the recovery period became shorter,' he would explain. 'It should have been the other way around.'

Kerry went through the motions of the National League between October '85 and March of '86. They won three matches, including one on a scoreline of 0-5 to 0-4 against Roscommon, and escaped relegation from Division One with a win over Kildare in Tralee.

P Ó Sé did not appear on any teamsheets.

He was back in training shortly after the League. By the time Kerry beat Tipperary in the Championship he was back in the usual spot. He stayed there for the Munster final against Cork. Kerry were going through the motions. It was enough. Kerry won a forgettable game by four points, 0-12 to 0-8.

The *Irish Independent* described the game in less than enthusiastic terms. *Even the clouds which clothed the mountains around Killarney shed a little tear yesterday. Kerry, arguably the greatest team ever, looked sadly ordinary as Cork still could find neither strength or character to end a decade of frustration and Kerry's reigns as Munster and national champions.*

It is probably a result of their conditioning over the last ten years that Cork find it so hard to even believe they can beat Kerry. Yesterday the champions showed that even they are affected by the ageing process but Cork were unable to exploit this obvious factor.

Meath provided a new challenge in the All-Ireland semi-final. Páidí, who had barely played a part in the Munster final, found himself facing a new danger. Bernard Flynn was a new kid on the block but he was unconcerned about reputation or surroundings. He was born to play in Croke Park. Their early exchanges were even. Then, just before half time and with the teams' level, the diminutive Meath kid shoved Páidí Ó Sé out of his way and kicked the ball over the bar.

It was Flynn's only score from play. He also kicked four frees, winning one by drawing a foul from his marker. Páidí survived but it had been a close call.

He was far more relaxed in the weeks before the final. He had become more wholehearted in his training and felt the better for it. The pub was busy. The collection of photographs was taking up more space on the walls. Visitors from Dublin particularly admired the montage from the 1979 final that captured his 'tackle' on Anton O'Toole.

It was a strange time for Páidí and his old comrades.

Páidí, Mikey, Ogie, Spillane and Powery were attempting to win their eighth All-Ireland senior football medal, a record, but there was surprisingly little hype. Tyrone had qualified for the final for the first time and that certainly commanded a lot of the attention in the media. They also had some exceptional players like Ciaran McGarvey, Kevin McCabe, Plunkett Donaghy, Eugene McKenna and Damien O'Hagan.

Páidí was marking Paudge Quinn, a fellow publican. Sean McNally was at left half-forward and his blonde head was popping up everywhere. Tyrone were the newcomers but they played like they were the old stagers. Jacko hit a penalty off the crossbar after two minutes and Tyrone began to believe.

The Kerry No.2 was doing okay, minding his patch, sticking close to Quinn. Donaghy was surprised by a quick line ball from McCabe and booted it high downfield.

Páidí watched.

Tom Spillane waited for the ball to drop. McKenna came from behind, Seanie Walsh trailing him. The two Kerrymen ran into each other.

O'Hagan burst onto the ball and headed for goal.

Páidí had a split second to make a decision.

He went to O'Hagan. The ball was handpassed to Quinn and he finished it neatly beyond Charlie.

Tyrone were six points ahead. They got a penalty. Kevin McCabe drove it over the bar. Spillane covered acres of ground, got on the end of a pass from Powery and flicked a goal. Mikey scored another. Tyrone lost McKenna to an achilles tendon injury. Without their leader they lost shape and the title.

Páidí had medal number eight. His performance in the final was lauded. *He certainly played his best game of 1986,* the *Independent* declared.

Tyrone's fifteen can hold their heads high this morning. Great credit is due for their efforts. Once again that mighty machine from Kerry has come through the most demanding test. Old men how are ye!

O'Dwyer rested some of the old men, including Páidí, for the pre-Christmas League games. He could not subject them to rigorous training and he remained blissfully disinterested in the League. Yet when the springtime came around in 1987 there were signs of life in some of the old dogs. Spillane was in flying form. Mikey was played some great football, especially in the League semi-final against Monaghan.

Without trying Kerry qualified for the final of the League. They played Dublin in front of an attendance of 35,181 on April 26, 1987. It was the last time Páidí Ó Sé would play in his beloved Croke Park.

Dublin won by 1-11 to 0-11.

O'Dwyer was already planning for the Championship.

The journey should have ended in Pairc Ui Chaoimh on July 26, 1987. Kerry were two points down as the game went into injury time. Páidí took a late free inside the Cork half. He wanted to land it on the edge of the square but barely lifted it off the ground. 'Bomber' tried to get the ball but it squirted away. After a frantic 15 seconds Mikey Sheehy squeezed the ball into the net. One point up.

Cork goalkeeper, John Kerins took a quick free out. Cork won a free. Larry Tompkins stroked it over the bar.

A draw.

They met a week later in Killarney. A Kerry forward line containing John Kennedy, Jack O'Shea, Pat Spillane, Mikey, 'Bomber' and Powery scored one point from play. Admittedly, Power spent more of the game on the bench than on the field having been sent off during the first half.

Cork won by 0-13 to 1-5.

It should have been more comfortable such was their dominance.

In the dressing room all was quiet. O'Dwyer was tearful as he spoke to his players. His words were recorded by Tom O'Riordan. 'You have given 13 wonderful years of service to the game. You have been fantastic in every way and I want to thank you all for your total loyalty and dedication.

Páidí and Maire Ó Sé with their daughters, Neasa and Siún.

*Páidí and his son, Padraig give a thumbs up
to life on and off the football field.*

Páidí and his eldest daughter, Neasa (above) – and Páidí and Neasa at an earlier meeting!

Maire, Siún and Páidí.

Páidí and Padraig.

Páidí and his children enjoy Central Park, New York City.

The best of American 'royalty', including Dolly Parton (above) have visited Páidí in his pub in Ventry over the years, but Páidí also loved visiting the United States himself – here he is in New York with his family and his nephew, Marc.

Páidí with Neasa, Siún, and holding forth himself.

Mickey Ned O'Sullivan leads the Kerry team during the pre-match parade before the 1975 All-Ireland final win over Dublin.

Páidí (right) with Paudie Lynch and Dublin's Brian Mullins close to the end of Kerry's storming All-Ireland victory in 1975 over Kevin Heffernan's All-Ireland champions.

The Dublin team that won the All-Ireland title in 1974.

Kevin Heffernan, who built the greatest Dublin team of all time in the 1970s, but failed to stop Páidí Ó Sé and Kerry from proving themselves the greatest football team of all time.

Páidí (second from left on front row) before Kerry reaffirmed their superiority over Dublin with victory in the 1978 All-Ireland final.

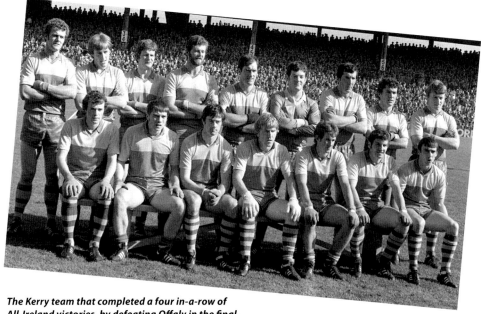

*The Kerry team that completed a four in-a-row of
All-Ireland victories, by defeating Offaly in the final.*

*Kerry's dream of a 'famous five' All-Ireland wins goes up in smoke as Offaly's Seamus Darby cracks the ball
over the despairing dive of Charlie Nelligan in the 1982 All-Ireland final.*

Páidí leads the Kerry team on the pre-match parade before the 1985 All-Ireland final win over Dublin.

Páidí is shoulder high, as Mick O'Dwyer awaits to congratulate his captain, after victory over Dublin in 1985.

The Sam Maguire Cup is lifted high after Kerry's victory over Dublin in the 1985 All-Ireland final.

*The Kerry 'Jubilee team' that won All-Ireland titles in 1984,
'85 and '86 is honoured during the 2009 All-Ireland final.*

*Jack O'Shea collects the ball as Kerry dominate Dublin and set off on another three in-a-row by defeating
their greatest rivals in the 1984 All-Ireland final.*

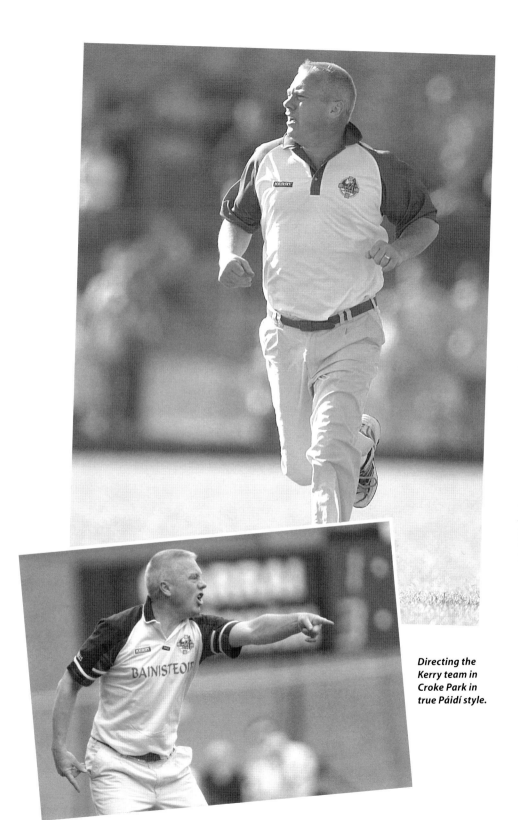

Directing the Kerry team in Croke Park in true Páidí style.

A family affair: Páidí hugs his nephew Darragh after they both led Kerry to the 1997 All-Ireland final win over Mayo.

Páidí enjoys the final minutes of Westmeath's win over Dublin in the Leinster championship.

Páidí at work in Croke Park as he delivers a Leinster title to the people of Westmeath in 2004.

'The Master' Mick O'Dwyer congratulates Páidí after West-meath's epic victory over Laois in the Leinster final in 2004.

Celebrating with his right hand man, Tomas O Flatharta after Westmeath's victory over Laois in the Leinster final replay in 2004.

Páidí and Tomas celebrate the Leinster triumph in South Africa.

Páidí has prayer and the people of Clare on his side as he is announced as county manager.

Páidí puts his faith in the Clare team before the start of the 2007 Munster championship.

GRADAIM AN UACHTARÁIN
PRESIDENT'S AWARDS

March 2013: The Ó Sé family after they were presented with the GAA President's Award for 2013 (from left): Páidí's wife, Maire, Liam O'Neill, president of the GAA, Páidí's daughter Siún, and his son Pádraig Óg.

Páidí and his daughter Neasa at the 2012 GAA GPA All-Star awards.

'I know some of you will be thinking of retirement but I ask you not to make any final decisions immediately. You have been a credit to yourselves and the game of football. It has been a privilege to work with this team and I just want to say thanks a million.'

O'Riordan spoke to 'Bomber'. 'I think it's time to pull down the tent and move on. The circus is over – it's time for a new act.'

He ruled out retiring. So too did Power. Seanie and Mikey could go on no longer. Their aching limbs screamed for mercy.

'What are you going to do Páidí?' everyone asked.

'We'll see in time,' was his answer. Deep down he knew. He couldn't stop. What else would he do without football.

In the *Irish Press*, Martin Breheny captured the mood. *Even true greatness falls prey to the clawing persistence of time. The greatest team ever to play Gaelic football heard the somber voice of fate telling them their time was up and although Kerry pleaded with their pride to give them one more chance it couldn't rescue them in this historic Munster football final replay in Killarney.*

He went on, *For Kerry it was the deepest of depressions as they tried to reconcile an awful performance with the magic which put them so high on the pedestal in the first place.*

For neutrals there was a strange sense of sadness. Nobody begrudged Cork their first Munster title since 1983 but it was difficult not to feel sorry for Kerry and their great band of players who had given so much to Gaelic football since they swaggered on to the stage with all their fresh faced enthusiasm in 1975.

—※—

Over the winter months of 1988-89 walkers on Ventry beach got used to a familiar sight. Páidí Ó Sé, publican and footballer, was getting back to business.

He pounded the sand and when he wanted to test himself more he pounded the surf. An Gaeltacht were going well in the West Kerry League. They hadn't won anything in years and there was a bit of interest building locally.

Páidí was playing at full-back and playing well. He was also feeling good, ready to have another crack with Kerry. Sean Walsh, his old pal and teammate, had replaced Liam Higgins on the Kerry selection committee as part of the fall-out from the 1988 campaign. That put a smile on Páidí 's face.

His club form was reported to O'Dwyer. He spoke to Walsh. 'We should bring him back in and have a look at him,' they agreed. Páidí 's return to training with Kerry was duly noted by the local newspapers.

Without Páidí, Kerry had put a run together. They lost the opening two games of the League but then went on a run of five victories in-a-row, with Meath and Dublin included amongst those conquered. They beat Antrim in the quarter-final and set up another big clash with Cork in the semi-final.

Michael McAuliffe had enjoyed a good winter. He had scored 4-8 in eight games. 'Bomber' had scored 2-7. Jacko was also going well. Spillane was Spillane. Maurice was having a bit of hamstring bother but was piling up the scores, 1-24 in seven games.

They had scored more than one hundred points, 102 (10-72) to be precise in eight games. And they had conceded 78 points (5-63). That was the statistic that interested Páidí.

Tom Spillane was playing full-back. Ger Lynch was in one corner. Ken Savage was getting a chance in the full-back line as well.

Over 25,000 spectators attended the League semi-final in Pairc Ui Chaoimh. Kerry scored just four points in 70 minutes. Maurice got three, two from frees. Spillane got the other. Cork scored 10 points, were comfortable winners. It didn't look good for Kerry.

Even during the good days Mick O'Dwyer had to face his critics. Now they were lining up while O'Dwyer tried to halt the slide. A month before the start of the Championship in 1989 Eric Browne, an Under-21 selector from Listowel, was severely critical of selection policy. He felt younger players were not being given a chance to establish themselves.

And he was also critical of the way Páidí and some of his teammates had been treated a year earlier. *These men, who have given 12 years of their lives to Kerry football, deserved to be told in person that they were being dropped. Hearing it on the radio and seeing it on the newspapers was just not good enough. Two great servants of Kerry football deserved some bit of courtesy.*

An Gaeltacht qualified for the West Kerry League final. They played Lispole in Pairc an Aghasaigh in Dingle on May 9. A good display and Páidí thought he might convince O'Dwyer that he was ready for a return; make up for last year and all that.

With five minutes remaining An Gaeltacht led by two points. The referee, Tommy Sugrue, awarded Lispole a penalty. Gabriel Casey drove it wide.

Páidí heaved a sigh of relief.

With two minutes left Páidí thought it was done. He had marked his old friend, Liam Higgins and kept him scoreless. Then Liam's brother, Denis appeared before him, ball in hand and heading for goal.

Two on one.

'Just like fucking Tyrone,' thought Páidí . It made up his mind.

He performed what can best be described as a body-check on Higgins. It was a sickening clash, involving heads. Higgins suffered multiple fractures to his head; Páidí almost lost an ear. His injuries required 32 stitches and an overnight stay in Tralee General. He woke to the news that he had also been sent off by the referee for his actions.

He recovered in time to resume training with Kerry in the few weeks leading up to the Munster final. But the feel-good factor was gone. He felt it the first night back. O'Dwyer's enthusiasm for his return had waned, if it had ever reached any sort of level in the first place. The two warriors had not communicated well since the summer of '88. Páidí still harboured hurt over his dropping; Micko was putting what he thought was the good of Kerry before personal relationships. They did talk, but it could not be described as communicating.

Páidí had lost valuable time. He knew it himself. This time he read the lines perfectly. Whatever chance he might have had of a comeback with a clear run to the Cork game, his injury had scuppered it.

Three weeks before the Munster final he was playing a club game in Kenmare. That morning he chatted with Maire, six months pregnant with their second child. 'Will you come to the match with me today ... leave Neasa with Beatrice?' he asked. She said yes.

On the way home that evening he turned to Maire.

'That's it … my last game.'

Veteran reporter, Eamon Horan and photographer, Martin Cleary travelled from Tralee to Ventry on Wednesday, July 5, 1989. Horan had built up a decent relationship with Páidí over the years and was trusted. A former champion handballer, he was always polite and unobtrusive when dealing with the Kerry players.

Páidí had an announcement to make.

On the front page of *The Kerryman*, published on July 7, 1989 under the headline *Paudie O'Shea hangs up his boots*. Horan quoted Páidí, *'I've decided to call it a day once and for all. My main reason for retiring is that I was not able to play football to the standard I wanted to play to. If I could not do that then it was time to call halt. I was preparing myself for the Munster final. I was dying to get another crack at Cork and I felt we could beat them this year.*

'Basically when I could not attain the proper level of fitness I desired, I said no to going any further.

'I suppose you could say I am both disappointed and glad at the same time. I am disappointed that I am not involved. Everything I do, even among my own family, revolves around football.'

In a tribute Horan wrote with great emotion about the player. *Over the years the grim-faced West Kerryman has been the bane of forward lines up and down the country: few defenders could tackle as hard and as relentlessly as Paudie could. In plain clothes he could deceive one. But once he togged out and put on that green and gold shirt then suddenly he assumed a physical stature which was as intimidating as it was unnerving.*

Thousands of Kerry followers have cheered the former Garda as he battled with might and main against the pretenders to football's biggest honours. It didn't matter whether it was Cork, Dublin, Tyrone or Roscommon who were providing the opposition, O'Shea was the rock on which many's the lusty attack perished.

And so Gaelic football says farewell to one of its most colourful and exciting stars. As they say, ins an teanga duchais – ni bheidh a leithead ann aris.'

Cork again defeated Kerry in the Munster final in Killarney.

Páidí took no pleasure in it. He was already looking to the future. O'Dwyer announced his resignation. Páidí began planning.

Away from football Páidí was fully occupied with the business. The family was also expanding. Siún was born on September 25.

And still Páidí could not leave football behind.

CHAPTER 8

On a warm summer afternoon the telephone behind the bar summoned attention. Páidí was on bar duty so he answered himself. An excited voice on the other end brought welcome news. 'Mick O'Connell's just landed in Dingle and he says he's on his way out to see you.'

It was just the tonic needed.

Páidí was not settling well in 1990 without Kerry football to occupy him. Yes, the business was going well and there were plenty of visitors traversing around Slea Head, dropping in to say hello and exchange a few yarns.

But Páidí found himself fidgeting. He wasn't happy, just could not get Kerry out of his system. Now, following the phone call, he had a welcome distraction. Something to focus on.

He heard the noises of boys playing outside the pub. Through the windows he spotted his young nephew, Marc, then just 10 years-old. There were five or six others with him. Naturally, they had a football. Páidí hatched a plan.

'Boys,' he called, 'one of the greatest footballers ever to wear the green and gold is on his way. His name is Mick O'Connell. And I am depending on you fellas to show what great footballers we have in West Kerry.'

Wide-eyed the kids listened as Páidí outlined his plan. He pointed to the gable end of the church beyond the boundary wall of the pub. Two stained glass windows would serve as goalposts, a sash the width of the wall acting as a crossbar.

In the middle of the crossbar was a rusty hook. It probably held a flower basket or some other decoration in the past. Páidí didn't know.

'What we'll do now boys is ... we'll take kicks from here and we'll hit that rusty yoke in the middle. If one of you does it even once that will impress O'Connell.'

Páidí decided to give a practical demonstration. He took the ball from Marc and steadied himself. He took a couple of steps and then kicked the ball.

He was off balance.

The ball screwed off his foot and flew into the stained glass window nearest the road, smashing it. 'Okay lads, get out of here. We'll leave it off ... I'll sort something.'

The youngsters heard nothing more about the incident and assumed Páidí had worked his magic with the Parish Priest. That lasted until the following Sunday and the weekly sermon. The wrath of the PP swept over them as he castigated the young boys of the parish for their lack of care for the House of God.

'They have great role models in this parish to follow and still they act like scoundrels.'

After mass the boys watched in astonishment as Páidí and the Monsignor stood side by side in serious conversation. 'It's a terrible thing,' they heard Páidí saying, 'but I guarantee you I won't rest till I find out what happened. And when I find out who it was – and I don't care if he's a blood relation – I'll make sure he knows the error of his ways.'

The Monsignor nodded, smiling benignly at Páidí . 'It was as if he knew he was being codded but it was alright because it was Páidí,' says Marc.

—⁂—

Dara O Cinneide probably should have known better. But he had excuses – he was young and was suffering from extreme pain and discomfort.

In such circumstances he allowed himself to be left in the care of the most unlikely medic of them all. Páidí.

It was the evening of September 10, 1995, and Kerry were celebrating victory in the All-Ireland Under-21 Championship. The dressing-room in Semple Stadium was packed with well-wishers and O Cinneide sought sanctuary in the showers.

During the first half of the All-Ireland final replay against Mayo he was involved in an accidental collision. He took a heavy blow to the right side of the face. Clearly shaken, he asked to remain on the field and the initial evidence suggested that would be a reasonable course of action.

He played the entire game and scored a crucial goal in the second half. But all the time the pain in his face intensified. Each time he put a hand to his jaw he felt the swelling worsen. By the end even speech was difficult.

'I actually believed my jaw was broken,' he says. 'I had a big lump, like as if a golf ball was wedged between my gums and my cheek.'

Arrangements were being made for the return to Kerry. 'They had organised a parade in Tralee. Imagine?' recalls O Cinneide. 'A parade for an Under-21 team. I suppose it shows how desperate we were at the time.'

Concern was expressed for the state of their young top scorer. Medical care had been properly provided but it was clear that there was a need for further examination. That was when Páidí, the Under-21 team manager, intervened.

'He nabbed me. Said "I'm taking care of Dara" and that was that.'

They got to the car.

Dara sat in the back, an ice pack held to his face, feeling just a small bit sorry for himself. Páidí looked around. 'If you think I'm taking you to hospital tonight of all nights you better think again.'

Dr Páidí had his own methods for diagnosis that would not have received the approval of the Medical Council.

They got as far as the Five Alley's bar outside Nenagh. Páidí ordered sandwiches. 'He thought if I could eat them that the jaw couldn't be broken,' O Cinneide explains. The sandwiches remained untouched until Páidí decided they could not go to waste.

They moved on.

In Castleisland they stopped at the Poet's Inn. Pints were ordered. O Cinneide was able to swallow fluid. His minder took that as a good sign.

Guinness was the right form of medicine.

And so the craic started. Locals wandered in. They were unimpressed by Kerry's victory. A local lad, highly rated within the GAA community of the town, had failed to make the team. They began to vent their ire at the manager. He listened silently and patiently for a while. Then he responded.

'Let me tell you why that lad wasn't picked. That lad wasn't picked because he is from Castleisland. And Castleisland is too far away from the sea and no player living too far away from the sea can be good enough to play for Kerry.'

They left quietly, sneaking an odd look over their shoulders until they were safely out of town. The only danger they actually faced was from the driver, Páidí, who was convulsed with laughter at what had just taken place.

Arrival in Tralee coincided with the beginning of the victory parade. They joined the rest of the squad as they were ferried through the centre of Tralee. Further exploration of the damaged jaw was delayed until the following day.

—៣៣—

In hindsight, though Páidí would only very reluctantly admit it, he was lucky that his attempts to become the Kerry senior football manager in 1989 and again in 1992 came to nothing.

The rejections hurt, surely, but they also stoked the fires of his ambition. Not only did he feel he had something to contribute, he also felt that he had something to prove.

After the splendour of the Golden Years, which had a period of relative continuity and harmony, Kerry football was in transition. The dominance of the senior team obscured other realities. At under-age level Kerry were not competing with the regularity expected in the All-Ireland series.

For example, Kerry won three All-Ireland Under-21 titles in a row between 1975 and '77 but did not win another title until Vincent Knightly led the 1990 team to success.

When the senior team broke up after the 1989 Championship a complete re-construction process had to be undertaken. A Kerry public and many within the upper echelons of the GAA in the county which had become sated by success also became impatient. The pressure on a manager like Mickey Ned O Sullivan and his young players was immense. They needed time and it was the one thing they would not be given.

Young players were asked to assume too much responsibility. That was no one's fault. It was necessary because they were the best players available. And the critics overlooked the fact that Billy Morgan had assembled an outstanding team in Cork, many of the players produced through an under-age system that had brought the county three All-Ireland Under-21 titles consecutively between 1984 and '86.

What happened in 1992 was freakish. The team had earned a reprieve by winning the Munster title in 1991. They beat Cork again in the semi-final of 1992 and faced Clare in the provincial final. No one predicted that Clare would create one of the greatest shocks in the history of the GAA. It was a staggering defeat that plunged Kerry into a crisis. Mickey Ned's term was over.

Páidí was a candidate again. Ogie also let his name go forward. Seamus MacGearailt was also in the frame and Con Riordan from Moyvane was a late applicant for the vacancy. Jack O'Shea, Sean Walsh, Tommy Doyle and Ger O'Keeffe all withdrew from the race. John O'Keeffe was coaching Limerick and was not available.

For some reason, be it superstition or suspicion or whatever we can only speculate now, Páidí did not attend the meeting of the Kerry County Board on September 14. Delegates probably had their minds made up anyway.

Ogie was the chosen one. Páidí polled in last place.

Ogie's tenure proved difficult. The transition was continuing. Meanwhile Páidí was encouraged to apply for the position as Kerry Under-21 manager. His confidence was brittle after being twice rejected for the job he coveted. The delegates, reluctant in September to trust him with the senior team, had by December gained sufficient confidence to give him the Under-21 job.

The timing was perfect.

Kerry reached the All-Ireland Under-21 final in 1993. They lost by one point to a Meath outfit that included Conor Martin, Enda McManus, Graham Geraghty, Tom Hanley, Jimmy McGuinness, Hugh Carolan and Trevor Giles.

A year later they lost to Cork but by 1995 Páidí had assembled a group of players who were comfortable in his presence. They liked him and were loyal to him. They listened. He was imposing his values and he found a young audience that was eager and willing to learn.

Being a Kerry footballer meant something. He drilled it into them. You behaved a certain way when you were a Kerry footballer. If you were marching behind a band you did so in an orderly fashion; you walked erect and with purpose. You walked the way Páidí himself had walked behind the Artane Boys Band.

They had all seen him do it, if not in person then on the Golden Years video, an item that was in every household in Kerry.

Dara O Cinneide remembers the lessons. 'He was always preaching the German mentality in sport. He would talk about Franz Beckenbauer and Boris Becker and the way they applied themselves to their sport, the discipline and the concentration, the order.

'He would also throw in Bjorn Borg's name from time to time but we weren't sure if he thought Borg was German too!'

Páidí would also use snooker player, Steve Davis as an example. 'Be cold, callous and calculated,' he would say.

'He wouldn't have liked white boots,' laughs O Cinneide. 'And he wanted everyone to wear the jersey inside the togs. He didn't like a fella lying on the ground if he got a belt. You weren't to let your opponent know he hurt you.' It was a theme that would be repeated throughout his career as a manager.

His enthusiasm for football lifted the players. They were constantly amazed by his recall of incidents, little moments in games. And he got to know the players so well, their mannerisms and other habits, that he could predict what they would do in certain situations.

'I've no doubt he had a photographic memory because he could remember shots I took, passes I gave, that I had completely forgotten and only recognised when I looked back at the film of a game.'

Páidí worked on their minds as well.

'This was a really bad time in Kerry,' admits O'Cinneide. Kerry reached the Munster senior final in 1995 but had lost again to Cork – Cork had won seven of the last nine titles, Kerry and Clare sharing one each. That surely ranked as a crisis. Ogie stepped down as senior team manager.

'There was a lot of negativity around the county. It was toxic at times. Young players were being told that they weren't good enough, there was no encouragement or support for the younger players trying to make the breakthrough. That much of the criticism was coming from players of the past didn't help the situation.

'Páidí knew he had to constantly address the situation. He told us simply – "we are a new team, a new generation. We don't belong to the famine years" – and eventually we believed him.'

Off the field they were enchanted by his stories, by the pranks he got up to and the fun he clearly got from football. He was good to them as well.

O Cinneide was a student in Limerick at the time. 'There wasn't much money around, that's for sure,' he says. 'We lived in fairly dingy flats and houses, the cheapest we could find. We didn't share just with other humans; there was all sort of animal life around the place.

'We didn't have much spare cash and we had to be careful how it was spent. This wasn't talked about. It was just the way it was and we got on with it.

'From time to time Páidí would arrive unannounced and for no particular reason. He would chat about football – I don't know that he was too bothered about what we were studying – and then before he left again would hand over £50 or £60. "Buy yourselves some Chinese," he would say and would be gone before you could say thanks.'

As the summer of 1995 progressed the manager's excitement grew. He had a talented bunch in his care that were responding to his urgings. His nephew, Darragh was maturing into a special player. The Hassett brothers, Mike and Liam, were playing well. He had talent everywhere – Diarmuid Murphy, Killian Burns, Brian McCarthy, Barry O'Shea, Niall Mangan, Charlie McCarthy from Gneeveguilla, Donal Daly, Denis Dwyer, Mark Moynihan, Johnny Crowley and Jack Ferriter.

They beat Cork, and then Donegal in the All-Ireland semi-final. They played Mayo in the All-Ireland final and nearly blew it. Mayo also had a serious team – John Madden, Ken Mortimer, David Brady, John Casey and Maurice Horan amongst them. The match was drawn. The replay in Thurles saw the team take flight.

Liam Hassett scored a goal after four minutes. Jack Ferriter got a second. O Cinneide's goal was scored at the start of the second half.

Kerry won by 3-10 to 0-12.

The Kerryman captured the mood. *This was a very sweet victory for Kerry and particularly so for team trainer Páidí Ó Sé and his selectors. It should help salve some of the recent wounds inflicted on Kerry football and gives promise of better times ahead.'*

The analysis read, *'Midfield proved to be a key sector in determining the outcome of this game. Dara Ó Sé and Donal Daly were a transformed partnership this time round and gave Kerry a distinct advantage throughout.*

'O Se had the game of his young life; he plucked some mighty balls out of the air and then ran at the losers' defence, causing waves of panic every time he pressed forward.

The newspaper also had words of praise for O'Cinneide.

Dara O Cinneide had a star-studded game at top of the left in the attack and the Gaeltacht player again showed that he is one of the brighter stars on the horizon as far as the future of Kerry football is concerned.

Páidí knew that night that the senior job was as good as his.

—◊◊◊—

When the appointment of the new Kerry senior football manager was ratified by a packed meeting of the County Board on Wednesday, September 20, 1995, life for Páidí Ó Sé and his family changed utterly.

His role as a newspaper columnist and his involvement with the Kerry Under-21 footballers had maintained a public profile for the man. But now he was public property.

Even the circumstances of his appointment were placed under the microscope. Páidí was named trainer, with Seamus MacGearailt as the coach. It was what Páidí himself wanted but immediately questions were being asked. *Does the Board not trust him to take charge on his own?* was the most frequent query.

Sean Kelly, the chairman of the Board at the time and currently an MEP, explained the position. 'It is not a co-management situation. What we are recommending to the board is that Páidí Ó Sé be appointed trainer to the Kerry team for the next two years. As trainer he is the boss and Seamus MacGearailt would be appointed as coach.'

That was that cleared up.

Then the question of three selectors arose. In his pre-selection discussions with the executive of the Board Páidí had discussed the appointment of Bernie O'Callaghan and the unrelated O'Connors, Jack and Tom. This, he understood, had been agreed.

But it took another two weeks before those names were accepted by the County Board. That ensured another two weeks of speculation and a little bit of controversy that a new management team did not want or need.

Then the football began. First up was Kildare in the opening round of the National League. They were managed by Dermot Earley. It was a menu from which the media feasted hungrily. Kildare won by three points in Austin Stack Park where the press box was packed way beyond capacity. *Páidí endures a baptism of fire*, was one headline.

The circus moved on.

It pitched camp in rural south Derry, the GAA heartland of Ballinascreen, also known to the community of another persuasion as Draperstown. For reasons lost in time the Kerry act took four separate train journeys on the day before the game to reach their overnight accommodation in Ballymena. It gave the new manager a chance to get to know some of the players better.

A League game on the last Sunday in October did not normally generate much interest. But Páidí's presence added to the spice.

As did the presence of the Derry manager. Brian Mullins.

Kerry won by 14 points. Mullins and Páidí embraced at the end. 'Are you going to haunt me forever?' the former Dublin hero enquired. Derry recovered to win the National League in May of 1996. Kerry were beaten in the quarter final by Cork. Winter does funny things in football.

Páidí was having the time of his life. He loved the trips to Killarney three times a week. The youngsters were fitting in nicely. And then he had Seamus Moynihan, Stephen Stack, Eamon Breen, Sean Burke, Billy O'Shea, Bingo

Driscoll, Genie Farrell, Sean Geaney. And he had Maurice Fitzgerald.

Maurice, with whom he had briefly played and who had coaxed him to Cork to coach UCC for two years, was playing great football. Páidí loved watching him practice and play. Maurice loved Páidí's humour and his passion. They were opposites in character and opposites attract.

Kerry played Tipperary in the opening round of the Munster Championship on May 19. It was not an auspicious beginning, even if Kerry won by 2-15 to 1-7. The *Irish Independent* reported thus: *Attempts to transmit just how close Kerry came to humiliation at Clonmel Sportsfield yesterday are completely undermined by the scoreline. Eleven points between them? You must be joking.*

'It may be that only those who were actually present at the rain-sodden venue can appreciate the extent to which Kerry courted disaster. They did not get their hands on the lead until ten minutes from time, a decidedly late hour, even by the standards set by the great Kerry team in some diffident Munster Championship outings.

And it took a 62nd minute goal by corner forward Dara O Cinneide to finally bury Tipperary. It was a painful death in the end. The subsequent procession of scores went some way towards soothing Kerry nerves which had been subjected to a terrible bludgeoning.

'The manner of the escape unhinged the Kerry men and no smugness was to be found among their number afterwards. Lovers of trivia will point to that much-heralded 1975 lift-off for the Kerry team at the same venue – a tale that gathered legs over the past week: acquired wisdom has it that lightning might strike twice.

Four weeks later they travelled to Dungarvan. They hammered Waterford by 3-16 to 0-8. The one moment of note took place in Lawlor's Hotel in the town late in the evening. Páidí had his nephew, Darragh and Dara O'Cinneide with him when they met the Waterford Ladies' Football team, then the outstanding outfit in the country.

'I've two good thoroughbred stallions here,' says Páidí to the ladies, pointing to his two footballers. 'We could start a right good breeding operation here.'

The two boys almost died of embarrassment on the spot.

They would get used to such scenarios.

Páidí was where he wanted to be. The TV cameras arrived. Ventry beach was glorious. Marty Morrissey was asking the questions. A fly buzzed over and back across Páidí's face. He did his best to ignore it. Marty asked, 'But what happens for Páidí Ó Sé, winner of eight All-Ireland medals, if Kerry lose on Sunday?'

Páidí paused briefly.

He flicked his hand.

The fly stopped buzzing.

'We won't lose at all.' Then Páidí exited the picture.

He was right. Kerry didn't lose. In his first season as manager Páidí had guided Kerry to the Munster title; only the county's second provincial success in 10 years.

It wasn't the greatest game of football. It wasn't bad either. Maurice kicked five points. Declan O'Keeffe made three outstanding saves, including one very late in the game when he dived at full stretch to deny Colin Corkery a goal.

Páidí was busy on the line. Sean Burke suffered a head injury and left the field on a stretcher. Maurice struggled towards the end with a leg muscle problem. Fortunately, Burke's injury proved not to be serious and he would be fit for the semi-final.

Cork had led by one point as the game entered the last 15 minutes when Colin Corkery pointed his third free. It would, however, be their last score. Liam Hassett levelled, Maurice added two and then Killian Burns sallied forth to score a rare Championship point. The three point margin, 0-14 to 0-11, was an accurate reflection.

The details, however, were lost on the Kerry public. They just savoured the success.

The Kerryman reflected the mood, *More classic games between the counties there may have been but for sheer drama, thrills, excitement and a titanic finish it would be hard to match Sunday's Munster SFC final at Pairc Ui Chaoimh as Kerry came of age with a memorable victory over Cork to take the provincial crown and, in so doing, they booked themselves a place in the All-Ireland semi-final against Mayo on August 11.*

The final quarter of this gripping game was contested with feverish intensity and, as play swung from one end of the field to the other, the rival supporters in the crowd of 36,405 roared themselves hoarse as they urged their team on for that all-important final surge that would win them the day.

In the end it was the delirious Kerry followers who had the final chorus as they hailed the new Munster champions.

There were, of course, a number of players who reached stellar heights on the day, but, overall, it was a superb team performance which finally ended Cork's three year reign as Munster champions and brought the Kingdom their first success over Cork in a Munster final since 1986.

It was a game of raw courage and physical endurance where the faint-hearted had no place. And when it came to the crunch, Páidí Ó Sé's players proved that they have come through a tough apprenticeship with flying colours and they are now set to tilt for even higher honours. With the kind of steely resolve and commitment that they showed on Sunday who is to say that they cannot reach the summit in the weeks ahead.

'Football's coming home,' the jubilant Kerry supporters sang beneath the stand at Pairc Ui Chaoimh, adopting the anthem written for the English soccer team at that summer's European Soccer Championships.

It was a presumption that would have to be put on hold.

The weeks ahead held unexpected twists and turns.

CHAPTER 9

Sixteen year old Marc Ó Sé, an aspiring footballer in a growing family tradition, was learning to drive during 1996. Lessons were strictly supervised by his mother and father, an introductory course of sorts to prepare him for when he became eligible to hold a provisional licence.

Naturally, like all teenage boys, he was anxious to expedite the process of learning by whatever means possible, including those that could not be revealed to his parents.

That is where Uncle Páidí became involved.

Late in the year the pair met in the dark of an evening as Marc headed home to finish some schoolwork. Páidí was heading towards his pub.

'How's the driving going?' asked Páidí .

A frustrated Marc outlined his problem. 'It's going grand but I need more practice.'

'Practice is the only way you'll learn,' agreed his uncle. 'Take my yoke whenever you need it.'

And so Marc did.

He would wait until Michael and Joan left Ard an Bhothair to run some errands in Dingle or, preferably in the mind of the youngster, further afield. The longer they were away the more time he had behind the wheel of Páidí's car.

The road around Slea Head and over the Clasach was quiet at that time of year. Through trial and error Marc improved his driving skills, though the lessons were harder on the clutch than Páidí would have wanted.

If the roads were too busy he would drive along the deserted stretches of Ventry beach; in quick time the seagulls sensed they were in mortal danger and found safer havens along the peninsula in which to forage.

As time passed the boy racer became bolder. Speed increased. Caution was replaced by daring.

'I was belting down the road one day ... thought I could take a corner.

'Couldn't ...

'All I remember is the car mounting the ditch and landing in the bog,' he confesses.

A local farmer arrived on the scene sometime later. He recognised the young footballer and took pity on him. The car was pulled from the bog.

'We'll say nothing,' said the man.

Marc was mildly relieved when he got into the car to drive back to Páidí's house. Then he started the engine. Even a rookie driver knew there was something wrong. The steering wheel commands were not being fully heard by whatever should have been hearing them and, in human parlance, the car hobbled home.

He told Páidí .

'Don't worry about it,' said his uncle, without inspecting the damage. He had bent a few fenders himself in his time. More than a few.

'We've all gone through it sometime.'

The following day Páidí was not quite so accommodating. The mechanic brought him unexpected and bad news. The car was not a write-off but the cost of repairs would run into significantly high figures.

Páidí thought about his problem. He couldn't approach his brother, Michael or sister-in-law, Joan because he would be in trouble himself for allowing Marc to drive the car. But Marc wouldn't know that and Páidí could use it to his advantage.

Marc was summoned to the bar. Páidí's face was full of thunder. Marc was nervous. 'You brought me back a wreck,' he accused. 'It's going to cost me a fortune to fix it.

'You'll have to make it up to me by working in the bar over the Christmas. And we can keep it between ourselves … and I won't tell your father and mother,' he said, a veiled threat implied.

Every evening the telephone would ring. 'Come on over now, I need you. We're run off our feet here.'

'He blackmailed me for the whole of Christmas,' says Marc. 'I was in the bloody place morning, noon and night. My mother was wondering what I was at. I told her Páidí was busy and that I needed to give him a hand. I was terrified she would find out what happened. And Páidí knew that.'

'Come on over, I need you.'

'I can't, I'm going to Dingle.'

'If you don't come over I'll tell your parents you stole my car and then crashed it.'

By New Year's Day Marc was 'broken'.

He confessed his sin to his parents.

The phone rang in mid-afternoon. Páidí.

'I'm not going over,' Marc shouted at him.

'I'm warning you!'

'Páidí … I've told them … now, fuck off.'

—⁊⁊—

'If you have just one pint they'll say you had 10.' How often was that phrase repeated and when was it first uttered?

Maybe its origin was on a flight home from the Canary Islands in January of 1997. It was certainly used in a conversation between Páidí and Sean Kelly, the chairman of the Kerry Board and the man who ultimately had appointed the Kerry senior football manager.

It was the price of celebrity, the fame that he had openly nurtured in order to enhance his business. Rumour and gossip became bedfellows, invading his private space and providing malice for his detractors.

Páidí's openness, his often garrulous nature, his easy embrace of the frolics and frivolities of life made him a soft target. His fondness for gaiety, the companionship of the bar room was just one part of his personality that, when presented as the whole, was a distortion.

He knew there were those in Kerry and elsewhere who considered him in the throes of lunacy. 'The mad bastard from the west,' often played up to that caricature, quietly laughing at those who misunderstood him. If they chose to mock then so be it.

He was bigger than that.

At other times it did him no favours.

He celebrated well after the Munster final of 1996.

He was proud of what had been achieved and he was not shy about showing it. He had spent years trying to convince the doubters that he was the man to restore Kerry to its rightful position and in his first season he had begun the process in a convincing manner.

Photographers naturally gravitated towards Ard an Bhothair. The pub was well populated throughout the day after the Munster success. Páidí was there for much of the day, revelling in the mood of joviality. He posed for photos with friends, with the Cup and with some of his players.

The happy scenes were printed in the local newspapers, reflecting the heightened mood of the summer in Kerry now that Cork had been put in their place and a journey to Croke Park could be planned. This is what Kerry football people lived for and they had missed it more than they ever thought possible.

Good man, Páidí. He soaked it up.

That was Páidí's mistake. It changed him. The memories of those weeks remained with him like demons, probably to the extent that the events became exaggerated in his mind.

It wouldn't have mattered if Kerry had beaten Mayo in the All-Ireland semi-final. There would have been no questions to answer then. And it might have helped if Mayo had gone on to win the Championship, which they should have. That year Mayo were the best team in the competition and were seconds from being champions when a late Meath point in the final forced a replay.

Nobody rated Mayo, especially in Kerry. Kerry supporters knew nothing of Colm McManamon and had hardly been impressed by John Casey when they saw him at Under-21 level. On the long journey back to Kerry on the night of August 11 they were very aware of the capabilities of that pair and the entire Mayo team.

A six point defeat was greeted with shock and awe.

The reaction was swift and sour. The manager was derided for what was considered a lack of control, a failure to maintain discipline. The evidence was damning, they claimed, and the celebratory photographs from the day after the Munster final were presented.

There he was in the centre.

Páidí, one hand on the Cup, the other draped around the shoulders of Muiris MacGearailt. Big smile on his face. Seamus MacGearailt, Charlie Nelligan and Killian Burns were also in the picture.

Charlie and Killian, a player, were holding pints.

In another picture Liam Higgins is the central figure. Dermot Hanafin, Sean Geaney, Mick Galwey and Billy O'Shea are laughing along with Higgins. Liam and Sean, a player, are holding pints.

In the right context there was absolutely nothing wrong with what was happening. A bunch of men celebrating a Munster Championship win, the first big win against the oldest of rivals in 10 years, was a perfectly natural happening. But it could be made to look bad. And when Kerry lost to Mayo they were plenty of people around who used those photographs as ammunition.

What should have been a summer of celebration had turned sour. The critics, and they were plenty of them after the defeat in the semi-final, turned their attention on the manager. It wasn't a pleasant time.

'All the stuff about the celebrations was completely overblown,' insists Dara O Cinneide. 'Of course we all had a few drinks on the Sunday night and there was a spill over into Monday. But there was an implication that it went on for a week ... even longer. And that just simply is not true.'

In fact, he recalls training with West Kerry on the Tuesday night after the Munster final and there was a full turnout of players. Similar training sessions were held all over the county and the excesses of the celebrations, whatever they were, perspired into the soil.

'The photographs,' explains O Cinneide, 'were taken on Monday. The newspapers weren't printed until the Thursday or Friday so there might have been an impression given that we were celebrating and drinking all week. At least that interpretation was put on it when we lost the semi-final.

'The implication was that Páidí was a loose cannon. He had fought for the job for years and then, when he eventually got it … he couldn't handle it. And that wasn't the case at all. But it had a big affect on him; he was a very wounded animal after that. The whole experience changed him and changed his approach to the role as manager.'

Kerry's victory over Cork had made them hot favourites for the semi-final. Mayo's pedigree was ignored. They had been in the semi-final three years earlier and suffered a 20-point humiliation to Cork, conceding five goals. They had struggled to beat London in the opening round. Some Kerry supporters had made plans for the weekend of the All-Ireland final.

But the Mayo manager, John Maughan – the man who masterminded Clare's victory over Kerry in 1992 – had his team exceptionally well prepared. Mayo were superior; stronger physically and more accomplished in attack. Only two Kerry forwards scored, Maurice kicking eight points and O'Cinneide one. Sean Burke scored a goal from centre half-back and Eamon Breen scored a point.

The reaction locally was reflected in the extensive coverage accorded to the game in *The Kerryman*. John Barry wrote: *It wouldn't be so bad if there were some redeeming features, something to nurture hope for next year, but sadly it all turned out to be an unmitigated disaster for Kerry.*

Páidí Ó Sé's men were chasing the game from the very start and such was Mayo's overall dominance that they should have won by ten or twelve points, not six.

It was not pretty to watch one team make another look so bad and remember, Kerry were the ones supposed to be dishing out the punishment.

They were 2/5 favourites with the bookmakers; they were the fancy of just about every commentator in the business, and, as well, they were coming out of the county with the best pedigree in the land and where football fever hadn't been as high for a long time.

The trouble about all that, of course, was that Kerry was being set up for a mighty fall if things went wrong….and, boy, did things go wrong.

Owen McCrohan, the newspaper's football columnist and biographer of Mick O'Dwyer was clearly stunned by the result. He wrote, *The bad days are far from over; indeed they may be only starting because on the evidence of Sunday's performance Kerry football is not just going through a transition period. The situation is far worse than that and it is quite possible that the bottom of the graph has not yet been drawn.*

He concluded, *All and all, it was a disastrous performance from a Kerry perspective. Not one shred of comfort can be salvaged from it and to suggest that the Páidí O Se honeymoon can be extended into the future is not being realistic. Life is not a dress rehearsal and the road back is going to be long and arduous.*

In his match report Eamon Horan wrote, *Not alone do you need to be fast but you also need to be big and fast. Kerry learned this unsavoury lesson to their regret in the white-hot combat of Championship football when they were outfielded, often outplayed and too often outflanked by Mayo.*

He went on, *This game was all about the hunger to win. Páidí O Se had said beforehand that he hoped that Kerry would be the hungrier side but this did not prove to be the case. Mayo played like a team who had not been at the table for a mighty long time and were prepared to devour anything and everything that came their way. They had an insatiable appetite or the game.*

Kerry, in contrast, played in fits and starts throughout, without ever getting up a full head of steam.

The fact that Kerry went on to retain the All-Ireland Under-21 title in September, beating Cavan in the final, almost went unnoticed. There certainly was no parade through Tralee that night.

Páidí was stung by the criticism. He questioned everything but mostly himself. He identified his mistakes, on and off the field. He possibly overreacted and was too hard on himself. Did it make him a better manager. 'Yes," says his nephew Darragh. 'And it probably made him a bit paranoid for a while,' says Dara O Cinneide.

They returned to training in October. The National Football League, regarded by many in Kerry as a sideshow, became a target. Páidí wanted to win everything, to develop the habit and to heal the wounds. 'We noticed a change in him,' says O Cinneide. 'He became a little distant; probably more demanding. We felt we had let him down and that meant that we worked harder.'

Páidí enjoyed the holiday in the Canary Islands. He shared a few beers with the lads, was something like his old self. But all the time he was thinking about the past and planning to make the future better.

He sat with Sean Kelly on the flight home.

'I'm sorry Sean,' was one of his opening lines.

'For what?'

'I let you down … I'm sorry. You gave me what I cherished and I didn't deliver for you.'

They talked for hours, covered every aspect of the management of the Kerry football team. Kelly provided all the assurances that Páidí needed. One defeat had not altered his faith in the manager.

They discussed Páidí's public profile and how it impacted on the Kerry team. 'If you have just one….'

Páidí vowed that would be one criticism that would not be thrown at him in 1997.

—⁊⁊—

The tannoy in Austin Stack Park crackled into life just after the start of the second half in the Munster semi-final between Kerry and Tipperary on June 29, 1997.

'Substitution on the Kerry team … Dara O Cinneide is being replaced by Johnny Crowley.'

It was a big call from the sideline.

Páidí made it. He had promised that he would be ruthless; that he would not hesitate when changes were necessary, that he would act with conviction and would not allow his judgment to be clouded.

And his move underlined that new approach.

O Cinneide was a Páidí stalwart. He was from An Gaeltacht. The manager had watched the kid grow up, spotted his talent very early. They travelled together, to training and to games. They laughed together, messed about.

They weren't laughing in Tralee that day.

The player walked to the sideline. He didn't look at the manager. The manager did not offer a consoling pat on the back. O Cinneide decided he would not 'have a hissy fit' but he would make his views known.

'We're struggling all over the field and what do you do ... take off a corner forward. Bloody typical.'

Páidí said nothing.

Early the following day O Cinneide was called to the phone. It was Páidí. Dara repeated his complaint as a greeting. 'Let's talk about it and see if we can sort it out,' said the manager.

Half an hour later O Cinneide had admitted he was injured and shouldn't have started. But like all young footballers, he hid the injury. He wanted to play and thought he would get away with it. Lesson learned.

Páidí created competition in his squad. No place was sacred. They had used different combinations during the National League. Pa Laide had made a very good impression over the winter; so too did a youngster from Killorglin, Mike Frank Russell.

The League had been a tonic. They played well in the knockout stages, beating Down and Laois to qualify for the final. The opponents would be Cork. Just under 29,000 supporters went to Pairc Ui Chaoimh on the first Sunday in May to watch Kerry win the county's first national title since 1986.

It was the only League title won on Páidí's watch but it was an important one.

Kerry were unimpressive in Munster, stumbling through the Tipperary game and being little more than efficient in retaining the Munster title, beating Clare in the final. Páidí was meticulous in his planning for the return to Croke Park and a semi-final against the new Ulster champions, Cavan. He chose a different hotel, one where the players would be sheltered from the supporters and could prepare without interference.

Mike Frank replaced Brian Clarke. Maurice and the kid combined five minutes from the end. Maurice won the ball in midfield; delivered a precise pass. Mike Frank slid by his marker and placed the ball neatly in the net.

Kerry pulled away to win by seven.

If the boatman sails his currach around the Blaskets once he knows the waters better the second time around. Today our team never forgot the lessons learned 12 months ago, Páidí said as he celebrated on the field, seeking out each player individually to offer his congratulations.

His promise to Sean Kelly on the flight back from the Canary Islands was being kept. Mayo qualified for the final again. This time, however, all was changed. Maurice, who had first played Championship football for Kerry when Páidí was still playing, performed heroics. They won by three points, 0-13 to 1-7, but it was much more convincing than that.

Even still Páidí held himself back.

He wanted to savour every moment. He had delivered. In two years he had dramatically changed the fortunes of Kerry. Two Munster Championships, a National League and, now, the All-Ireland.

From the moment he had told Maire back in 1989 that his playing days were over Paidi had dreamed of this. His self-belief never wavered. Despite the rejections, the claims that he did not have the qualities necessary, and the frustrations he suffered as summer after summer went by and silverware remained within other borders, he always believed that he was the right man to bring Kerry out of the wilderness and back to their rightful place in football's hierarchy.

He didn't sleep that night. He called to see Dwyer who was staying in the Burlington Hotel. They drank tea and talked football.

Back at the Tara Towers hotel in Booterstown later in the morning he picked up the newspaper. Miriam Lord, the colourful and talented feature writer, had penned a piece about the occasion in the *Irish Independent*.

He had a good laugh when he read it.

Restoring some lost pride to Ireland's must cultured footballing county was what they wanted to do. Páidí was there for the great days in the seventies but was he ever as pumped up on the field of play as he was on the sideline yesterday.

All afternoon, barrelling up and down, patrolling the margin like a neurotic bull terrier looking for an argument.

A man would be afraid to lose a match with the likes of Páidí doing the training.
He liked that.

—⚏—

The West Kerry car admitted a new passenger when Páidí steered the 1998 model towards Killarney. Tomas O Se, his nephew and younger brother of

Darragh, had been promoted to senior ranks.

Having close family involved did not worry the manager. He had inherited Darragh from Ogie Moran's squad and Tomas had been one of the best under-age players in Kerry in the mid-1990s. He was on the minor team in 1996 that lost to Laois in the All-Ireland final and had come through the ranks impressively.

Uncle Páidí didn't do any favour for his nephews. In fact, Tomas had to work harder than others and it took some time for him to establish himself and prove his worth.

For example, Kerry were struggling to complete their full-back line in the build-up to the 1998 Championship. They were due to play Cork in the opening round. The Hassett brothers, Mike and Liam, had withdrawn from the squad following a disagreement with the County Board when Mike was not awarded an All-Ireland medal for the 1997 victory. Mike would comfortably have slotted back into the defence after recovering from injury.

After a forgettable League campaign – Kerry were relegated – Páidí and his selectors, including the new County Chairman, Sean Walsh from Moyvane, still had not resolved the problem at corner-back. Killian Burns was injured. Tomas was a natural wing back but many players had been converted before, including Páidí himself.

When the team to play Cork in Killarney on the first Sunday in July was selected the No.2 shirt was handed to Tomas. He would line up beside Barry O'Shea and Stephen Stack in his senior Championship debut. In front of him were Seamus Moynihan, Liam O'Flaherty and Eamon Breen.

That looked like solid protection for the youngster.

It wasn't enough. Aidan Dorgan was threatening to tear Kerry apart. Before half time Páidí made the call. Tomas was withdrawn. Eamon Fitzmaurice took his place. 'I never played in the position again so that tells its own story,' Tomas explains.

It fed the critics, however.

There were quiet accusations that the manager was favouring his family. The fact that Tomas did not get a run again in the 1998 Championship did not appease those who continued to search for faults. And their search intensified when Kerry lost their All-Ireland crown at the semi-final stage to a Kildare team managed by Mick O'Dwyer.

Looking back any suggestions that Páidí favoured his nephews are easily discounted. The oldest nephew, Fergal, had played under-age football for Kerry and featured in the National League in 1997 but was never promoted to full Championship status.

Tomas took some time to earn a regular place but eventually became one of the outstanding players of his or any generation. He was named Footballer of the Year in 2004. Marc, the youngest brother, also took a couple of seasons to make the breakthrough and was chosen as the Footballer of the Year in 2007.

Allegations of nepotism, however spurious, were only part of the baggage that Páidí had to carry after losing to Kildare. He was heavily criticised for the fact that Karl O'Dwyer had been allowed to transfer out of Kerry and played such a part in defeating the champions.

The fact the O'Dwyer had been dropped from the Kerry panel three years before Páidí was appointed manager somehow got lost in that argument.

The manager never responded.

He might have defended himself. A late goal by Denis O'Dwyer had been disallowed by the referee, Michael Curley, because the Kerry forward was deemed to be inside the square before the ball. It was a marginal call. On another day it might have been permitted. But Páidí did not seek solace from that. It was a game Kerry should have won. They scored just four points playing with the wind as an advantage. That simply was not good enough.

Sean Walsh, the chairman, defended him. 'That was a defeat that he took badly,' Walsh remembers. 'It was a huge disappointment. He thought he had the team in peak condition. It turned out that they weren't.

'It wasn't easy for him playing against a team coached by his old mentor. He found it strange having Mick in the opposing camp. They had been through so much together. There was talk about a strain on their friendship when Páidí finished playing but they were tight by the time of the 1998 semi-final.

'For months afterwards he examined what went wrong, why the team hadn't performed like he expected them to. He had his critics but we (the County Board executive) were fully behind him.'

However harsh his critics were, there was no one harder on Páidí than the man himself. He berated himself for what he perceived as his own failure. He felt he had been slow to make changes; that he had been spooked by the presence of his old mentor on the sideline. He had worked hard on some aspects of the battle, like securing the dug out to the right of the Hogan Stand tunnel.

Why did that matter? Because Páidí believed that it was the dug-out Micko favoured. Should he have bothered with something like that? Probably not, he said himself in the wake of the defeat.

He resolved that he would change his approach; that he would become more meticulous in planning for every game.

He decided that other changes were needed. He brought in his old teammate, John O'Keeffe to look after the physical training. However, the spark that had been so apparent throughout 1997 seemed to die in the early part of 1999. 'Quite simply' says Sean Walsh, 'we were beaten by a better team in the Munster final.'

Kerry led by 2-2 to 0-5 on a wet and difficult day in Pairc Ui Chaoimh; Aodan MacGearailt had scored the two goals. In the second 35 minutes Kerry scored just two further points. Cork scored 2-5. Neither Maurice Fitzgerald nor Dara O Cinneide registered a score. It was that kind of day.

Owen McCrohan in *The Kerryman* was not impressed. *God be with you Kerry, as the tinker said to the Cork judge. Being beaten is one thing, but what happened in Pairc Ui Chaoimh on Sunday represents more than just the end of a cycle of Kerry dominance in Munster – it was complete, abject humiliation.*

Kerry's tame, limp exit from the Championship race was hard to stomach. As the game entered the closing minutes with Cork coasting by six points and the victory cheers ringing around the stadium, the men in green and gold cut a forlorn sight.

Comprehensively outplayed all through the second half and flattered by a three point lead at half time, Kerry were getting lessons from opponents who had done their homework well and who had left no doubts as to their worthiness to wear the mantle of champions.

Tom O'Riordan wrote, *At the finish Kerry could not offer even a hint of an excuse, no matter where they looked or how they viewed the encounter not least when Cork came out for the second half fired up to such a degree that once they lit the fuse they left a trail of destruction behind them.*

Sean Walsh consulted with his fellow executive members during the month of August. 'We didn't look for another manager and no one else asked for the job,' he explained to local reporters when Páidí was re-appointed in the first week of September. John O'Keeffe also became a selector as well as team trainer.

Buoyed by the vote of confidence Páidí attended the All-Ireland final between Meath and Cork in late September as a newspaper analyst. He sat in the press area, mingling and chatting with the men he actively avoided through the summer months. 'Tis a pity you're not as talkative for the rest of the year,' they joked.

Even then he was already planning the new campaign. His column the following morning would contain messages for Cork. He was quietly provocative, laying down a marker.

He was critical of the Cork forwards in the final. *When Cork needed their forwards to keep them in touch in the first half and to drive home their advantage in the second, they were found wanting. In fact, there were at least three men up front who didn't want to know and only the wire fencing around the pitch was keeping them on the field.*

Páidí then went on to name Michael Cronin, Mark O'Sullivan and Don Davis.

And he was not finished. *Mick O'Dwyer used to tell me there were three types of footballer. Players who want to make it happen, players who want to watch it happen and players who don't know what the hell is happening.*

If you can get rid of the third type and join up the second with the first you'll have a team that can win.

Yesterday Cork didn't strike that balance while Meath showed just how valuable it is when every player is pulling his weight.

He then concluded, *After viewing a poor enough final, especially from Cork's point of view, I realise we must do some serious soul-searching in Kerry. No doubt Meath deserved to win the Championship, they were the best team in it, but Cork's ultimate failure begs the question, what are the rest of us at?*

All I can say for now is that Cork will get little sympathy from us in Killarney next summer.

All of this was coming from a man who was regarded in the media and amongst many of his players as paranoid about how the Kerry team and management portrayed themselves publicly.

Reading the words the following morning the players didn't know whether to laugh or cry. Typical Páidí.

Unpredictable and full of surprises.

CHAPTER 10

No one admired the beautiful skills of Maurice Fitzgerald more than Páidí
Ó Sé.

And reading that sentence will cause a rise in blood pressure amongst
some gentle folk in all corners of this land that will create concern amongst
the country's already overworked cardiologists.

Páidí was first mesmerised by Maurice when the then kid from Cahirciveen
was called into Kerry training sessions in late 1987.

Although 14 years separated the pair in age and they hailed from distant
corners of Kerry, they immediately bonded. Their characters were different
in many ways but they shared two important traits – a great sense of humour
and a perfectionist approach to Gaelic football.

Although their playing careers interlocked for only the briefest period they
got to know each other much better when Maurice inspired an invitation
from the University College Cork, GAA Club to Páidí to coach their Sigerson
Cup team for two seasons at the beginning of the 1990s.

And when Páidí became Kerry senior football team manager in late 1995
he knew one thing for sure – one of the first names on his teamsheet would
be that of Maurice Fitz. Páidí created the environment in which the dazzling
skills could be displayed to the widest audience.

It led to the show-stopping performance in Croke Park in the Autumn of

1997 when Maurice gave one of the greatest, if not the greatest, individual displays in the history of All-Ireland finals.

Yet just three years later Maurice was unable to get a starting place in the team and spent his last two years with Kerry as a frustrated replacement before calling time on his career.

So what happened?

How did it all go wrong?

Or did it all go wrong?

There are two distinct sides to the debate. On one side is the claim that Páidí managed the skills of a player entering the twilight of his career with aplomb, introducing him from the bench with precise timing to torment the opposition.

The conspiracy theorists, on the other side, have a variety of complaints that Páidí did not recognise the genius or that he did not want that genius to overshadow Páidí's own role in Kerry's successes. Neither withstand scrutiny. Páidí was a vocal admirer of Maurice's talent and it would have been madness not to exploit it to Kerry's and Páidí's advantage.

Could Páidí have handled the situation better, if not in 2000 when Maurice was recovering from serious injury, then certainly during 2001? In hindsight it is easy to answer 'possibly' but that does not mean that Kerry would have been even more successful.

Maurice was in his 30s by then, had given 14 years of service to Kerry. He did not need the heavy training that was the norm at the time. It can be argued than an exception could have been made for an individual so gifted with talent. But Páidí was not the first football manager, and this includes all codes worldwide, who did not believe in making exceptions no matter how talented the individual.

The only certainty in the debate is that there will never be agreement between the two bodies of opinion.

It is a pity that when the careers of both men are discussed that there is so much emphasis on the supposed 'rift' between them that emerged during 2000. The circumstances were complex and neither man wished to fan the flames of controversy at the time or when their careers were over and there was time to reflect.

Maurice broke the same ankle twice in a six-month period, the first time in a club game in the autumn of 1999 and the second time in a challenge game for Kerry in the early part of 2000. That shortened his period of preparation for the Championship, in which Kerry had been drawn to play Cork in the Munster semi-final in mid-June.

He started on the bench. Dara O Cinneide and Mike Frank Russell tortured Cork for 35 minutes. Kerry led by 2-9 to 0-5 at half time. Cork staged a comeback and reduced the deficit to two points. Páidí called on Maurice with 15 minutes remaining. He went in to partner Darragh in midfield.

The ship steadied.

Maurice was again a substitute against Clare in the Munster final. It was a comfortable game that did not spark controversy.

Darragh O Se was the big talking point. His display was described as 'spectacular'.

This was the best performance from O Se since the 1997 All-Ireland final, wrote Tom O'Riordan, *not just in his high fielding but with his work rate and distribution which saw him set up several scores.*

On August 20 the flame of controversy was fuelled by Maurice's brilliance. Kerry engaged in a monumental battle with Armagh. Maurice was introduced early in the second half and scored a spectacular goal, soloing in from the Cusack Stand, skipping past four Armagh players including Kieran Hughes and John McEntee.

He soloed with his right foot and in the next stride struck the ball with his left foot into the corner of the net past Benny Tierney.

There was more to come.

Kieran McGeeney kicked Armagh into a one point lead. Kerry were awarded a free for a foul on Denis O'Dwyer. It was 40 metres from the Armagh goal. Maurice had not taken a free for Kerry in a year. He took this one and drove it over.

The match was drawn, 2-11 each.

Eugene McGee was straight to the point in his match analysis. *Class was conspicuous by its absence yesterday with a few very notable exceptions. And bearing that in mind it was astonishing that two of the classiest forwards in football, Diarmuid*

Marsden and Maurice Fitzgerald, were left sitting in the dug-out for the entire first half.

In a game where unforced passing errors and erratic shooting were dominant factors, one would have thought that both should have been in the game after 15 minutes, if not from the start.

At least Páidí's burden was shared in that assessment.

Seamus Moynihan was having a brilliant season; Mike Frank Russell was scoring freely; Declan O'Keeffe was superb in goal. All anyone was talking about was Maurice.

The newspapers carried reports that he was 'certain' to be selected for the replay. It then emerged that Maurice had suffered a toe injury in the drawn game and had not been able to train. He was again kept in reserve for the replay against Armagh and made a big contribution when Kerry won in extra time.

Mike Frank was in mesmerising form. He kicked 2-3, all from play, one of the greatest scoring performances in Championship history. And still the talk was of Maurice. *Much of the credit for their revival must go to Maurice Fitzgerald who came on as a sub in the 39th minute,* wrote Martin Breheny.

He may have only scored two points but he was at the heart of Kerry's more creative play including picking out Russell with a superb pass for Kerry's first goal.

The clamour for Fitzgerald's inclusion from the start increased before the final against Galway. Pages of newsprint were devoted to the issue. At Kerry's media day Maurice was the focus of much attention. He declared himself one hundred per cent fit. That sparked many headlines.

Páidí and the selectors kept to their plan.

The headlines blared *Fitz gamble puts Kerry boss Ó Sé in firing line.* Team managers from other counties were quoted expressing their surprise. Mikey Sheehy was quoted giving support to Paidi and the selectors. 'The team management were the only ones qualified to make a proper judgement,' he said.

'In fairness to the selectors, they have got it right so far this year. Obviously it is tough on Maurice and we all know what a wonderful talent he is. He can make more out of one pass than many others can make of four but we've got to accept that the selectors have called things right in other games. Otherwise Kerry wouldn't be in the All-Ireland final.

'Anyway with five subs it's not all that important who starts and who doesn't. You can move very quickly if the occasions demands and I'm sure Maurice will be involved at some stage on Sunday.'

Maurice came on in the 48th minute but did not get much chance to make an impression at corner forward.

The All Ireland final ended in a draw, 0-14 each.

The replay was played on a Saturday evening, October 7. Maurice came into the game after just 28 minutes. This is how the *Irish Independent* reported on his contribution. *Kerry's dominance of the closing quarter was almost as pronounced as their superiority in the opening 25 minutes of the drawn game 13 days earlier. Quicker and sharper to every breaking ball they worked the gaps and angles perfectly.*

Nobody did it better than Maurice Fitzgerald. The debate about whether or not he should have started can end here and now. He is still a front line player for Kerry, as he proved with a wonderfully intelligent contribution in the final 20 minutes.

Fitzgerald sees gaps where others see roadblocks and while he may lack the speed and energy of some younger Kerry colleagues, his subtlety and poise more than compensate. Indeed, it is the perfect topping in an exciting Kerry attack.

Páidí had guided Kerry to the Promised Land once again.

Kerry 0-17, Galway 1-10.

And everyone was talking about Maurice.

—◊◊◊—

Sean Walsh observed the growing controversy over the selection policy with the natural concern of a custodian. He could see the point of view shared by Páidí and his management team. They felt they were getting the best out of Maurice by bringing him into games during the second half. And the results, especially Maurice's part in achieving those results, vindicated what they were doing.

But, like any footballer, Maurice wanted to play from the start. Kerry football had history in this regard. Remember the chairman's namesake, Sean Walsh, back in 1976. Super-sub. How he hated it. But it was effective.

The chairman hoped that the growing controversy would not seep into the camp. He admits today that it was only a worry for a very short time. What he observed re-assured him.

'One point I would make is that with Maurice Fitzgerald, you were dealing with a total gentleman,' says Walsh. 'Never once did I hear him say anything about not being picked. I have vivid memories of all those games - semi-finals, semi-final replays, the All-Ireland final and replay. Maurice would be togged out going around the dressing room having a quiet word with every player.

'He would stop with the younger lads especially, offering words of encouragement. He would calm nerves before a game. At half time he was quietly complimenting players, offering bits of advice without intruding too much. He was a huge team man.

'There was never any obvious sign of friction or annoyance on his part. In training he was always in good form. He participated in everything. He had a lovely sense of humour and there was never any sign of that leaving him.

'Maurice had great friends on the team. He wouldn't dream of letting them down because of some personal agenda. If you read everything that was appearing in the media about Maurice you would have been certain that there was friction in the camp. If everything that was said was true then you couldn't imagine that the atmosphere was so good. But the fact is that there was no difficulty at all between Maurice and Páidí.

'That was Maurice. He was in that dressing room for the betterment of Kerry football. He had a huge influence during that Championship.'

—◊—

The storm did not abate after 2000. It actually got worse. During the early months of 2001 the Maurice saga dominated the sports pages of the national newspapers. It was unrelenting. It must have, by then, seeped into the consciousness of the players. It had to have been an irritant to the manager and his selectors.

It was a distraction that would not go away, no matter what Páidí said.

To get a flavour of the time it is best to dig into the files. The extensive coverage is quite extraordinary. Significantly, through it all Maurice never went public. He maintained a strict silence and did not implicate anyone or lay blame anywhere.

The Irish Independent on February 27 reported:

Kerry football fans were in shock last night amid growing speculation that Maurice Fitzgerald's future involvement at inter-county level is in serious doubt.

Reports that he was to leave the Kerry squad swept through the Kingdom yesterday following his failure to travel to Roscommon for last Sunday's crucial Allianz Football League game.

Fitzgerald played at centre-forward on the Kerry team which lost heavily to Offaly in Tullamore two weeks ago, but was omitted from the side for the clash with Roscommon last Sunday.

He spent some days in the US between the two games but returned home last Wednesday to find that he had been left off the team for the Roscommon clash.

Fitzgerald played for the full 70 minutes against Offaly but was named at No 21 for the trip to Hyde Park. His failure to travel has fuelled the rumour mill that he is set to end a glittering career during which he built up a reputation as one of the best forwards of his generation.

Kerry manager Páidí Ó Sé said last night that he was not in a position to make any comment until he had spoken to the player.

Fitzgerald informed him on Friday that he would not be travelling to Roscommon on Sunday, but it's understood he gave no further hint as to future plans. Fitzgerald was in Dublin yesterday, which ruled out any talks with his manager.

Ó Sé, when contacted, said: "I'm not in a position to say anymore because I think it would be unfair until such time as I speak with Maurice."

However, sources close to Fitzgerald have claimed that he was very unhappy at being omitted for the Roscommon clash.'

The following day, the same newspaper had an update.

The Maurice Fitzgerald retirement storm looked to have blown itself out last night, following discussions between Kerry manager, Páidí Ó Sé and his unhappy player.

Rumours that Fitzgerald had quit inter-county football after being left off the Kerry team for the Allianz Football League clash with Roscommon last Sunday swept through the country on Monday but a calmer atmosphere prevailed yesterday.

Manager and player had a full and frank discussion, after which Ó Sé said he was hopeful that Fitzgerald would continue while expressing regret at the circumstances which led to the controversy.

'I regret not consulting with him before he went to America regarding the game against Roscommon and also regarding how he wanted to play as many games as possible to build up confidence and continuity,' he said. 'I explained my position to him. I'm hoping that Maurice will put all this behind him and get back as soon as possible.'

Ó Sé said he was extremely hurt by some of the comments that were made about his relationship with Fitzgerald. "They are all totally untrue. I never had any problems with Maurice, whatever other people might want to think. The last thing I want is any hassle with anybody. I want to look ahead and try to get things back on track for the long season ahead. We have a lot of work to do, judging by our recent performances."

Fitzgerald, who was named in the subs last Sunday, refused to travel to Dr Hyde Park for a game which Kerry lost by 0-11 to 1-5 to plunge them into a relegation crisis.

They must beat Dublin in Killarney next Sunday to have any chance of surviving in Division One.

It now appears as if the outbreak of détente has diffused the situation. Fitzgerald had spent a few days in the US prior to the Roscommon game but returned home on the Wednesday night to learn that he had been omitted from the team, despite playing for the full 70 minutes against Offaly on the previous Sunday week.

Kerry hope to select their team tonight and it could include Fitzgerald, if he is willing to return. Liam Hassett is a slight injury doubt but Dara Ó Cinnéide, who missed the game against Roscommon, is expected to be fit.

And still it was not over.

On March 20 it was reported: *Maurice Fitzgerald has not yet resumed training with the Kerry football squad, refuelling speculation that the after-tremors of the recent controversy are still rumbling on.*

Having been omitted from the team for the Allianz FL game against Roscommon on February 25, Fitzgerald declined to travel to Hyde Park, leading to an outbreak of claims that he would not play for Kerry again.

Fitzgerald made no comment, although there were plenty of "sources close to the player" who did nothing to power down the rumour mill.

'Kerry manager, Páidí Ó Sé, spoke to Fitzgerald at the time and assured him that

he was a valued member of the Kerry squad. The foot-and-mouth crisis subsequently intervened, prompting a cancellation of matches and training for a period.

However, the Kerry squad have now returned to training but Fitzgerald has not yet joined them.

Ó Sé said yesterday that he was still hopeful that Fitzgerald would rejoin the panel and reiterated that, as far as he was concerned, there was absolutely no animosity or problems between them. "I'm getting tired of saying that now but I'll say it again and again if I have to. All I want is the best for Kerry football. We have a very important period coming up in April when we face three League games, all of which will be crucial, not just in terms of staying in Division One but also as a build-up to the Championship.

"I want to have every player available, including Maurice (Fitzgerald). There's a very big task ahead and we need everybody pulling hard in the same direction," said Ó Sé.

Finally it seemed there was an end to the saga.

The following day, March 21, the news was more positive

The Maurice Fitzgerald "will he, won't he?" saga was finally put to rest last night when he returned to Kerry training thus ending weeks of speculation that he may well have opted out of the inter-county scene.

Fitzgerald took part in a full session with the emphasis on stamina under trainer John O'Keeffe, with Páidí Ó Sé keeping a watching brief.

Phew.

It was over.

For the moment.

—⚹—

Ask any young footballer today what was the greatest score he has ever seen and it is likely that he will choose Maurice's pointed free in the final seconds of the 2001 All-Ireland quarter final replay against Dublin.

Maurice, however, came off the subs bench to score it and that opened up the great debate again.

He played in all three games in the provincial Championship that year but was substituted in the Munster final victory against Cork. This is how *The*

Kerryman evaluated his performance. *Maurice Fitzgerald and Noel Kennelly were substituted and, in Fitzgerald's case, it cannot be said that he left his imprint on the game.*

Páidí and the selectors left him on the bench for the All-Ireland quarter final against Dublin, played in Thurles. At the end of a pulsating game Darren Homan scored a goal to give Dublin the lead for the first time. Johnny Crowley, superb on the day, missed a chance to equalise. The Dublin goalkeeper, Davy Byrne, rushed his kick out. The ball screwed off his boot and went out of play. Kerry had a sideline kick, 45 metres from the Dublin goal with the referee, Mick Curley, looking at his watch.

Maurice took responsibility.

The flag was in his way, the linesman was in his way, the Dublin manager Tommy Carr was in close proximity and the words he was saying were hardly encouraging. Maurice ignored it all. He was in a world of his own, oblivious to the mayhem around him. Páidí would not have wanted any other player to be in that position.

He sent the ball high across the face of the goal and watched as it coasted in the wind, drawing inside the far post in a glorious arc.

He started on the bench the following week, was introduced, scored a point and Kerry won. The controversy reached the Letters Pages of the national newspapers. On August 13, the following appeared in the Irish Independent.

Sir - The time has arrived for the Kerry County Board and the Kerry team to make a choice, Paudie O'Shea or Maurice Fitzgerald. If O'Shea remains at the helm, Maurice's future at inter-county level is in serious jeopardy. The players know and if they are prepared to admit it, the County Board know also that Maurice is more vital to Kerry's prospects than is O'Shea.

Consider the facts. Maurice won two All-Irelands for Kerry and on Saturday enabled them to remain in the hunt for a third. What is O'Shea's claim to fame as a manager? He has treated shamefully the greatest forward of this or any other era. Hardly something of which he can feel proud. O'Shea should be stripped of his authority as a team selector forthwith. His actions in respect of Maurice Fitzgerald clearly reveal flaws of an unacceptable level.

John O'Shea, Monkstown, Co. Dublin.

John was well known to all involved.

The former sports journalist with the *Irish Press* who had founded the third world charity GOAL and turned it into a global phenomenon, John had close ties with Kerry and knew all the parties involved.

His letter prompted replies. On August 17 the following appeared.

Sir, I was horrified to read John O'Shea's recent letter, which was highly critical of the Kerry County Board and, in particular, Paudie O'Shea regarding Maurice Fitzgerald.

Like you Mr O'Shea, I think Maurice Fitzgerald will go down as one of the greatest forwards of all time but has yet to perform in this year's Championship for the full 70 minutes despite being given the opportunity.

Paudie O'Shea is a leader both on and off the field who does not bend to any pressure be it media or public. He is also a manager who has brought All-Ireland success at both senior and under-21 level.

The commitment and leadership Paudie O'Shea has given to Kerry football and the youth of the Kingdom over the last 25 years is unlikely to be seen again.

Proof positive of Paudie O'Shea's management skills can be seen in Kerry's two recent All-Ireland successes. The influence of Maurice Fitzgerald cannot be denied but the Kerry team won those titles and not just Maurice.

The decision by Paudie O'Shea to hold Maurice in reserve and make use of his talents as an impact player proved vital and wise.

Finally, I hope with a name like O'Shea, John from Monkstown will enjoy the rest of Kerry's All-Ireland campaign and celebrate with our highly successful County Board and team, including both Paudie and Maurice.

Paddy Mulvihill,
Chairman, Moyvane GAA Club.

Three days later the subject was again raised in the Letter's Pages.

Sir, I am amazed at John O'Shea's brutal attack on Kerry manager Paudie O'Shea for his treatment of Maurice Fitzgerald.

He asks what is Paudie O'Shea's claim to fame as a manager. I answer: he has won two All-Ireland medals as a manager of a Kerry team. My question is how many all-Irelands had Maurice Fitzgerald won before Paudie O'Shea became Kerry manager.

He had played for eight years for Kerry and they hadn't won any All-Ireland Championships before O'Shea took over and he had played under three different

managers, Mick O'Dwyer, Mick O'Sullivan and Ogie Moran. Since Paudie O'Shea
came on the scene, Kerry has won two All-Ireland's and are going for a third.

I have nothing but good time for Maurice Fitzgerald but you shouldn't denigrate
Paudie O'Shea as a manager. He has been a very successful manager for Kerry and I
am amazed at John O'Shea's tone of letter.

Jim O'Shea,

Co Kerry.

—⚭—

Páidí had other worries as he prepared the team for the All-Ireland semi-final. Tomas had been sent off against Dublin and would miss the game. Both Tomas and Darragh had been heavily criticised on television for the physicality they brought to the game. Their uncle had never before spoken much about his nephews, but he was angry and worried.

He was worried because he felt that some referees were being influenced by TV critics and that players were at greater risk of being carded or dismissed.

Páidí was not critical of Pat McEnaney who had dismissed Tomas. 'He is one of our top referees and I'll respect any decision he makes.

'My problem concerns the pressure referees are coming under from commentators who unfairly single out some lads and imply they play a rough type of game and need careful watching.

'We're all human and if referees keep hearing that certain players are flying close to the edge, it's very hard to ignore it. Commentators can do a lot of damage to a player's reputation with a few carefully chosen words.

'I just don't think it is fair that referees are being put under pressure by people wo are sitting back and watching games and then reaching conclusions which, in many cases, have no basis in fact.'

He had another substantial concern. Despite the sequence of results and the drama in which the team was involved, the manager felt that they were drifting. He found it hard to pinpoint the problem but he was uneasy. The team was not operating with the fluency they had brought to the 2000 campaign. He thought they might be vulnerable, especially against a rugged team like Meath, All-Ireland champions from 1999.

On or off the bench, Maurice Fitzgerald could not summon the wizardry to save Kerry against Meath. In what was Kerry's worst Championship performance during Páidí's years in charge they lost heavily, 2-14 to 0-5.

Kerry supporters departed Croke Park very early. The second half had only begun when the drift began. The Meath crowd loved it. It wasn't often Kerry were made feel so uncomfortable in the stadium they called their home from home.

It was an annihilation.

Consider this verdict from *The Meath Chronicle* newspaper beneath the heading *King Dumb!*

Awesome! Monumental! Staggering. It doesn't really matter which superlative you use because words alone cannot do justice to Meath's remarkable performance in Sunday's All Ireland SFC semi-final at Croke Park.

Never before has the Kingdom of Kerry been brought to its knees in such emphatic fashion.

Kerry, allegedly the best team in the land and a county which has long held the reputation as the connoisseurs of the game, looked like lost sheep and there wasn't a shepherd in sight to help them find their way home. Make no mistake about it, this defeat will damage the Kingdom severely.

Picture a featherweight boxer trading punches with a super-heavyweight and you might get a clearer picture of the dominance which Meath enjoyed in this game.

In his *Sunday Independent* column many years later Páidí admitted that the defeat was one that haunted him. He wrote:

In my own managerial career, one day stays with me: the All-Ireland semi-final against Meath in 2001. I knew things weren't right on the morning of the game. I sensed that there was something wrong with the atmosphere among the players in the hotel and on the bus -- they weren't fired up at all. I sensed it, but said nothing.

In the fall-out which followed our defeat, I spent many hours going over every little thing, every small detail of our preparation and I wonder now could we have had the players fresher. Did we get the balance wrong? I should have weighed up the amount of work we did in getting players fit against the amount of rest they should have had.

When a team is over-trained physically, it will eventually be found out. When the chips are down, they will play what I call punch-drunk football – like a boxer on his last legs just lashing out, relying on memory alone.

I often think of Tom O'Riordan, the journalist and former athlete. He came down one time to Ardfert in the early 1960s in the midst of an intensive training regime and didn't put his spikes on for 10 days. He then went back to Dublin to compete in a cross-country event in the Phoenix Park and broke the Irish record.

When we hear talk now of player burn-out, have you ever noticed how it nearly always centres on the debate over excessive training? We rarely hear a complaint that a young fella has had too many matches - mostly that he has had too much training. The move to ban collective training at inter-county level was a good one but we shouldn't lose sight of the fact that what's needed is less training and more football.

In 1982, John O'Keeffe had a lot of miles on the clock but he still trained as hard as ever – pushing himself all the time. After one session, myself and Tim Kennelly said to Micko that what John needed was a night at the Rose of Tralee to relax. "You're right," came the reply, "but ye don't."

My advice to managers this year is simple: remember to keep your team fresh for when it really matters.

Maurice Fitzgerald did not play Championship football again. He announced early in 2002 that he would not be making himself available for selection.

Páidí's final words on Maurice were spoken during an interview he gave to the *Sunday Independent* in the latter part of 2003. Discussing all the great players he had seen Páidí said, *I want to put it in record that I have always had the height of respect, irrespective of these fly-by-nights who are above in Dublin, these old smart alecs who aren't worth mentioning in print, who think that I have disrespect for Maurice Fitzgerald, because I haven't, because he is right up there with the best of them.*

CHAPTER 11

'Pride lads,' Páidí said.

'What is pride?

'I'll tell you now. Pride is when your mother puts your football boots out on the window ledge on a Monday and the dirt is still on them. And when people go past the house they don't see unwashed boots. They see boots with the Croke Park sod on them.

'That's what pride is.'

He had seen such an expression of pride in his own home. Beatrice didn't waste words when an act could better illustrate her emotions. When Páidí 's bag would be returned after an outing to Croke Park she would remove his boots and leave them outside on the window-sill for all to see.

During the Summer of 2002, an emotional roller-coaster of a time for Páidí and the extended Ó Sé family, he preached to his footballing congregation a lot about that sort of pride; pride in your family, in your home place and the people around you.

Above all, he talked about pride in Kerry and its place in football's firmament.

'I have no doubt,' says Dara O Cinneide, 'that his greatest triumph as a manager was in turning our season around that summer and getting to the

All-Ireland final.'

But, you will protest, Kerry didn't win the championship. How could it be his greatest triumph?

'Yes, that is the great shame. Because it would have been poetic if we had won the title. But that cannot take away from the fact that he was brilliant during those months.'

As County Chairman, Sean Walsh watched that season unfold he was more astonished with every passing weekend. 'In all the years Páidí served as manager I don't think Kerry played better football than that team played in the championship after losing to Cork,' he declares stridently.

'No one could fault him for the fact that we didn't win the final. He could have done nothing more.'

It had taken Páidí and the players a long time to get over the mauling suffered in the 2001 semi-final against Meath. The mauling they got at home, from supporters and the local media, was as rough as they had anticipated.

There was no hiding place.

They could not mount a defence because they did not have one. They spent a gloomy winter and an even gloomier spring tending to their wounded souls and damaged egos. Life as a Kerry footballer or manager was not supposed to be like that.

Marc Ó Sé escaped the melancholy. He had only operated on the fringes of the panel in 2001 and was busy securing a place on the team in the early stages of 2002. Páidí had kept a close eye on his progress. Young Marc was a tidy footballer and Páidí felt he could make a fine corner-back.

Marc had been banished from the West Kerry car late in 2001. It wasn't a form of punishment. He had lessons to learn and Páidí was making sure that those lessons would be imparted by the best teacher of them all, Seamus Moynihan.

Kerry were travelling to play Meath in a challenge game one non-descript Sunday afternoon. They gathered, as usual, in Killarney. Some thought they were meeting just so that someone could count the numbers and make sure that they had enough players travelling. Páidí had more important matters on his mind.

He took Marc aside and then called Moynihan over. 'Anything you need to know about playing in the full-back line you will learn from this man. Stick with Seamo ... and you won't go wrong.'

The car broke down on the way. 'At least it gave me more time to listen to Seamus and learn,' Marc chuckles at the memory.

The Munster championship was played on an open draw basis in the summer of 2002. The luck of the draw pitted Kerry against Cork at the semi-final stage, assuming Kerry would take care of Limerick in the first round. Despite their wounds, emotional as they were, Kerry would not be getting an easy ride in the new championship.

Marc Ó Sé played senior championship football for the first time on May 12, 2002, in the Gaelic Grounds in Limerick. He wore the No.2 jersey. Tomas was in front of him. Darragh started on the bench and came on during the second half to help Kerry secure an unimpressive four-point victory.

Another newcomer that day kicked one point.

His name was Colm Cooper.

The three brothers started a championship game for the first time together on June 16 in Fitzgerald Stadium against Cork. Darragh was Kerry's captain. Their father Michael did not attend all games that his sons played but he vowed not to miss this one. It was special. He travelled to Killarney and looked on with pride, reporting back to their mother immediately after the game that all had gone well. The lads had done well and no one was hurt.

It had been a terrible game; Kerry and Cork kicked eight points each, a miserable return on a miserable day. He didn't bother telling her that.

'It was a draw,' he told Joan. 'They'll be out again next weekend, probably Saturday.'

Michael died suddenly the following Tuesday at the age of 60.

The football community united in grief and provided comfort for the desolate family. Michael was buried on Thursday. Tough decisions had to be made. Darragh spoke with his mother. 'What should we do about the replay?' he asked.

'You dad would have wanted you to play.'

And they played. The game was delayed for 24 hours. That helped just a little. Kerry played poorly. Only three points separated them at the end but that flattered Kerry, a team described as 'lack lustre' in most reports on the game.

In the past the players could have escaped for a few weeks, drowned their sorrows or found comfort elsewhere away from football. But the introduction of the qualifier series in 2002 meant that they would be back in action within a fortnight. And Páidí knew that if their form continued to drift, their interest in the qualifiers could be short-lived.

Before leaving Cork that night Páidí had made some decisions. He had seven days to rescue their season. He brought the players and selectors together.

His message was brief. 'We meet tomorrow night in Killarney. And between now and then I want each and every one of you to think about this team and where we are headed. Because I don't think we are going to a good place.'

—⁓—

Páidí did a lot of the talking on the Monday night. He mostly listened on the Tuesday night when they got together again to continue their discussions in Tralee. 'We were rudderless, going nowhere and in those meetings we admitted that to ourselves,' says O Cinneide. 'We were playing terrible football

'A lot of us had been going for a long time ... seven years with Páidí. We were, as he would describe it ... in 'happy lounge'. We were content with our lot, wearing the green and gold and representing Kerry. But we weren't playing Kerry football. And that was the message Páidí wanted to get across.'

Páidí addressed his own weaknesses. He changed routines at training, tried to make it fresher and more interesting.

He changed the way he talked to the players, the manner in which he got his message across. He spoke to the players collectively but he also talked to them individually. He addressed issues quietly and precisely.

And he used a bit of fire and brimstone.

'Ye know lads why they brought in these qualifiers ... this back door, don't ye?

'They brought it in to make the weak strong and the strong weak. They're

fed up of us in Kerry winning All-Irelands. They don't want us anymore …
they think we have enough.

'Well I'll tell you what I think. I think we should break down that fucking
back door and show them that it will take more than that to stop Kerry
winning All-Irelands.'

Páidí was reinvigorated. So was his team. They drew Wicklow in the
qualifiers. Poor Wicklow.

The manager made changes. Seamus Moynihan returned to the full-back
position. Páidí had been severely criticised for playing Moynihan in that
position in the past. It was argued that a player with so much ability was
wasted in such a restricted role. He had succumbed to the fervour to release
Moynihan.

In an ideal world he would have played one of his favourite footballers at
centre half-back or midfield, anywhere where Moynihan could display his
full repertoire of skills. But in this Kerry team there was a problem position -
full-back, and Moynihan was the answer.

Páidí became more decisive. 'I think you might use the term ruthless,' says
Marc today. 'He was driven; no one questioned him that summer.'

Moynihan took the No.3 jersey. John Sheehan was promoted and started
in the half-back line. Donal Daly returned to partner Darragh at midfield.

Sean O Sullivan and Eoin Brosnan were handed the 10 and 11 jerseys, with
Noel Kennelly on the left wing. Dara O Cinneide was berthed at 14, flanked
by Mike Frank and Cooper. It was a formidable attacking combination.

There was some controversy over the staging of the game. Wicklow, with
the former Dublin goalkeeping star, John O'Leary as their manager, felt they
were entitled to a home venue. The game was fixed for Portlaoise.

Wicklow protested. The GAA authorities refused to budge. Páidí was
asked for his opinion. 'We'll play it anywhere they like.'

'We weren't going to show any mercy. We knew we would beat Wicklow
and we wanted to beat them by as much as we could,' explains O Cinneide.

They scored 5-15 in Portlaoise.

Eoin Brosnan scored 2-2.

Mike Frank pitched in with 1-3.

Even Tomas got in on the goal scoring act.

Wicklow scored seven points.

Next they got Fermanagh.

Again, no mercy, 2-15 to 0-4.

It was brutally efficient. The opposition was not the strongest but it was easy to see that Kerry were back on track. 'He was quite brilliant,' Sean Walsh says. 'Páidí became the dominant force in our lives. He would call me six, seven times a day … full of ideas, checking on arrangements for match days. He made sure nothing was left undone.'

He practised his team talks endlessly. He mixed the calm and measured with the fiery. 'At times you left a team meeting emotionally drained,' remembers O Cinneide. 'But in the dressing room before a game he got it just right that summer.'

They were drawn against Kildare in the final round of the qualifiers. This was a true test. Kildare had players of real quality who had tormented Kerry just four years earlier – Brian Lacey, Glen Ryan, Ken Doyle, Anthony Rainbow, Dermot Earley, John Doyle, Tadhg Fennin and Martin Lynch.

Kerry won by 2-10 to 1-5.

Eight days later they travelled to Croke Park. Galway, the reigning All Ireland champions, awaited in the quarter-final. There was something special about these Kerry-Galway games. The players knew each other well.

The two games they played two years earlier to decide the 2000 championship were amongst the most celebrated of the modern era. Tomas Ó Sé had described them as amongst the most enjoyable games he had played because of the quality of football produced by both teams.

Not everyone was anticipating a game of beauty.

In the *Connacht Tribune* their reporter Francis Farragher, once a Galway selector, had words of warning for Galway. *What must also be borne in mind is that Kerry, despite their reputation for pure footballers are far from angelic when it comes to stymieing opponents. Kerry are subtle masters of the art of the judicious foul or tug to prevent opponents from getting into any sort of rhythm.*

On the night before the game Páidí changed the normal routine of having

a meal and a team talk in the hotel. He brought the players on a bus journey.
To Croke Park.

Teams would not normally have access to the stadium on the night before
a game but Páidí had convinced one of his legendary contacts to have a gate
opened.

They walked as a group onto the playing pitch. They gathered around the
manager and he spoke. Again he emphasised Kerry's tradition. He talked
about pride. He asked them to think about how they had embarked on this
journey and what memories they would have forever. 'It was very special,'
says O Cinneide.

The Galway team was familiar. Gary Fahy, Declan Meehan, Tomás
Mannion, Sean Og de Paor, Kevin Walsh, Michael Donnellan, Ja Fallon,
Derek Savage, Padraig Joyce and Matthew Clancy had played many times
against Kerry. It would be a real test for the new Kerry.

They won by 2-17 to 1-12.

'I don't think that at any stage in Páidí's time as Kerry manager that the
team played better football,' Sean Walsh insists. 'He was immense through
all those weeks.'

In his newspaper column Mikey Sheehy heaped praise on the team.
*Without question this was the best performance by a Kerry team since the All Ireland
final of 2000.*

*All you can do is look for superlatives to describe it. Kerry were absolutely brilliant,
absolutely scintillating and it's going to be awful difficult to stop them from going all
the way now.*

There's no weakness in the squad and it is never easy to say that about any team.

*I have stated before that Darragh Ó Sé is the best midfielder in the country but I am
adding now that he is the best footballer in the country.*

*He gave a truly incredible display. For every minute of the 70-plus that were played
he was in there doing his stuff in tremendous fashion and he capped it all by scoring
a great point. Darragh Ó Sé has awesome power and just makes space for himself so
easily. He is a powerful rallying force for the team and his delivery of the ball is superb.*

*His brother Tomas was, I thought, the player who might have vied with him for the
man of the match award. He too gave a majestic display.*

Francis Farragher also paid his tribute.

Say what you like about Kerry but they are pure and natural footballers, their trade learnt almost from the cradle and finely honed along the way to produce players of real quality and high entertainment value.

The fun, for want of a better word, was only starting.

—⚏—

Páidí was never comfortable with the tradition of playing club matches while the county team was contending in the championship. He understood the needs and desires of clubs and their players but he naturally worried that some of his county men might come to grief in what were extremely competitive and often very physical matches.

His discomfort was all the greater in the middle of a hectic championship schedule imposed on Kerry through the qualifier series in 2002. All his carefully laid out plans, his meticulous preparations were at risk when a round of club games were fixed for the weekend following Kerry's victory against Galway.

One of those fixtures was particularly attractive – An Gaeltacht versus Austin Stacks. The match would be played in Gallarus and Páidí made the short journey from his home to watch his four nephews line out. Marc was at full-back, Fergal at right half-back, Tomas at centre half-back and Darragh was, as usual, in midfield. Aodan MacGearailt and Dara O Cinneide were also involved.

Páidí spent some time chatting with Bertie Ahern and Pat Rabbitte who were enjoying their traditional August break in West Kerry. He was nervous, restless and had to keep moving. He found a spot to watch the game. He was following play when he heard some shouts from the far end of the field. He looked to see what was happening.

A Stacks player was on the ground.

The umpire had his arm raised.

'Did ye see what happened?' he asked those around him.

No one had.

He saw the referee speaking to Darragh. 'Someone get that lad out of there, he'll get himself in trouble,' muttered the Kerry manager.

He heard another roar from the crowd. The referee was showing a red card.

'Who's gone,' he said, his voice rising.

No one was brave enough to answer.

Aiden Corkery reported the details in *The Kerryman*: *This game will be remembered for a long, long time but never for its result. For the record An Gaeltacht won the encounter but the score was secondary to an incident in the sixth minute when Kerry's captain Darragh Ó Sé was sensationally sent off for allegedly elbowing Stacks defender Brian Dennehy.*

Although in years to come hundreds will probably claim they saw the foul the reality is that only a small number of people clearly saw what happened. With the ball at the other end of the field, most of the crowd – as well as the referee – missed the incident.

However, umpire James Lyons didn't miss it and raised his arm to get Castleisland referee Tom McCarthy's attention. When McCarthy finally spotted the raised arm the umpire's version of events was sufficient enough for McCarthy to call Ó Sé over and furnish him with a red card.

Ó Sé and the entire crowd were visibly shocked particularly when the full significance of the sending off began to sink in.

The news that Ó Sé could now miss the All-Ireland semi-final swept through the crowd which only added to the anger of the home supporters.

As he walked with his head bowed towards the sideline the home crowd voiced their disapproval at the referee.

It's doubtful if a sending off in the county senior championship ever provoked as much controversy as this.

After the game referee Tom McCarthy received a Garda escort to his car, while a small and sometimes volatile crowd surrounded the Press area where the incident was being discussed on local radio.

A straight red would mean a four-week suspension. The Kerry captain might miss the big showdown with Cork. A furious and frustrated Páidí departed Gallarus in silence.

The dismissal dominated the sports news locally and national. It was the lead story on the local newspapers. Kerry's magnificent resurgence in form was forgotten. The red card obscured everything else.

The manager found solace with his players.

They gathered on the following Tuesday and the banter was merciless. Darragh's pugilistic skills were the butt of irreverent jokes. His protestations of innocence were met with peals of laughter.

Saint Darragh, man of peace.

Then they trained, as hard as ever. They could not control what happened in the committee room so they would not worry about it.

Events in the committee room worked in Darragh's favour. There had been frantic activity in that room. Advice was even sought from the GAA's central authorities at Croke Park. The crux of the matter was that the referee had not seen the incident himself. Others who attended the game and saw the incident insisted it was no more than a yellow card offence.

Six days after the game it was announced that the red card had been rescinded. Naturally, the news was greeted with a degree of scepticism. There wasn't a lot either Páidí or Darragh could do about that.

—◊—

Tomas didn't receive a red card against Cork but he did get a four-week suspension after Kerry humiliated the old foe in the All-Ireland semi-final.

It was a matter of considerable mirth amongst the players once it was clearly established that it would not force him out of the final, although Tomas did have difficulty seeing the funny side of it.

Three days after the game the GAA's Games Administration Committee viewed a video of the game in which there were a number of scuffles between players. Tom O'Sullivan and Fionan Murray had been dismissed after one flare-up. Colin Corkery followed them shortly after.

Tomas was ordered to appear before the committee to answer a charge of striking. It was dealt with swiftly and without a great deal of fuss. The four-week ban ended on the night before the final. It was much ado about nothing.

Nothing could take away from the warm glow of satisfaction. The Kerry team that had failed to raise a performance in two previous games against

Cork produced one of the great performances of the championship. Cork left the field a broken team having conceded three goals and 19 points.

Eugene McGee, the journalist and newspaper proprietor who had been Offaly manager on the famous day in 1982 when they prevented Kerry from winning the famous five in-a-row championships, described the victory in his column: *The most relaxed group of people in Croke Park yesterday were the four Kerry selectors John O Keeffe, Eamon Walsh, John O'Dwyer and Eddie 'Tatler' O Sullivan. They had the best chairs in the house along the sideline and looked for all the world like doting parents watching their sons playing an Under-21 game. They never had a worry throughout the game and anyway if there was any sweating to be done the manager Páidí Ó Sé was more than happy to oblige as he patrolled the sideline.*

Kerry had scored 14 goals and 76 points in five games, a remarkable return. Marc remembers the atmosphere. 'It was my first full year with Kerry and I had never experienced anything like it. Páidí was so inspiring. He led us … he carried us with him. It is hard to describe but all I can say is that I have never experienced anything like it since.

'It's just a pity we could not finish it off.'

'It would have been poetic if we had gone on to win the All-Ireland,' says O Cinneide. 'Darragh as captain, Páidí as coach and in the year that Michael died. But it just wasn't to be.

'But even if we didn't win the All Ireland we played the best football of our lives getting to the final. And we were very close to winning it.'

They led by four points at half time, and were still four points ahead after 54 minutes. Then Oisin McConville orchestrated a little magic to ease through the Kerry defence and get the only goal of the day. Armagh led for the first time in the 63rd minute when a Steven McDonnell point made it 1-12 to 0-14.

Ten more minutes were played and no one scored. Eoin Brosnan sought salvation with one last effort. The ball seemed to be heading over but drifted to the left.

Amidst the delirium that followed Armagh's first ever All-Ireland triumph Páidí and the players remained on the field. They watched history unfold as Kieran McGeeney bowed his head, closed his eyes and contemplated for a moment before lifting the Sam Maguire Cup to the skies.

Páidí knew how that felt.

He smiled.

He simply said, 'I wouldn't begrudge them. I never like losing an All Ireland but losing to Armagh and Joe Kernan, you couldn't lose to a nicer team and a nicer man.'

CHAPTER 12

The offices of the *Sunday Independent* on the fourth floor of Independent House on Dublin's Middle Abbey Street were quiet in the day or two following Christmas of 2002. It is not a time of year favoured by journalists, sports journalists especially, with little happening to assist them fill empty pages.

GAA writers try to vanish around that time of year. No one answers a phone. Footballers and hurlers tend to take holidays. There is no action and that means that there is very little to write about. But there must be someone on duty. That Christmas the duties fell to Kevin Kimmage, a native of Dublin with a strong family background in cycling and who had enjoyed success himself as a cyclist. As a journalist, however, his beat was Gaelic Games.

He chatted with his sports editor about various ideas, individuals who might be worth interviewing. Retrospective pieces, maybe. Or looking forward? Anything that might be interesting during these slow weeks.

Somebody like Darragh Ó Sé.

'He doesn't do many interviews, does he?' commented the sports editor, Adhamhan O'Sullivan.

'Doesn't do any,' confirmed Kimmage.

'How will you approach him?' asked O'Sullivan.

'I'll ring Páidí.'

At 10 o'clock that evening Kimmage duly rang the Kerry manager. They shared small talk, exchanged seasons' greetings, the usual.

'What can I do for you Kevin?' Páidí asked.

'Do you think there's any chance Darragh would do an interview with me? I know he doesn't usually make himself available for interview but I was wondering would you ask him for me,' enquired Kimmage.

'Interview me,' came the unexpected reply. His tone suggested to Kimmage that there wasn't any other option.

'But it's Darragh I would prefer.'

'Interview me ... I'm telling you.'

'When?'

'Tomorrow ... lunchtime.'

Normally such an invitation from a personality with the profile enjoyed by Páidí Ó Sé would be regarded as a privilege for a sports journalist. But Kimmage was wary and with good reason.

The two men had met for the first time six years earlier, in May of 1996. Kerry were preparing to play Tipperary in the Munster Championship, Páidí's first Summer outing as Kerry senior football manager. He was obviously a ripe subject for an interview. Kimmage had tried to make contact by phone, making a number of calls to the number he had found for the pub. Mobile phones were not widely in use at the time. The new Kerry manager was proving elusive.

The journalist set off on a speculative trip by road for Kerry, stopping by the public phone boxes in Mountrath in County Laois to try to get in touch. This time he was successful. 'I wonder would it be possible to get an interview with you?'

'Of course ... of course. Come on down and you can stay in my place,' was the enthusiastic response.

Kimmage arrived late in the evening.

Páidí was behind the bar, serving thirsty customers, locals and tourists. Introductions were made all around and the journalist was heartily welcomed. 'I didn't know him from Adam but it turned out to be a great evening,' Kimmage says. 'He got me drinking ... pints of Cider for half the night.

'It was great fun. He was full of chat, telling great stories. I thought "this is great stuff, I'm going to get some interview here".

'Then, around two or three in the morning, when there was only the two of us left in the bar, he decided it was time for the interview. And everything said up to then, all the great yarns and insights, were off the record. I couldn't use them.

'At first I wasn't worried. I thought that with a few questions I would prise some of the stories out of him again. I turned on the tape recorder and the shutters came down. Nothing. He withdrew into himself.'

Páidí's answers were short, almost clipped.

The jovial, generous host of the hours just past was gone, replaced by a football manager who was minding his words very carefully. If alcohol was meant to loosen the tongue it had managed to do the exact opposite to Páidí.

'I went home the following day disappointed,' remembers Kimmage.

At the beginning of 1997 the newspaper and the journalist decided to give it another go. Páidí had won a Munster Championship. Maybe the pressure would be off and he would be willing to open up. Maybe when the Championship was not so near Páidí would be prepared to provide an insight into his extraordinary character.

Contact was made. Once again, Páidí was welcoming. He agreed to do the interview and Kimmage prepared himself. 'It was even worse than the first time. He gave me nothing,' recalls Kimmage.

'I decided there and then that I never wanted to interview him again. I liked him. He was so brilliant as company but he was so protective of everything. Off the record he was full of life and energy. Once the tape recorder was turned on he changed completely.'

So between Christmas and New Year at the end of 2002, Kimmage faced a dilemma. He knew he would have an early morning departure from Dublin to make it to Ventry by lunch. And past experience had taught him that there might not be anything at the end of the journey to make the effort worthwhile.

He rang a mutual friend.

'Páidí's in mighty form,' Kimmage was told. The decision was made. Very early the following morning he began the journey that would have a sensational outcome.

—◊◊◊—

For a man who spent all of his adult life in public view and as one of the very few from the protected world of the GAA to be accorded celebrity status in Irish society, Páidí always had an ambiguous relationship with the media.

His approach in the early years of Kerry's successes – the mid-to-late 1970s – was balanced. He was respectful and suspicious in equal measure. He gave interviews but was cautious with his words.

As the years progressed he became more relaxed. He became acquainted with almost all of the journalists who wrote about Gaelic football. It was a very small group back then, with the personnel hardly changing during his playing career, and there was an easy alliance between the media and players.

He enjoyed the annual visits of men like Paddy Downey and Sean Kilfeather from *The Irish Times* and Peadar O'Brien from the *Irish Press*. They were men who liked a drink and were very good company, with a lifetime of yarns to impart. Downey and O'Brien were polar opposites in character – Downey the urbane, bow-tie wearing and eloquent son of West Cork; O'Brien an impish Dub from the northside with a sharp sense of humour – and great friends.

Kilfeather was a native of Coolera in Sligo, not far from Ballymote where Beatrice had spent her early years, and was a great conversationalist.

Those who did not bother with alcohol, like RTE's Mick Dunne, Donal Carroll of the *Irish Independent* and Jim O'Sullivan from the *Cork Examiner*, were also welcome guests and often stayed longer in Páidí's company than intended. There were also a growing number of younger journalists about the same age as Páidí appearing on the scene and he felt at ease with them.

As his playing career ended and he ventured into management the media began to change. There were new newspapers, national and regional, and the numbers reporting on Gaelic Games increased dramatically. The revolution in broadcasting and the granting of local radio licences brought a different dynamic. Páidí's caution returned.

Some accused him of paranoia in the way he dealt with the media and the way he instructed his players to handle themselves with journalists. Páidí never denied that!

He actively encouraged some players to avoid publicity altogether. He chose those he exposed very carefully. Páidí knew that players like Billy O'Shea, Maurice Fitzgerald, Seamus Moynihan, Dara O'Cinneide, Killian Burns and Declan O'Keeffe were well able to handle themselves on Press days before big games and left the responsibility to them while others were absolved from responsibility.

'Some of us were not entirely comfortable with it,' explains Dara O'Cinneide. 'I was one of those. I told him it didn't suit me but he thought I could handle myself and he ignored my protests and put me out there.'

As his managerial career progressed, however, he became even more cautious and protective. Páidí the Manager was a different person than the man who served behind the bar or put up the posters advertising events taking place in the bar.

That led to some ill-informed claims that Páidí was hogging the limelight for himself; that he didn't want any individual to enjoy a higher profile than he himself enjoyed. Such expressions furthered the distance between Páidí and elements of the media. He trusted those close to him but was extremely wary of anyone else.

As a businessman he quickly learned the value of PR and that is where the ambiguity was most pronounced. He needed publicity for his business, for boosting tourism on the Dingle peninsula. He had created a phenomenon in Ard an Bhothair that thrived on the creation and maintenance of his own image.

Páidí the promoter and Páidí the entertainer courted the media; fed it and dined on it. Páidí the footballer and Páidí the manager skirted on the edge of the media, engaging but maintaining a barrier.

It was a very delicate balancing act and very hard to pull off successfully. On one occasion he lost his balance and, typically in the life of Páidí, the repercussions were tumultuous.

He made a few lifelong friendships amongst the journalists and photographers that lasted through the most turbulent years of management of Kerry. From time to time he would discuss his caution with those friends. They would argue long and hard. Eventually the journalists would stop. Páidí could not be changed.

He was more comfortable speaking 'as Gaeilge' and the most enduring interviews were conducted with Radio na Gaeltachta and a man who would become one of his close friends, Martan O'Ciadhra.

Mícheál Ó Sé was also a very close friend and a journalist. He took Páidí aside once and admonished him for what Mícheál felt was his 'over protective nature' towards his players when dealing with the media. 'I told him that his players were well able to look after themselves and that there was no need to be so worried about the media,' says Mícheál.

'He rummaged around a desk and came out with an article from years back … his own playing days. It was an interview Jack O'Shea had given before an All-Ireland final in which Jacko was quoted as saying that Kerry would win easily. "Do you know what happened," he asked me. "We were bet and Jacko had a poor game.

'"If one of the greatest players that ever laced a boot can be affected by publicity of that sort then I'm going to be careful".

'I argued that it was a one-off. He rummaged again and produced more examples. I knew then I was battling a lost cause,' Mícheál admitted.

During the summer of 1997 I was working for a new newspaper dedicated to sports, *The Title*, which had been launched a year earlier by the former Meath footballer and journalist, Liam Hayes. Before our launch Páidí had sent me one of his notes wishing us success. We hadn't met for a while so when planning a visit to Dublin he called me and we arranged to meet.

After casually mentioning the phone call to Liam Hayes, he asked would I conduct an interview with Páidí which we could carry sometime in the next few weeks. I rang and got the response I expected. 'No problem.'

We met in The Berkeley Court just after six the following evening. His regular travelling companion was Derry Murphy. Derry had some business to attend to and asked what time he should get back. 'Don't be too long,' said Páidí. Ominously.

Our interview was delayed by a succession of admirers stopping by to shake his hand. He rose to greet the former Taoiseach, Albert Reynolds. Eventually I had the chance to switch on my dictaphone and ask the opening question.

He replied, 'In Kerry we start out every year with the same ambition; to win the All-Ireland. That is what the people expect. And that is all I have to say on the matter.'

He stood up. I protested.

'Come on P ... that's not an interview. Jesus, I can't go back to the paper and fill a two page spread with one line.'

'Make what you like of it,' he responded. 'That's all I'm saying. Now are you coming for a drink or are you going to stand there looking like an eejit for the rest of the evening.'

We went to the bar, had a few drinks and talked for hours. He described his frustration, sometimes anger, at the level of criticism both his players and himself were subjected to in the local and national media. It fuelled his suspicious nature. We argued about the rationality of his approach.

He could not be moved.

At the end of the evening as we parted, he said, 'I bet you've got enough for your spread now.'

I had.

Part of the contradiction was that Páidí was a regular analyst during the early 1990s on radio and had begun contributing a ghost-written column for the *Irish Independent*. He had not been shy in criticising Kerry. He had been particularly critical of Mickey Ned O'Sullivan in 1990, a matter of great regret later in his life.

In 1994 he was also critical of Denis 'Ogie' Moran and his Kerry management team, which included Seanie Walsh as a selector. 'The Bomber' had been recalled, a move that Páidí openly criticised.

There was mutiny amongst the Heavies.

Seanie Walsh recalls, 'One evening after a game in Killarney we were sitting in Jack C's bar. The mood wasn't good. We were all disappointed. Bomber was with me and a few others, and he was unusually quiet. After about an hour Páidí walked in and 'Bomber' jumped up, pointing his finger.

'Páidí had been very critical and we felt that he had been out of order, that he could have laid off. 'Bomber' was going to have his say. "You're offside Se," he told him. "Ogie's your friend ... Seanie's your friend. You played with these guys, you went to war with them and this is how you treat them."

"Bomber kept it up for what seemed like a few minutes. The bar had gone quiet, looking at the two boys. When 'Bomber' finished there was silence for a few seconds. Then Páidí calmly put his hands on 'Bomber's' shoulders and said, "now Bomber ... that you've got that off your chest, what are you having to drink?"

'What could you say to that,' says Sean, wistfully.

They had that drink and all was forgiven.

One of Páidí's closest friends in the media was Aengus Fanning, the editor of the *Sunday Independent* from 1984 until his death in 2012. Fanning was a native of Kerry and had played minor football with the county in the late 1950s alongside Mick O'Dwyer. He became a familiar visitor to Ventry. Urbane, with greying fair hair always worn long and swept back, nattily dressed, he enjoyed the rogue in Páidí and the sense of fun that always seemed to be around his friend.

Fanning's newspaper was not always kind to the famous. At times it was vicious. But Páidí was almost always well treated. In fact, Fanning as editor actually collaborated with Páidí on his column when it was switched from the daily newspaper to the Sunday edition. They would socialise together on holiday in Spain, clearly enjoying each other's company.

Critical words about the Kerry manager would appear from time to time. One example appeared in a May 1999 edition of the newspaper which was speculating about Kerry's Championship prospects. The largely negative article, which quoted extensively from Jimmy Deenihan and Seamus MacGearailt, concluded with the comment. 'If Kerry are to succeed this year, they must play without the paranoia which their manager displays.'

The words were penned by Kevin Kimmage.

They reflected Kimmage's own unhappy experiences when trying to interview the manager. Having vowed never to try and interview him again the journalist never expected that the vow would be broken at the instigation of Ó Sé himself.

It was typical of how things happened for Páidí Ó Sé.

—〽—

The atmosphere was festive, welcoming and convivial when Kevin Kimmage arrived in Ard an Bhothair between noon and lunchtime. His host and subject, Páidí Ó Sé, was in relaxed mood, looking forward to a holiday in South Africa with the Kerry players and GAA officials. It would be a break from the pressures of business and football.

There was a good crowd in the pub for such an early hour and Kimmage did not see his host at first. Then he heard the familiar voice.

'Kevin, come over here.'

Páidí was in company but gave his full attention to the journalist. 'Listen, we'll do that interview soon but I have one condition.'

'Oh no,' thought Kimmage, expletives occupying his thoughts, 'here we go again, another bloody wasted journey.'

'What's that?' he asked.

'That you'll sit down here and have a pint with me,' requested Páidí.

Kimmage remembered the last time he had sat drinking pints with the man. It had been a long night and morning. On this occasion he had to drive home. He would have one pint. Páidí ordered him a Bulmer's. A pint of Guinness for himself. They drank them and then walked across the road to Páidí's home where the interview took place.

It was said later, by friend and foe, that what transpired was the result of Páidí indulging too much in pints. Kimmage refutes that. 'Drink was not an issue,' he insists.

The interview was wide-ranging, reflecting on the past, looking forward to the future. Ó Sé was being open and honest, comfortable in his surroundings and lacking the caution that normally stunted such exercises.

Early in the chat Kimmage quite naturally asked about the level of criticism aimed at the manager following what had been a mere one point defeat to an Armagh team that was generally recognised as above the ordinary.

Páidí talked about wanting 'to restore lost prestige'.

'What do you mean by lost prestige?' the journalist asked.

The response was typical Páidí-speak. Unfortunately for him.

'We didn't win the All-Ireland last year so it didn't matter whether we lost by one point or 50. That's not acceptable to Kerry supporters,' he said.

Then he added, 'People will say that we are great losers and all that. We are gracious in defeat but, deep down, Kerry people don't like to lose.

'Being Kerry manager is probably the hardest job in the world because Kerry people, I'd say, are the roughest type of fucking animals you could ever deal with.

'And you can print that.'

They both laughed.

Kimmage recalls, 'My initial reaction ... well there were two actually ... was that it was a great quote and that this was going to be the best interview I'll ever do.'

It was a great quote but soon afterwards the interview began to stall. 'He started to clam up a bit,' says Kimmage. Páidí mentioned 'going with my own instincts'. What did he mean by that?

He wouldn't expand. Kimmage surmised that Páidí was saying he would have played Maurice Fitzgerald if he got his own way. In fact, his regret was not introducing Tadhg Kennelly into the squad for the final. Kennelly was contracted to the Sydney Swans in the AFL but had arrived home for a holiday in the late summer.

After 45 minutes the interview ended. Kimmage returned to Dublin. 'I went away disappointed after a promising opening. It was better than before but not what it could have been.'

The *Sunday Independent* did what Páidí asked. They printed his comments, word for word, on January 5. Kimmage didn't sensationalise it or even emphasise it. He just used the quote in the context of the interview. But the words jumped off the page.

The reaction was immediate and generally hostile. His opponents seized on the opportunity to attack the manager. Only one interpretation of the words was accepted and that was that the manager had insulted the supporters.

The interview was forensically dissected. Comments about taking a more 'hands on' approach to training were interpreted as a direct criticism of the methods of team trainer, John O'Keeffe, his former teammate. He talked about bringing new ideas, innovations, into training in 2003. Again, this was interpreted as a slight on O'Keeffe and the attacks on the manager increased.

On the Monday evening following publication Kimmage got a phone call at his home from the office. It was a warning. 'They're going bananas in Kerry.'

The Examiner newspaper and *Kerry Radio* had seized upon the words and the interview became a sensation. Kimmage was interviewed on radio. He supported the manager. 'Does anyone seriously believe after all he has done for Kerry football that he has no respect for the supporters?' he asked. But, the damage was done.

Páidí had actually arrived in Cape Town on the day of publication.

It seems that he was concerned about the interview though whether it was the 'animals' quote or not that concerned him remains unclear. He met Dara O Cinneide, himself a journalist with Radio na Gaeltachta. 'I'm after giving an oul' interview at home,' he told O Cinneide, ' … and I'm a small bit worried about it.'

O Cinneide promised he would have a look at it. He went to a local internet cafe and found the article online. 'I read it,' explains O Cinneide, 'and I didn't think there was anything in it to worry about. To this day I don't believe that what he said should have caused the trouble it did.

'I told him there'd be nothing about it. Jesus … was I wrong about that!'

The peaceful environment by the side of the hotel pool in South Africa was interrupted by the ringing of mobile phones and text alerts. O Cinneide received a number of texts from his parents. The word began to spread.

Trouble was brewing.

Páidí was charged, tried and sentenced to hanging before he even got a chance to launch a defence. He was in holiday mode; switched off. He didn't understand the strength of the storm brewing at home.

The Kerry County Board issued a statement. 'The Kerry County Board disassociates itself unequivocally from the remarks made by Páidí Ó Sé. We apologise to all the people who were offended and assure them that we do not in any way condone them.'

Páidí knew that statement was being issued but still felt it was much ado about nothing. Had he been at home he might have been able to gauge the level of controversy and reacted immediately. But he was cocooned, out of sync. It took him a couple of days to come to terms with the fact that his words had created a storm that was showing no sign of abating.

A former teammate, Ger Power, was highly critical of Páidí. That prompted his old friend, Liam Higgins to jump to Páidí's defence. Higgins found a new target for criticism – Kevin Kimmage.

'The man had a few pints in him and he was caught by a crafty Dublin journalist,' Higgins said on Terrace Talk, the *Kerry Radio* GAA chat programme.

'I never had a problem with Liam Higgins,' says Kimmage today. 'He was standing up for his mate. What else would he be expected to do.'

The Supporters Club in Kerry demanded clarification and an apology. As the pressure mounted Páidí had one ally at home that he could rely on. The Parish Priest of Dingle, Monsignor Padraig O Fiannachta, a renowned linguist and friend and counsel to Páidí, explained his interpretation of the words. 'In west Kerry, the term "animal" is not as offensive as it is to perhaps the more Anglicised, uppish people in towns like Killarney,' he said.

Páidí was spoken to by friends, both in South Africa and from home.

It was agreed that he should respond. A statement was issued through Radio na Gaeltachta, which was forwarded to Radio Kerry. It stated:

'I wish to clarify a few important items with regard to my interview in the *Sunday Independent*. I have always had the highest admiration for the Kerry supporters. What I meant in the article about the Kerry supporters is that they are very hard to please, always demanding the highest standards because they are very proud people.

'From time to time, I unfortunately go about describing things the wrong way and I apologise to the people of Kerry if I have hurt, disturbed or upset them in any way.'

His statement directly addressed John O'Keeffe.

'He was the one man I wanted and pursued for that job from the very beginning. He is the main cog in the Kerry machine and I have no question mark of any kind over Johnno's physical training techniques. As an individual he is a man of the highest integrity.'

Still the storm did not abate. The interview became the main item on the talk shows on *Kerry Radio*. A number of polls were taken and all suggested that the Kerry public wanted the manager to resign.

Local and national newspapers were full of reaction. Comments made in an interview in the *Irish Daily Star* then surfaced. Páidí had said in that interview that he knew on the Thursday before the All-Ireland final that

Kerry would not win because the players 'were not tuned in.'

He added that he had spoken to Brian Cowen in Government buildings about his concerns. The critics lashed back, 'What was he talking to him for; what does he know about Kerry football?' Indeed.

The advice sought from the Government minister did not concern football or tactics; it was about leadership and how to get the best out of the people in your command. In that context his visit to the then Minister for Foreign Affairs was perfectly legitimate and understandable. The critics did not point that out.

In Cape Town the chairman, Sean Walsh, and Páidí spoke daily. It was agreed amicably that the issue would be addressed immediately on their return to Ireland and that they were better off staying quiet until then.

One morning towards the end of the holiday they met in the hotel foyer. Páidí had been approached to do an interview with RTE. The GAA commentator, Marty Morrissey was holidaying in Cape Town at the time and called to the hotel and suggested the interview to the embattled manager.

Páidí was inclined to do it.

Walsh did not agree. 'I think you should leave it Páidí,' he said. 'We've been out here for 13 days and we've been in the papers back home for 11 of them. It's best leave it alone.'

'Chairman,' said Páidí, 'I think it will give me a chance to tell people what I meant.'

Páidí admitted later he should have listened to his chairman.

The interview did not go down well. He admitted, 'It probably added more fuel to the fire because during that holiday I wasn't short of fuel myself.'

The controversy escalated.

John O'Keeffe issued a short statement saying that he would not be taking a scheduled training session on the Saturday morning after the players returned from South Africa. 'There will be a meeting with management and the air has to be cleared,' he told *The Kerryman*.

O'Keeffe, Ó Sé and Chairman Walsh did meet the following Sunday. The meeting lasted two hours. Explanations were offered and accepted. The old teammates were never going to scrap for too long once they came face to face.

Anxious to bring the issue to a close Walsh called a press conference for the Austin Stack Park pavilion for Monday night, January 20. Neither the manager nor his trainer was asked to attend. Walsh had the Kerry GAA Secretary, Eamon O'Sullivan and PRO, Willie O'Connor with him as he read out two statements from the manager apologising to both the supporters and the trainer.

He also read a statement from O'Keeffe accepting the apology.

O'Keeffe's statement read, 'Following recent meetings with the Chairman of the Kerry County Board and my fellow selectors and a private meeting today with the team manager, I am pleased to confirm that I will continue to serve as physical trainer/selector to the Kerry senior football team.

'I welcome the unequivocal statement from Páidí Ó Sé confirming his total confidence in me. I am gratified to note his remarks concerning the physical training programmes I have prepared and implemented as being "consistently appropriate and effective."

'This has been a difficult time for me and my family and I wish to record my appreciation for the constant support of the officers of the Kerry County Board and my fellow selectors. I do not intend to make any further comment on this matter and I would urge everyone to focus on making Kerry the All-Ireland Senior Football champions in 2003.'

That effectively brought the turbulence to an end, much to the relief of everyone involved. Reflecting now, 10 years on, on the animals quote, Walsh says, 'I never had an issue with the use of those words. That was Páidí. People have to realise that there was no greater Kerryman, on or off the field, than Páidí. He was passionate about Kerry football, about Kerry and the Kerry people. Some people wanted to take the words he used their own way; for me those words were never a problem and they were not the reason he was removed as manager a year later, I guarantee that.'

The affair was quite effectively summed up in *The Kerryman* by Owen McCrohan who wrote, *A few erratic words delivered in a convivial atmosphere had the whole county tearing itself apart with sixty-five per cent of callers to the station (Radio Kerry), apparently, expressing the view that the manager should resign. This was an extreme reaction and showed the depth of feeling that had been aroused. But resign? For what?*

Páidí Ó Sé has done a lot of good for Kerry, both as player and manager, and one silly mistake should not be enough to hang him. He is a passionate football man who doesn't indulge in polite drawing room conversation and his robust personality is well known. His problem is that on occasion, he speaks without thinking and sometimes he puts his foot in it. He has to be more careful in future.

Lessons will be learned from what transpired in a Ventry pub over the festive season when loose talk was projected literally into print not by "a crafty journalist" who was trying to set him up but rather by somebody who was merely doing his job efficiently.

It read far worse than intended but that's the nature of the business. The written word is deadly and can be contorted and distorted to suit the minds of those who read it.

For sure, the hysterical reaction that followed was way over the top. There was no malice at work when Páidí Ó Sé sat down to accommodate a visiting journalist who had made the long journey from Dublin when he could have gone missing or said "call back another day".

His finer instincts, traditional West Kerry hospitality, the mood he was in, his innate good nature, all of these probably infringed on his better judgement.

Unwittingly and through nobody's fault only his own he became a victim of circumstances for being tactless in his choice of words. Already he has paid the full price for a mis-adventure that will make him more wary in the future. Or, at least, it should.

Later that year Kevin Kimmage was relaxing at home when his telephone rang. 'It was Páidí,' he recalls, ' … full of chat and good humour. He said if I ever wanted to interview him again just give him a call. He had no issues with me.

'That summed him up.'

CHAPTER 13

The sun had almost set behind Table Mountain, now silhouetted in the distance, as Páidí led his merry men in revelry on the long white beach of Bloubergstrand on the shores of Table Bay, just north of Cape Town.

It was an idyllic setting for a final night of ribaldry at the end of a two-week team holiday. They had luxuriated for some of that fortnight in the Hans Merensky Lodge and Country Club in the Kruger National Park and were completing the holiday by the sea.

Wives and girlfriends had left for home a few days earlier, flying into the storm generated by Páidí's interview. The last few days in South Africa was for the Kerry squad alone, along with selectors and a few officials. It was a time for strengthening the bond; re-energising and focussing on the year ahead.

This was the environment in which teams were nurtured. Footballers did not always form lifelong friendships with the men they played with. But through shared experiences on the field and on holidays like this one to South Africa in January 2003 they developed trust, discovered a commonality that was unique to the group.

It was experiences like those Páidí enjoyed himself as a player, on Kerry's world tour in 1981 and on various trips to America and to the Canary Islands, that cemented and sustained the team he played with from 1975 to 1988.

Páidí took charge for the final night. A barbeque was arranged. The best cuts of South African beef were ordered; fresh fish from the sea was procured from a local source. The manager had the boys to himself and he was determined that the final party would be the best of them all.

A jazz band was hired and the merriment began. Páidí was at the centre of everything, laughing and joking, encouraging the quieter lads amongst them to get involved and joking with the jokers.

At one stage in the evening as the band played, *Strangers on the Shore* Páidí headed for the ocean. He waded into the waters, arms flailing against the waves as if brushing them aside. Like Bull McCabe in the final scene of John B Keane's classic, *The Field*.

On the beach a nervous Sean Walsh looked frantically around him. 'For Christ's sake will somebody go and stop that lunatic from drowning himself,' he pleaded.

Moments later Páidí re-emerged beaming.

'Had you going there chairman … had you going," he repeated, chuckling delightedly.

—◊◊—

Sean Walsh didn't know Páidí well before he was elected chairman of the Kerry County Board in January of 1998. His knowledge of the man was confined to football experiences and Walsh had been a member of the Kerry executive that appointed the manager in September 1995.

Walsh had played against Páidí, though never as a direct opponent. The chairman had played on two county Championship winning Feale Rangers teams in 1978 and 1980, alongside Tim Kennelly, Jimmy Deenihan and Johnny Mulvihill. 'Johnny marked Páidí whenever we played against him and Páidí always said Johnny was the hardest man he ever had to mark.'

They met in several junior Championships when Walsh played for Moyvane against An Gaeltacht. 'He was a larger than life figure to us,' recalls Walsh. 'As a player he had this great charisma about him.'

He brought that charisma into his management. The two men began to travel together to various events – meetings, functions, funerals – and they got to know each other. A firm friendship formed, though at all times they realised that they needed to respect their roles as chairman and manager.

'We knew the parameters,' explains Walsh. 'We knew what could be done and what could not be done. There were certain limits to what I could agree to do; limits to what could be expended. He respected that and never used our friendship to go beyond that.'

The chairman always looked forward to a journey with the manager. Those were always lively adventures that seemed to pass quickly. 'The journey was over so quickly. He was a great conversationalist ... a great story teller.'

Páidí's contact list was a constant source of wonder. The Taoiseach, opposition leaders, churchmen of renown, the country's leading businessmen, the best entertainers – you never knew who would be ringing Páidí or who Páidí might need to contact during one of those journeys.

'You never ceased to be amazed by the way he attracted people to him from all walks of life,' explains Walsh.

Páidí delivered for the chairman and the chairman delivered for Páidí. 'He demanded high standards on the field and off it. As a chairman I had to match those standards. He could ring me once a day or he could ring 10 times. But there was hardly a day went by that he did not ring.

'There was always something to discuss. He was alway thinking about the job, how to be better and how to make things better for the players so that they could give of their best.

'He could be demanding at times. And there is no chairman worth his salt who will say "yes" to everything a manager asks for. Otherwise you would cause all sorts of financial problems for your county. There is a budget and it is your responsibility as the chairman to ensure that you remain within that budget.

'Páidí respected that. Of course he tried to stretch it at times. I wouldn't have expected anything different. But there was no off-the-wall stuff. He was very measured and he understood my position. I have to say I never got a request from either Páidí or the players that I considered excessive.'

It was during the early days of their relationship that Walsh was forced to deal with a thorny sponsorship issue. Kerry had a long association with the sports gear company, Adidas. Páidí himself was very close to the company and the people working in it and wore their gear all the time. But, the GAA banned the use of the gear and Kerry had to look elsewhere. Walsh negotiated a deal with O'Neill's, the Irish sportswear company.

It led to the one minor disagreement between the two men that Walsh looks back on with some amusement today. It was typical Páidí.

Kerry were hosting a media day during 1998. It was the first outing for the O'Neill's gear and, as such, an important day for the company and the Kerry chairman. The photographers arrived in Fitzgerald Stadium in abundance. The TV cameras were there too. It was a PR man's dream gig.

Páidí wandered around in his new tracksuit top, chatting and joking as usual. A TV journalist requested an interview pitchside. Páidí said yes.

The cameras started rolling. Páidí took off the tracksuit top. The shirt underneath was emblazoned with the adidas logo.

The chairman and the manager crossed paths later that afternoon. 'Don't ever pull a stunt like that again,' growled an angry Walsh.

'What stunt?' asked Páidí, eyes flickering in blissful innocence.

'The shirt.'

'What… Ah chairman, shure I was sweatin' in the heat.'

The chairman's ire did not last.

'What could you do,' he reflects. 'That was pure Páidí.'

Páidí never called him Sean. It was always chairman. After Kerry's holiday in China it became Chairman Mao. 'I always felt respect for my position. Sure, he could have a laugh and make jokes. He was always full of fun. But when it got serious and I had to act according to the office I always got full support and respect from Páidí.'

That friendship extended over the years to Maire and to the children; it also encompassed the nephews. The chairman's number was in all their contact lists; theirs in his.

That did not make life any easier for anyone as the Championship season of 2003 came to a close.

—〰—

Once the storm over Páidí's now infamous interview abated in early 2003 a certain calm settled over the Kerry football camp. They were refreshed after the winter break and the soothing effects of the warm South African sun.

No one could have forecast the storm that was brewing, its epicentre in the north of the island. It would spread over the entire land and wreak havoc in the further parts of the south west.

Kerry played Tipperary in the Munster semi-final and despatched them with relative ease. Cork had fallen at the first hurdle in the province. Kerry played Limerick in the Munster final. They weren't great, just adequate but another title was won. It was the eighth Munster title of Páidí's managerial career.

Back in Croke Park, on the August Bank Holiday Monday, they met Roscommon. They were coasting when they conceded three goals. It was sloppy. Páidí was furious. They had let their guard down. It could have cost them dearly and that wasn't good enough.

He had watched the quarter-finals the day before. Tyrone, the new Ulster champions, had 19 points to spare over Fermanagh.

They looked lively, quick and hard.

They played with a lot of players behind the ball, moving forward in a swarm. It wasn't a style of football Páidí would have enjoyed but he was happy his players could deal with it. They were vastly experienced, with buckets of talent.

On August 24 Kerry arrived in Croke Park and were suffocated.

Darragh Ó Sé was the best fielder on the pitch. He could win the majority of the ball in the air. The problem was when he returned to earth. Three, four, even five players swooped down upon him. He had nowhere to go; he couldn't even see another Kerry jersey.

The same thing happened to Dara O'Cinneide.

And Eoin Brosnan.

Then Eamon Fitzmaurice. There were white shirts everywhere. Someone along the line shouted, 'Is anyone counting how many players they have?'

'We were steamrolled,' recalls Sean Walsh. 'No one had seen anything like it before. It is a bit like what Donegal did in 2012. It was the first time anyone had seen that type of football; every time a player got the ball he was surrounded by a crowd of players. There was no time to do anything.

'They came to Croke Park with a plan … knew how they wanted to play. And they executed it perfectly. We were well beaten by the better team.'

Tyrone won by 0-13 to 0-6.

Páidí and his players went home frustrated and angry.

This was not how it was meant to be.

The manager was measured in his response. 'Tyrone got a lot of men behind the ball. It's the first time I have ever played against a team with these kind of tactics. But it's in the rules.'

He was asked if he considered that type of football cynical.

'If it's cynical or not they are in the All-Ireland final and that's what matters. It's immaterial what I think of it. What they did worked today.'

It was left to GAA writers to give a verdict on Tyrone. In the *Irish Independent* Martin Breheny wrote, *It was a day which pointed Tyrone towards the stairway to heaven and Kerry toward the hell of another football semi-final disaster. And it left the rest of us feeling that if God decides a spell in purgatory is required, he will reduce it by 70 minutes in lieu of yesterday's punishment.*

'Neutrals in the 58,687 crowd – not to mention the hundreds of thousands who watched it on television all over the world – were made to suffer through an abomination of a game, one where the pernicious forces of negativity destroyed every flowering instinct quicker than a powerful weedkiller.

The newspapers also focused on an incident at the end of the game. A spectator, bedecked in Kerry colours, had left the stand and breached the security cordon around the field. He confronted Páidí.

A blow was struck. Páidí did not react.

It was the final indignity.

Páidí and Maire decided to take a break.

On the Tuesday after the game they flew to Spain. Just before boarding the flight at Farranfore, Páidí took a phone call. It was the first of many that would question his future as Kerry manager.

In Marbella over the next few days they ignored what was beginning to happen at home. They knew there would be flak. Three big defeats in three years would have the critics loading their weapons.

Páidí reflected. He chided himself for not being ready for Tyrone. He thought he was prepared and the team was prepared. He had been mistaken. Did that mean he was losing his touch, the edge he always sought?

Was it time to go? Maybe.

Then he began to think about countering this new style. Could he re-invent his team and come back in 2004 and show them that Kerry were not as one dimensional as they looked in the semi-final?

He didn't want it to end this way. There had been so many good times. He had made promises to restore Kerry's reputation and he had kept them. But if he left the job in the wake of this defeat, would all the good things be forgotten. Should he rally the troops one more time and squeeze one more All-Ireland title out of them before he took his leave.

It was tempting.

Back home there were as many people encouraging him to put his name forward again as there were those calling for his head.

The defeat and the issue of the manager's future prompted the editor of *The Kerryman*, Dingle native Declan Malone, to make the future of the Kerry team the subject of their editorial the following weekend, an unusual step that reflects just how seriously the sport registers in the minds of the people in the county. It was a placatory piece that focussed largely on the huge effort made by the players in preparing for the Championship.

Then it turned to Páidí. *'Much will now be written of Páidí O Se and his future plans. The Kerry manager has been at the helm for eight campaigns and in that time he has transformed Kerry's football fortunes. When Páidí O Se took over the county had gone five years without capturing a Munster Championship and 10 years without a treasured All-Ireland crown.*

Within one summer we were restored to supremacy in Munster, while the second year of the Ventry man's command brought Sam back to Kerry after an 11-year absence.

For a county bred to success on the Jones' Road venue, this 11-year gap constituted a famine. But Páidí ended it. Indeed during his term of office Kerry won six of eight Munster titles and two All-Ireland titles.

Outside of legends Sean Boylan and Mick O'Dwyer there is no manager in the game today to match that record of achievement. For the past eight years Kerry have been challenging every single summer for major honours. Great credit is due to Páidí O Se for this.

So the manager must reap some of that due and be left to reflect for himself what his footballing future holds. He has given his all for Kerry, both on and off the field, and his next move must be his own.

Criticism is all very well if it is measured and qualified but it must never be forgotten what these players and men have given for Kerry.'

Much of what was said publicly was favourable to the manager. Former players like Mikey Sheehy, Jack O'Shea, Eamon Breen and Liam O'Flaherty spoke out in support. They felt it should at least be left up to the manager to decide what to do. But it was also only natural that reservations would be expressed, even within the squad.

Páidí would have understood that.

When the matter was discussed at the highest level in Kerry GAA, however, the mood was a little different. The consensus was that it was time for change. Páidí had restored pride and prestige to Kerry football. They would forever be in his debt. But it was time to move on. In three consecutive Championships they had lost big games to Meath (semi-final), Armagh (final) and Tyrone (semi-final).

A new voice, maybe a new approach, was needed. They would seek a new manager.

And that is when the problems arose.

As chairman Sean Walsh had the responsibility of informing Páidí of the Board's decision. Before he got a chance to do so a third party, to this day unidentified although a sufficient number of people are certain who it was, called to Páidí to relay the news. Páidí's disappointment was also laced with some anger at the manner in which the message was delivered.

The reaction of others carried greater fury. It was felt that Páidí had been badly treated; that he deserved to make his own decision about his future. And even if that was denied him then the decision not to re-appoint him should have been relayed in a more formal and respectful way.

A local issue became national news. The fate of Páidí Ó Sé was plastered over the front pages of the national newspapers; it was the lead story on television and radio news. Páidí appeared on chat shows. He was a headline act.

That all made an already unpleasant task much more difficult for the chairman. He had befriended Páidí and the extended Ó Sé family. It would not have been easy breaking the news in normal circumstances but the growing controversy and the publicity surrounding the issue put both himself and Páidí in an extremely awkward position.

Walsh telephoned Páidí on October 2. It wasn't the easiest conversation they ever had though it was courteous.

They agreed to meet in Dingle the following Monday. The conversation lasted for more than an hour. It was civil, a conversation between friends the content of which they both wanted to be kept confidential.

Two days later Páidí held a press conference in Killarney. Tom Long joined him. So did Liam Higgins and another friend, Peter Callery, a solicitor in Dingle.

The message was clear. Páidí would not be seeking another term as Kerry senior football team manager.

To this day Sean Walsh is emotional when he discusses the events of those weeks. He would have handled it differently; he had planned to handle it differently and to have spoken to Páidí before anyone else had a chance. But the 'unauthorised' third party scuppered the chances of that.

'It was a very difficult time for Páidí and it was a difficult time for me,' Walsh reflects. 'It was difficult because I considered him a good friend. I considered Maire a good friend. I was fond of the children and of the lads (Darragh, Tomas and Marc).

'At the time the executive of the Board felt that a change was needed. I was chairman and it fell to me to tell Páidí. Having so much admiration for him and time for him it was unfortunate that I had to do it but that is what I was elected to do. It would have been negligent of me not to do it.

'I know people were not happy with me and maybe to this day they're still not happy with me. But I am glad to say that Páidí and I remained friends and to this day I have remained friends with all of the Ó Sé family.'

In his delivery to the press conference, Páidí described Walsh as 'a man of the highest integrity. I like him and get on well with him.'

He escaped to Spain again.

While in Marbella he did an interview with his old pal Aengus Fanning. His 'sacking' was the main subject, though he did expand on other aspects of his life. Fanning wrote about 'assassins' plotting against Páidí. He described his friend in colourful tones.

Ó Sé's personality is extravagant, larger than life, he talks loquaciously, his presence is big and dominant, and his ego is built to proportion,' wrote Fanning. *He is classically the type of man who would miss the warning signals, the quiet rhythms of the assassins' murmurs, the hints that he was about to be ambushed. The shock he got still hurts deeply.*

The interview also broached the 'black dog' depression that Páidí had talked about in a television interview the previous month.

He had at that time explained, *Every footballer gets depressed when he loses. He is not a footballer if he doesn't get depressed. Any player that hasn't got a problem or that doesn't get down after losing a match, losing an All-Ireland or losing a semi-final, he's not a player at all. I do, I get really down if I have a bad night with the team, if training goes bad for me on the night, if players are not responding, yes, I do get very down and depressed. I become very hard to live with.*

I mean, I become very hard to be tolerated at home because I become grumpy when things go against me. Maybe I'm a bit of a spoilt child. I don't know. Maybe my mother spoilt me too much when I was small. But certainly my wife doesn't spoil me because she stands up to me. I do get down when I lose. I am very bad loser. I make no bones about it.

He also expressed a fervent wish to put the entire matter behind him and to get on with life. *I haven't come off the papers for the last three weeks. I am on every paper every day for the last three weeks. I'm on the television. That isn't my choice. I am actually the dead opposite. I am constantly being reminded by my family "Get off the bloody papers, because Páidí, that's not Páidí Se".*

He wouldn't be staying out of the papers for too long.

CHAPTER 14

Kinnegad is a sleepy little town these days. Nestling just inside the border of Westmeath, within touching distance of both Meath and Offaly, it is as sombre as it is tranquil. Sometimes, depending on the wind, you can hear the hum of traffic going east and west on the nearby motorway.

Once, not very long ago, all that traffic was filtered through the broad street that makes up the linear settlement that had been an important transport hub in the centre of Ireland for centuries. Inns and hostelries became familiar and popular stopping off points for travellers of all ages.

It was a town that was described variously. Locals often referred to Kinnegad as 'the crossroads of Ireland' and it was that. Weary motorists towards the end of the Twentieth Century would often call it 'the traffic jam'. It was that too.

There were many meeting points, the most popular of which was Harry's. Located in the centre of the street, just beside the imposing church, this hotel catered for generations of Irish men and women, boys and girls.

Just down the street was Jack's.

Across the road was The Dunner Arms, run by the hospitable Paddy Dunne who played football for both Westmeath and Galway and who welcomed football, hurling and racing fans with enthusiasm.

Further on, just beyond the turn off for Athlone and Galway, on the

Mullingar route on the right hand side of the road, is Denis Coyne's public house. It remains the same warm and welcoming place it always was, though Denis says it is less busy these days. There were summer Sunday nights when there wasn't even standing room in Coyne's and accents from a broad spectrum of Ireland mixed with the locals.

Football and hurling supporters returning to various points west of Ireland would mingle and share stories. Sometimes players would stop as well and were not given any special treatment. Everyone was equal. Horse racing folk would also stop by. It was convivial, it was fun. It truly was middle Ireland.

Coyne's hasn't changed but everything else has. Harry's is gone, replaced by a new hotel. Jack's has been renamed. The Dunner Arms is no more.

The traffic is gone as well. But Kinnegad has history; it has stories to tell. None of those stories is more spectacular, more fantastic or more enjoyable than that which began in Coyne's bar one late September morning in 2003.

Denis Coyne was doing routine chores behind the bar when the phone rang. He suspected it would be football business because football took up far more than the little leisure time he enjoyed in life. It was a commitment he gave easily.

The conversation that followed would be far different than anything he would have anticipated, or even concocted in his dreams.

Denis had been chairman of the Westmeath Football Board for six years at the time, one of many posts in which he would serve the Westmeath GAA community through his lifetime. On the other end of the line was his vice-chairman, Des Maguire from Mullingar.

'Páidí Ó Sé would love to come and manage us,' said Des.

Denis was momentarily stunned. He asked Des to repeat what he had just said. 'You're joking me surely,' he said simply.

Even when Maguire had confirmed the content of his message, Coyne found it hard to believe. 'I've just spoken to him … I just rang him and asked him,' insisted Maguire. 'If he gets the boot in Kerry he says he will come to Westmeath.'

Coyne decided he would have to speak to the man ultimately responsible for all GAA matters in Westmeath, the county chairman, Seamus O'Faolain.

He too was flummoxed. He also had concerns. Páidí was still the Kerry football manager and it would not be good manners to be seen to be interfering with matters internal.

'There isn't to be another word about this,' commanded the chairman.

'I understand,' said Coyne. 'But if he is no longer Kerry manager next week what should we do?'

'Come back to me then,' said O'Faolain.

When the conversation ended both men remained pre-occupied. 'I just thought "what if...."' recalls O'Faolain today.

—␣w—

Matters pertaining to Westmeath football never excited the attention of the nation prior to 2003. The GAA within had endured its own managerial crisis that summer when the football team manager, Luke Dempsey, regarded as the author of unprecedented under-age success for the county over the previous decade, had failed to gain the required support for an automatic re-appointment and had resigned. It barely registered on the national consciousness given the level of interest in matters further south.

Westmeath football existed in the wilderness.

The county's only claim to fame, some might say infamy, was the fact that it was one of just three counties that had never won a provincial Championship - Wicklow and Fermanagh being the other members of that unlikely elite.

Despite Westmeath's lack of success at inter-county level there was a very strong football tradition within its borders. The club scene was always strong and over the years the county provided a number of schoolboys who attended St Mel's College in Longford, one of the most powerful schools in football from the 1930s to the 1980s. For a brief but unforgettable period in the 1970s and early 1980s Carmelite College of Moate won Leinster and All-Ireland titles.

None of this had any impact on the fortunes of Westmeath. Clubs and schools were separate entities. The county teams lacked tradition. Comparisons with their neighbours, Meath and Offaly were unfavourable.

Wearing the county jersey was not always regarded as an honour.

Denis Coyne had served as County Board chairman in the latter half of the 1970s. There were Sunday mornings when he recalled calling to players' homes and getting them out of bed to ensure that Westmeath had enough players to fulfil a National League fixture.

It wasn't unusual to have just 16 players available for a game and the only supporters who attended games were those who drove the players. Few despaired because only a small few cared. They approached a Championship weekend like kids preparing to visit an amusement park. 'The annual outing' it was called.

Rarely was there a second outing during the summer.

Westmeath football did have its smattering of heroes over the decades – men like Sean Heavin, Mick Carley who won two Railway Cup medals with Leinster in the early 1960s alongside some of the game's most famous players, Dessie Dolan Senior, Willie Lowry and Michael 'Spike' Fagan. It was Fagan who showed the warrior spirit of Westmeath when plucked from obscurity to play International Rules football for Ireland against Australia in the 1980s. He became a national hero, his geniality as well as his sporting prowess endearing him to everyone.

The most famous Westmeath GAA figure of all was not a player but a referee. Paddy Collins was also the long-serving secretary of the Westmeath County Board. Collins became football's most respected referee during a career that spanned the 1970s and 80s, and took charge of the All-Ireland finals of 1976, 1981, 1984 and 1989.

All of those men provided some of the inspiration that kept the game alive. Behind the scenes men like Denis Coyne worked tirelessly even though they were aware that rewards were unlikely. Their only reward was the fact that they kept fielding teams even though they were not competitive.

They continued to provide the outlets and the opportunities for young men to play football. The county won Leinster minor titles in 1939, 1952 and 1963 but had not reached a senior final since 1949. Appearances in minor finals in the province continued to be sporadic but by the start of 1995 there were small signs that something positive was afoot. Former player, Luke Dempsey had been appointed to manage the minors. He instilled belief in his young charges and they created history. After beating Laois to win the Leinster title they went on to claim All-Ireland glory.

Westmeath celebrated wildly. Tens of thousands of supporters welcomed the teenagers back to Mullingar. They were feted as heroes. Gaelic football, often the third choice of young men behind soccer and rugby union, was suddenly the game to play.

Dempsey was promoted to Under-21 manager. Many of the players moved with him and four years later, in 1999, Westmeath won the All-Ireland Under-21 title for the first time. The final against Kerry was played in Limerick on Saturday evening, May 5. The Kerry senior manager, P Se, was one of the almost 10,000 people in attendance.

The Kerry team was defending the title won in 1998. Michael McCarthy, Tom O'Sullivan, Tomas O'Se, Tommy Griffin, Aodan MacGearailt were seasoned county players already. They were joined by Tadhg Kennelly, Sean O'Sullivan and a kid named Paul Galvin. Ian Twiss had secured a place in the starting fifteen. It was a formidable team and no one expected them to lose.

The final score was Westmeath 0-12, Kerry 0-9.

Luke Dempsey had got into the heads of the players. In a speech two nights before the final at the training base in Ballinagore, Dempsey had given an inspirational speech. Denis Coyne recalls his own reaction vividly. 'I got into the car to drive back to Kinnegad that evening absolutely convinced we would beat Kerry,' he says now. 'It was an alien feeling ... Westmeath beating Kerry! But I believed it would happen.'

The victory, said Dempsey that evening, proved there is 'no logical reason why Westmeath cannot go on and win Championships at senior level. Today's win augurs well. With the proper structures in place we can go on and compete at the highest level. I hope we can go on to even greater things.'

Westmeath would go on to greater things. Dempsey would make a contribution to that. But he would not be around to savour the success from the inside.

His elevation to the post of senior manager was inevitable. Westmeath had brought in managers with All-Ireland winning experience during the 1990s. Brendan Lowry was a member of the Offaly team that denied Kerry five All-

Irelands in-a-row in 1982. Barney Rock won an All-Ireland with Dublin in 1983. They were two of the most celebrated forwards of the 1980s and they played a part in the process of improving Westmeath's status.

Dempsey, a schoolteacher based in Rochfortbridge, was a calm, thoughtful and meticulous man. He kept his emotions on an even keel. He brought organisation to the camp, order and discipline. But Meath were his bogey team. For three years in succession Meath blocked Westmeath's progress in Leinster. The greatest frustration was in 2003 and it would lead to changes in Westmeath that would be seismic, to say the least.

Westmeath beat Carlow in the opening game of the Championship by five points and qualified to play Meath in the provincial quarter-final on June 1 in Croke Park. Westmeath started poorly and were five points down at half time.

They fought back to level the game and the teams were 2-13 apiece in the final moments when the referee, Michael Curley from Galway, awarded Westmeath a free. Meath's veteran player, Graham Geraghty vehemently protested the decision and Curley brought the ball forward. In most circumstances this would be advantage Westmeath. But by bringing the ball forward Curley actually narrowed the angle for free-taker, Dessie Dolan. He missed.

It was a huge moment.

Doubts began to creep into the minds of players. They had another chance but a few inside the camp were worried. They feared this team would never beat Meath. Some began to doubt the manager. At half time during the drawn game, despite his team having played relatively tamely in the first half, Dempsey had been calm and controlled, as usual. Before the players left the dressing room, however, Jack Cooney, a selector, made a loud and impassioned plea to the players. Banging his fist off a table he demanded an improvement. It was fire and brimstone, not the Dempsey way. This time it seemed to work.

The team was flat in the replay and well beaten.

In the All-Ireland qualifier series they lost to Monaghan. The whispers about the manager became louder. Dempsey heard them but decided he wanted to stay. In newspaper interviews he explained why. 'I've come too far and put in too much work at this stage to give it up. I feel we were only a scrape of paint away from reaching a Leinster semi-final against Kildare. That's too small a gap to walk away from given the problems we had this year.' Those problems included injuries to key players at key times during the year.

Dempsey went on, 'I really don't think we could be as unlucky again. Once I have the respect of the players and backing from the county board I'd like to carry on.'

And that is when Luke Dempsey's problems began.

Some of the players felt that the time had come for a change of management. A few others, including a number who had been with Dempsey since the heady days of 1995, felt he should be given another chance. The manager decided that it was better to meet with the players, thrash out their thoughts and see if they still supported him.

The meeting went well. The players gave him a vote of confidence and as he drove home to Rochfortbridge that night Dempsey was already thinking, planning for another campaign.

In Kinnegad Denis Coyne was called to the telephone.

A player, whom Coyne does not identify, told him there was a problem. He outlines what happened next. 'He said, "Denis we've just met with Luke and told him that we're backing him. But the truth is we think he should go. We need something different. Can you do something about it?"'

It was an awkward situation for Coyne who had worked closely with Dempsey for many years. To this day, he accepts ruefully, he is regarded as the man who 'sacked' Luke Dempsey, the manager described at the time by the county chairman Seamus O'Faolain as 'the best manager Westmeath has ever had, we owe him a huge debt of gratitude.'

The Westmeath Football Board met on the night of Wednesday, August 13. The appointment of the team manager for the following season was at the top of the agenda. Dempsey was on holidays in Portugal unaware that the matter was up for discussion. Denis Coyne spoke to the meeting. The phone call from the player was relayed. Other delegates expressed some reservations about continuing with Dempsey at the helm.

The decision was taken. Dempsey would not be immediately re-appointed but would be one of a number of candidates interviewed for the position. 'We're not ruling anyone in or out,' Denis Coyne later explained to the media.

Two weeks later the decision was taken out of their hands. On August 27 Dempsey announced that he would not be seeking re-appointment. Without the full and unequivocal support of the Football Board and an element of doubt about the position taken by the players, he felt he could not continue.

It was, in many ways, very similar to what was happening in Kerry at the same time. It did not attract in any way the same level of interest nationally. In fact, Dempsey's departure was completely overshadowed by the events in Kerry.

And as Denis Coyne and an appointment committee began to search for a successor they were able to carry out their business in anonymity. Many names were linked to the job – Dessie Dolan Senior, the former Down manager Peter McGrath and former Meath star forward, Colm O'Rourke. At no stage in the proceedings was the name Páidí Ó Sé mentioned.

—⁓—

On the morning of October 8 Denis Coyne was relaxing with a cup of tea in the back lounge of his pub and reading the *Irish Independent*. There was extensive coverage of Páidí Ó Sé's press conference held the previous evening in Killarney. Des Maguire's phone call of the previous week had never left his mind. His eyes scanned the pages.

And something caught his attention. Páidí would be appearing at the launch of some festival or other in the Dublin pub, The Merchant, owned by the unrelated O'Shea family. A plan of action formed.

Way back at the beginning of the 1980s Coyne had become friends with two West Kerry natives who lived for some time in the Kinnegad area. Alistair Fitzgerald and Teresina Higgins were married in 1982 and Denis, his wife Eithne, and a number of other people from Kinnegad made the journey to the Dingle peninsula for the wedding. Teresina is a sister of Liam Higgins, the two-time All-Ireland winner who was at the time a Kerry selector. Liam was also one of Páidí's closest friends.

The wedding was held on the Saturday after the All-Ireland final when Kerry folk were still recovering from the shock of losing to Seamus Darby's late goal. 'That was the first time I met Páidí,' recalls Coyne. 'We all pretended we were from Offaly. It was being said that there was one guest missing from the wedding. His name was Sam. It was all good fun.'

More than 29 years later Alistair and Teresina had moved to Dublin but still kept in touch with their old friends in the midlands. Alistair, an accountant, also had connections with the O'Shea family. Denis decided to give him a call. He explained that there was some evidence that Páidí would be interested in coming to Westmeath.

Alistair's initial response was curt. 'Are ye all gone mad?' he asked.

Or words to that effect

Denis persisted and Alistair agreed he would speak to Páidí in The Merchant on the evening of Thursday, October 9. The following morning Denis got the response he hoped for. 'That man wants to talk to you,' was the simple message from Alistair and he passed on Páidí's mobile phone number.

The conversation that followed between Coyne and Páidí was relatively brief. Coyne admits to this day that he was still a bit taken aback by the prospect of Páidí coaching Westmeath. Just a week before Páidí was front page news, his position in Kerry a regular item on primetime television. He was battling to hold on to the job of Kerry football manager. Now Denis Coyne was about to ratify his appointment as Westmeath manager.

'I'd love to manage Westmeath,' Páidí confirmed. 'But we'll keep a lid on this until Monday. I have a couple of people to speak to.'

Coyne agreed. Páidí would attend the funeral of Padraig 'Jock' Haughey, brother of the former Taoiseach and himself an All-Ireland winner with Dublin in the 1950s in Dublin on Monday, October 13. He was flying by helicopter to the Citywest hotel and the two men arranged to meet for an hour on Monday afternoon to finalise whatever arrangements needed to be made.

Denis Coyne rang both Seamus O'Faolain and Paddy Collins to update them. The excitement was already building but both men agreed that no word of the impending appointment would be leaked until Coyne contacted them on Monday evening.

However, they learned very quickly that, when it came to Páidí Ó Sé, keeping the lid on things was not that simple. Late on Saturday morning O'Faolain rang Coyne. 'I thought this was supposed to a secret,' he said.

'Well I told you the way I saw it,' said Coyne.

'It's on the front page of the *Examiner*,' reported an exasperated O'Faolain.

A specially convened meeting of the Westmeath Football Board was called for the following Wednesday. There was a full turn-out in Cusack Park. Various aspects of the appointment were questioned by delegates but it took just 15 minutes for the appointment to be ratified. *The Westmeath Examiner* newspaper reported extensively on the content of the meeting.

The question of remuneration was raised. The *Examiner* reported: *On the latter St Mary's (club delegate) Christo Bradley was informed that the financial arrangements had not been put in place but the chairman did advise the meeting that Páidí's initial response to the question of expenses was that he would not be "too hard" on money.*

Delegates were also concerned about the distance between West Kerry and Westmeath. The newspaper revealed: *When quizzed by Mr Oliver Costello of Moate All Whites, Mr Coyne said that the question of travel was one that would have to be given close scrutiny. Stating that a Westmeath camogie team had taken six hours to travel to the Ventry area the previous weekend, Mr Coyne said that a person had contacted him to say he would be prepared to fly Páidí to and from Kerry for the fuel money alone. A further difficulty, according to Mr Coyne, was that Farranfore Airport closed at 5.0 p.m. in winter time.*

Páidí's footballing pedigree did not convince everyone of the merits of his appointment. *When Killucan delegate Mr Des Briody suggested that the former Kerry ace knew nothing about footballers across Westmeath, Mr Coyne said he would listen to people before making up his own mind.*

The appointment for a two-year term was formally proposed by the delegate from the Rosemount club, P.O. Keenan and seconded by Christo Bradley. Two days later as a helicopter deposited Páidí onto the lawns of the Bloomfield House Hotel, outside Mullingar, accompanied from West Kerry by Derry Murphy, hundreds of supporters had gathered near the Greville Arms hotel in the centre of the town where a press conference had been arranged.

Páidí's old friend, Tom O'Riordan had travelled from Dublin to report on the event for the *Irish Independent*. *Such was the excitement surrounding the arrival of the Kerry legend, traffic in the town came to a standstill,'* reported O'Riordan. *'Local fans cheered loudly when he stepped up on the stage and Ó Sé got the crowd going further by punching the air like a man who had just brought home the Sam Maguire Cup.*

The press conference lasted 45 minutes. When it concluded Páidí stood up, removed his jacket, and pulled on a Westmeath jersey. The photographers went into a frenzy. The attendance erupted, clapping and cheering. No one had ever seen the like of it before. This wasn't just sport, it was showbusiness and it was well handled by people who did not have a lot of experience of handling this sort of situation.

Páidí outlined his thoughts. 'Westmeath have gone close to winning big games in the past. I'm not going to set myself up by promising anything but I will say that I intend to do my utmost to bring success to Westmeath. It will mean hard work. That is definitely the key to success on the sporting field. There are no short cuts to success and I'm confident that when I come here and meet the Westmeath players that they will understand very quickly where I'm coming from and what I want to achieve together with them.'

Newspaper speculation began about the cost of the appointment. Denis Coyne reflects that it was never an issue. 'People kept saying to me that Páidí would cost us a fortune. And it was different paying a mileage rate for a man coming on a 400 mile round journey from Ventry compared to a man living in the county.

'But it was not Páidí who cost us. It was the regime he introduced. Of course, for us it was going to be a gamble. But from the earliest days we spotted benefits. There was unprecedented interest in our team. That was positive. We had to do something different and appointing Páidí was certainly different.

'The people responded. Why wouldn't they? We had a legend of the game with us. Eight All-Ireland medals. Manager of two All-Ireland winning teams. We had to soak up all of that experience and knowledge. It would cost us, of course. The first thing we did was bring about 40 players to Sunderland for three days to see how they did things there.

'It opened our eyes, especially the eyes of the players. This was an opportunity we would not have had before. Páidí was a friend of Mick McCarthy. That was new to us.'

Páidí and his friends.

Westmeath would never be the same.

CHAPTER 15

On a cold Sunday afternoon in November 2003 in the south Dublin suburb of Templeogue two men honed from the wilds of West Kerry stood together, watching a game of football intently. They were silent mostly, occasionally exchanging short sentences about the fare being served.

There weren't many onlookers and those who were passing by didn't linger. The football wasn't that bad – it wasn't great, it should be pointed out – but the members of the St Jude's club had other matters to occupy them, juveniles to coach, pitches to cut, that kind of thing, the ordinary mundane tasks required of any club membership.

Dublin were hosting Westmeath. It was a non-descript match that would have received no attention at all except for the fact that it was the first outing for Westmeath since Páidí Ó Sé had been appointed their manager in a blaze of publicity just a month earlier.

The new boss had only had a brief introduction to the players. He was still busily building up his management team. Taking charge of Westmeath that afternoon were two of the selectors recently appointed, Paddy Collins and Jack Cooney.

Collins, one of the most respected and popular referees in the history of Gaelic football, was well known nationally. He was also secretary to the Westmeath County GAA Board. Cooney had been an excellent player in his time and had acted as a selector in the previous administration.

They had put together the team for this game, made up largely from the panellists from the 2003 Championship who remained available. It wasn't difficult to persuade them to turn up – a new manager, especially one as famous as Ó Sé – was sure to generate interest.

Standing on the sideline alongside the new manager, the pair slightly detached from everyone else, was an unfamiliar figure. Tall, erect and composed, the opposite to Ó Sé in almost every way physically, he would become very familiar to the players especially in the coming years.

Tomas O Flatharta was Páidí's new wing man.

They knew each other for most of their lives. They played football together in West Kerry and shared two passions above all others, football and the Irish language.

O Flatharta was from Tiorabhain, a cluster of houses just over a mile outside Ballyferriter on the road to Dunquin. Tiorabhain is also the home place of the former Siobhan Ferriter who married Stephen Fahy when he was posted as a Garda in Ballyferriter and their daughter Maire married Páidí.

He had moved to Dublin to pursue a successful career in banking. He transferred his football allegiance to the Kilmacud Crokes club and was a member of the squad which won the All-Ireland club title in 1995. But he never lost touch with his roots and was in regular contact with Páidí.

Significantly they met in Croke Park at the All-Ireland final in 2003. O Flatharta had been hearing rumours, from both Kerry and from Kerrymen around Dublin, that there were moves to get rid of Páidí as Kerry manager. The subject was raised in Croke Park.

'Don't worry,' Páidí reassured him. 'I'll be fine.'

'Just go carefully,' advised Tomas.

Páidí remembered that conversation when he began to take stock of his new post in Westmeath. Tomas, he thought, was ideally placed in Dublin to help out. What precise role he would fill could be decided later. 'I need someone looking out for me in this one,' Páidí told those closest to him. 'And the one thing I am sure is that I can rely on Tomas.'

He phoned O Flatharta on his mobile.

'Will you come down to Mullingar with me to pick a few selectors for this job?' was the request framed more like a command. Tomas protested that he didn't know the people, didn't know anything about Westmeath football and didn't see how he could be of much help.

'Come on anyway.'

Shortly afterwards Páidí asked him to be a selector. This was when the Celtic Tiger was roaring at his loudest. Bankers simply did not have time to be helping to run inter-county teams. 'I was working until 6.0 pm and sometimes later every day,' explains O'Flatharta. 'It was flat out. And there was no motorway to the west then. It could take you two hours to get to Mullingar ... I told him that.

'I'll get a helicopter to pick you up,' Páidí insisted.

'I work in the city centre ... where will you land it?'

'Did you ever hear of Leopardstown?' He had an answer for everything, rational or not.

Páidí rang him every day, cajoling him. When the house phone rang late one evening he expected it would be Páidí again. But the voice was different, quieter, older and more refined. 'Hello Tomas ... this is Kevin Heffernan.'

Heffo, the legend, was helping the Dublin County Board organise management teams for the Dublin under-age structures. He wondered if Tomas would be interested in becoming involved with the Dublin minor team. At any other time he would have jumped at the chance, especially at the request of a man he admired greatly. But the Páidí factor weighed heavily.

Darragh Ó Sé was despatched by Páidí to apply pressure. When they spoke, Tomas asked Darragh what he thought the outcome of the adventure might be.

'All I can say is that if you go with him for two years you'll have the best craic ever. Other than that I don't know how it will work out.'

Tomas went to his boss in AIB and explained his situation. Could he combine his work with football? 'If you come in earlier you can leave earlier,' was the response. It clinched the deal.

It brought him to St Jude's that November day, a club against whom he had often played. This was a far different experience. Ten minutes into the second half Páidí Ó Sé let out a sigh of desperation. He turned to his friend. 'Jesus Christ almighty … what have we let ourselves in for?'

'We … ' laughed Tomas. 'There's no "we" here. It was you got us into this.'

Páidí, however, was working hard. He was putting together a management team of stout individuals. Mick Duffy became team co-ordinator. He was involved with the Supporters' Club as well. It was a good combination. Dr Gerry O'Flynn, Seamus Brown, and Jimmy Marshall were amongst those brought on board. They liked Páidí, dedicated themselves to him.

A trainer was needed. It would be a massively important role. 'You do it Tomas,' he said one evening.

'I've never been involved with an inter-county team before, what would I know about training them,' he replied.

'Jesus Christ, you're as fit as a fiddle yourself … in great shape. Whatever you need just ask for it and you'll get it. Don't be worrying about it. I'll back you all the way.'

Páidí reflected on his own playing days and Mick O'Dwyer's obsession with fitness. Modern standards were higher again. He knew there were good footballers in Westmeath but he was not happy with their fitness. That was the priority. He sat down with O'Flatharta one evening and outlined his plans.

'These guys are not in the shape they needed to be. I want them to be the fittest team in Ireland. I don't care about anything else. Fuck the League. Get them fit so that when I start getting ready for the Championship they are as fit as they possibly can be! The Championship is the target. Nothing else … nothing, matters.'

Mick Galwey, the former Irish rugby international, was contacted. He immediately pointed them in the direction of Liam Hennessy, an internationally recognised fitness coach. A former athlete, Hennessy has worked with Irish Olympic teams, the Irish rugby team, soccer teams in the English Premiership, and with Tipperary, his native county, when they won the All-Ireland hurling Championship in 2001.

'Liam was fantastic,' says O'Flatharta. 'He advised me on every aspect of physical preparation. It was a great learning experience. He helped me draw up programmes for both the gym and the training field. The sessions were unreal. The players never saw it coming. It was a big shock to them.'

Denis Coyne attended those early sessions. He too was shocked. He remembered reading about the reactions in Kerry to the early sessions undertaken by Mick O'Dwyer, the view widely held that he would kill the players. This was far worse.

'I would go out to Ballinagore where the team trained and it was something we had never seen in Westmeath before,' recalls Coyne. 'It was a whole new culture. I saw fellas crawling across the field on their stomachs, using only their elbows and knees to propel them forward. They couldn't use their hands or feet.'

There were a few other surprises in store. Páidí arrived one evening and asked the Football Board officers present for a chat. 'I need a 100 metre sand track installed over there by the side of the pitch.' The players wondered what was going on over the next number of weeks as workers prepared the track. They would soon find out.

Dessie Dolan, who would be one of Páidí's best players in Westmeath, still grimaces at the memory. Páidí had the entire panel sprinting backwards on that track, the sand sucking their feet into its purgatory. 'It was torture,' says Dolan.

'Páidí would tell us stories of how Mick O'Dwyer ran them from wire to wire. And then he made us do it … for hours. Sprinting full tilt. Absolute torture. You would feel sick in your stomach just thinking about it. We thought we had worked hard and that we were fit before he came to us. But he brought it to a completely new level. He worked us to the bone.'

The physical approach was not the only change introduced. The new regime also tackled the mental approach and that was just as difficult for the players. There were used to a culture whereby if training started at 7.30 in the evening you turned up at 7.30. And if you needed physiotherapy or some other attention you got it then. It meant you might not be ready to join training until an hour later. That would change.

'It became clear very quickly that if you wanted physio then you arrived at 6.00 or 6.30 at the latest and the physiotherapist would be available,' Denis Coyne recalls. 'Your treatment was properly scheduled and there was no waiting around.

'And if training started at 7.30 you were on the pitch at 7.30. They wouldn't tolerate you being a minute late. No excuses. It may seem like a small thing now but at the time it was the start of a complete change in attitude towards how you prepared.

'We had never seen anything like it in Westmeath.'

—⁓—

If anyone had any doubt about the impact the appointment of Páidí Ó Sé had on the wider public in Westmeath then the doubts were dispelled in the early weeks of 2004. Some local wags claimed that only the Pope in St Peter's Square was attracting a bigger audience on a Sunday afternoon.

On January 4 Páidí's Westmeath gathered for its first competitive outing, an O'Byrne Cup game against Louth. It was the sort of billing that would have sneaked into the diary section of the national newspapers on a Saturday and received an expanded scoreline on Monday.

A couple of stiles into Cusack Park would be opened. The Gardai would not be much bothered and the people attending would be expected to steward themselves.

More than 4,000 spectators turned up. Publicans and shopkeepers who had not anticipated such a post-Christmas bonanza found themselves short-staffed and run off their feet. The press box in Cusack Park was overflowing. Local officials were stretched to the limit meeting the unexpected demands.

On the field there was drama too. The visitors, Louth, did what all gatecrashers do to a party. They tried to spoil it. In injury time Louth led by two points. Ger Heavin, one of Westmeath's trusted lieutenants, narrowed it to one. Seven minutes of injury time was played by the referee, Dave Coldrick.

Páidí and the selectors had summoned Joe Fallon into action five minutes before the end of normal time. He repaid them when scoring the equalising point. Páidí headed for the dressing-room.

'Hold on,' he was told, ' ... there's extra time!'

Westmeath went on to win by four points. 'We were a little bit jittery,' was Páidí's post-match understatement. 'I suppose I felt a bit under pressure myself because it was a first competitive game. All we wanted was to get them past the post and it will make the training ground an easier place for us on Tuesday night.'

Seven days later the hordes descended again on Cusack Park. They beat Kildare by eight points. Another week later the turnstiles registered 5,100 paying customers attending the Westmeath versus Carlow O'Byrne Cup semi-final. The coffers of the Leinster Council were bulging with unexpected booty.

Three games, three wins, three cheers for Páidí O Se and Westmeath, wrote the GAA Correspondent for the *Irish Independent*, Martin Breheny before adding a more cautious note, *not too loudly, though, as that might create the impression that they had hit the new season on full throttle. Not so. There was as much chaff as wheat embedded in their O'Byrne Cup semi-final win.*

Whoever was in charge of the fixtures tapped into the mood. The final, against Meath on January 25, was fixed for Cusack Park. Denis Coyne takes up the story. 'People paid in at the stiles and we had a safety limit of 15,000. The estimated attendance was over 18,000.

'People came from everywhere. It was a fine day and everyone came to see Páidí. It wasn't just Westmeath and Meath supporters. They came from all the surrounding counties and it was just to see him. It was almost unsafe except that the atmosphere was so good. Everyone was there for one reason ... Páidí.'

Tomas O Flatharta had never seen anything like it. 'I met people who told me they would never normally go to a game like that but they wanted to see this guy. They were fascinated by him.

'And, you know ... he hardly noticed. He kept saying to me "get them fit." Nothing else entered his mind.'

Meath won after extra time.

Some Westmeath supporters muttered darkly about another defeat to their bogey team. 'Might be for the best,' said Páidí. 'Keep everyone's feet on the ground.' And he would remind his friend, 'I want them fit for the Championship.'

Dessie Dolan says, 'It was a whole new world for us. Nobody ... officials, supporters or players, had ever experienced anything like it. I remember when he was first appointed the players were wondering what was happening. We were all fully aware of what had happened in Kerry and we didn't know what was bringing him up to us.

'Then there was the whole announcement, the excitement. It was like something you would see on Sky Sports. It was headline news and it was happening in Westmeath. It was happening to us. There was a great buzz throughout the county … it was infectious.

'Just by being there he gave the players a bit more relief.

'And when he started communicating with us you were immediately struck by the amount of experience he had and especially the know-how. He talked so much sense when he talked football. He talked about trust. And that is something we bought into.'

—◦—

Páidí Ó Sé, OBE.

Out Before Easter

No one is quite sure of the origin of the special OBE attached to the Westmeath manager in the mid-spring period. It was the sort of pun he himself would have enjoyed in other circumstances. There is a school of thought that it all began in Kerry as Westmeath's campaign in the National Football League during the months of February and March stuttered along.

Some folk in the county were clearly following his unlikely sojourn in the midlands with a sense of mirth if not malice.

It could have also come from within Westmeath.

As early as mid-March Denis Coyne heard the first rumblings of discontent. Operating within a very competitive Division One in the NFL – Kerry, Tyrone, Dublin, Cork, Mayo, Fermanagh and Longford made up the section – while going through a ferocious fitness campaign was a difficult combination. Relegation became a concern for supporters and some officials. Not for Páidí.

They opened the campaign with a draw against Cork, lost to Longford and then drew with Fermanagh. Dublin came to Mullingar and won by five points. The next game, against Kerry, was the one Páidí did not need or want.

Not at that stage. Not at any stage really.

On March 14 the new Kerry manager, Jack O'Connor brought Kerry to Mullingar. Darragh, Tomas and Marc were playing. Páidí had never faced such a situation, never envisaged one like this. He was edgy all week. When he arrived in Mullingar he was quiet. He didn't engage with anyone; kept to himself.

During the game he sat on the bench, never moved. Those closest to him, including O'Flatharta, understood but were still startled. Páidí was always on the move. He normally couldn't sit still for more than a few minutes. Here he was hardly able to get up at half time to go to the dressing room with the players. A small number of Westmeath supporters in the attendance became restless. This was not what they expected.

Kerry won by two goals, 2-10 to 0-10.

His loyalty was to Westmeath, was it not?

He explained himself in an interview a few days later. 'Unknown to a lot of people yesterday was, apart from bereavements and other situations, the hardest day of my life. Other people can apply themselves differently but my mind was in turmoil.'

Adding to the sense of unrest was that the manager was attending only a handful of training sessions at that time. O'Flatharta was in charge from game-to-game. Some people, officials and supporters, were uncomfortable with his absence. Was he taking them for granted? Was he really interested?

'I knew,' says Denis Coyne, 'that was how it would be.'

'He told me that from the beginning. The distances to be travelled were huge. Páidí had a business to run as well. He told me he would not worry about the League; it was all about the Championship. I took him at his word. I trusted him.'

O'Flatharta was similarly dismissive of Páidí's absences. 'In fact, I was ignorant of what people were saying, that there was even talk of getting rid of Páidí. I trained the team and then went back to Dublin. Páidí had told me he wouldn't be there all the time and to do what I was doing. I was happy with that.'

However, he found himself having to address the issue. The players began to get restless and anxious. They found Páidí's absences confusing.

They found his distance uncomfortable. They were accustomed to managers paying close attention.

Páidí had not yet even attempted to form relationships.

He was elusive, a nomad.

The team captain David O'Shaughnessy met O'Flatharta one evening to voice the concerns of the players. 'Look David ... Páidí doesn't give a shit about the League. When Championship time comes around you will see a different man and we've got to be ready for him.'

The Football Board chairman was approached. 'We've got to get rid of him,' he was told. 'These people were genuine Westmeath supporters and there was no malice in what they were saying. We weren't winning games and we were struggling against teams that our supporters expected us to do well against. I wouldn't say the numbers wanting to get rid of him were huge but there were a significant body of people.

'I rejected it all,' Coyne says. 'We appointed Páidí for a two-year term and I was determined we would stick to our side of the agreement. He had always kept me appraised of what was happening. It might not have been the way others did their business but Páidí never left me in any doubt about what he was doing and I was happy with that.

'People might have thought I was under pressure but I never felt it. I knew the team was in good hands with Tomas. He was working very hard.

'And every time I met Páidí he was positive, really active and animated ... always planning. Except that one day against Kerry. And I understood that too. Páidí made no secret of where his loyalties lay. He was a Kerryman through and through. We knew that when we appointed him. We had to stick with him and give him a chance.'

Reflecting now, Dessie Dolan doesn't believe the manager's regular absences had any major impact on the players. 'Everyone realised the vast distances that he was travelling and, anyway, there were compensations for his absence. It did seem a bit strange for a while that training would start at half past seven and forty minutes later he would be leaving because he had to get to Dublin to get a flight home. But we got used to it.

'The thing was that Páidí was bringing a lot more to Westmeath than just the physical aspect of training. He was changing our whole mental approach. He was constantly testing us … working on our attitude. Why hadn't we won anything before; what was the difference between the maroon and white, and the green and gold? He wanted us to start to think like winners.

'Results weren't going well for a while but we had the feeling all the time that Páidí had no interest in the League. It was all about the Championship. And when the Championship came around we saw a different man.'

—〜〜—

On March 21, 2004 the Westmeath footballers travelled to Omagh for a National Football League game against Tyrone. This was the big time. Tyrone were the All-Ireland champions. All the marquee names were there – Canavan, Dooher, McMenamin, Jordan, Gormley, Cavanagh. Except for one. Cormac McAnallen had died suddenly, at the age of 24, less than three weeks previously.

It was a sombre occasion in many ways.

The Tyrone players responded to pay tribute to their fallen comrade in the best way they could. Westmeath were put to the sword. They didn't score in the first half. Tyrone led by 2-7 to 0-0 when Dessie Dolan scored Westmeath's first point of the day from a free in the 45th minute. The match ended Tyrone 2-11, Westmeath 0-6.

Westmeath were bottom of the table after six rounds, their interest in Division One football seriously threatened.

As the bus left Healy Park there was a giddy air amongst the players. 'The match was already forgotten,' remembers Dessie Dolan. 'We were chatting and laughing amongst ourselves, and the one thing we weren't talking about was the match. Someone asked for a DVD to be put on. A comedy.

Bad Boys 2 or something like that. We were ready to settle down and have a bit of craic … young lads out for a good time."

Bad Boys indeed.

Páidí exploded.

'Ye should be ashamed of yourselves,' he roared from the front of the bus. 'Do ye even care what just happened here today? Have ye no respect?

'Ye were fucking hammered out there … and look at ye. Laughing … and joking. By Jesus, I didn't see much today to be laughing and joking about.

'You boys are going to have to toughen up.

'Otherwise … we're wasting our time.'

The rant did not go on for long but the message was clear.

The DVD stayed in its cover.

The screens remained blank. And the laughing and joking was replaced by silence. In that silence the players began to think about what had happened; about the manager and his demands. And they began to think about what might be achieved if they followed the manager's advice.

In Ballinagore two nights later they suffered. Training was 'brutal'. The message from the bus was repeated without words. Just deeds.

On the first Sunday in April, Westmeath beat Mayo by six points in Mullingar in the final round of the League. Other results worked in their favour. Westmeath retained their Division One status based on scoring averages.

They trained in Cusack Park on the Tuesday night. Everyone was on time. It was a bright evening and the mood was positive. The medical team worked on a few niggles. Paddy Collins and Jack Cooney took note of progress reports. Tomas O Flatharta chatted with a couple of the players.

'Where's himself?' someone asked.

When the players began to arrive out onto the field in twos and threes they saw him. In a cream jersey, collar up, and shorts. Kicking frees from fifty yards.

Strutting. Laughing.

Joking.

Bouncing.

Championship mode.

CHAPTER 16

In the middle of the white-washed dressing room beneath the Hogan Stand, sound-proofed by concrete, Páidí stood in defiance.

He had placed a trusted sentry by the door.

'No one gets in … no one,' was the clear instruction.

His eyes blazed with fury as he looked at the players, one after another. The little metal table in front of him was in danger of being shredded. With every belt of his fist, each successive one being delivered with greater ferocity, the table hopped a couple of feet off the ground and landed with a clanging noise that reverberated through the room.

Westmeath had just drawn the Leinster football final, letting a three point lead slip. As the players trudged off the field all of their old insecurities returned. Páidí looked at the glum faces passing him on their way to the tunnel. He heard someone mutter 'here we go again, another Westmeath cock-up.'

Páidí 's composure evaporated.

Words spilled forth, as Gaeilge as well as English, a few of them unintelligible such was the passion with which they were expressed.

Pausing for just a moment to catch his breath, he noticed the silence. No one even twitched. All eyes, bar a few that were staring at the floor, were focused on the manager. The backroom team had stopped their work. Officers of the County Committee retreated into corners as if in search of sanctuary.

The players sat or stood, some gear discarded.

They were rapt. It was his time, he knew.

'Lads,' he roared, ' … do you want to be losers all your lives. Do you want to be joining the usual brigade of fucking losers wearing the maroon and white that have left Croke Park in years gone by? Because lads, there's been plenty of them and ye'll have plenty of company.

'Or do you want to be different.

'Do you want change things?

'Rip up that fucking stereotype and try to be history makers? Do you want to become ambassadors for Westmeath?

'Do you want to be men who will be talked about for years to come … the men who changed everything?

'It's your fucking choice. You have six days to make it.

'Losers or legends … it's up to you, but I know which one I want to be.'

That was Sunday, July 18, 2004.

—◊—

In the early days Páidí called all of the players Joe.

He was adapting to changed circumstances. The new faces bewildered him for a time. So he called them all Joe because the first player he spoke to in the county when he arrived was Joe Fallon.

He spoke to Joe because they conversed in Irish.

At the time it didn't matter. The new manager wasn't interested in individuals at the start. Changing the collective mindset was his priority. It took him some time to work it out. Páidí believed he was better than everyone else when it came to football. He grew up in an environment where footballers went out expecting to win. Not hoping.

In his home place Páidí was surrounded by winners. He was brought up in that mindset. He was a winner himself.

Eight All-Irelands as a player.

Two as a manager. In his adopted county people just didn't think like that. He grappled with that reality; couldn't make sense of it.

'Páidí ,' said Seamus O'Faolain one day, ' … there's only one man in Westmeath with an All-Ireland medal and that's Sean Cleary.'

'Sean from Galway,' as Páidí correctly identified, a member of the famous three in-a-row team from the 1960s, was teaching in the CBS in Mullingar. There might have been Celtic Crosses in every village and townland in his native Kerry but they were rare items in Westmeath.

He called to see his friend Brian Cowen in Tullamore one afternoon. 'He talked about the need to get these guys to believe that they could be as good as anyone,' Cowen remembers. 'Tradition is a word that is used so often in such circumstances. We talked about tradition. When you analyse it tradition is doing something well more often than anyone else, that's all it is.

'He needed to get it into the heads of the players that they could develop the skills and then, with his experience, find the mental toughness that at the highest level of the game is usually the differentiating factor. It is that belief that, at a certain point, you push on; that when you're five points up you don't think that these fellas are going to come after you but that you're going to go seven up.'

Páidí realised that it would take more than talk to get them to believe. They had to be made feel special. So he organised weekends in Inchydoney Island Lodge and Spa, the five star resort in West Cork. There was no expense spared. 'We began to live the lifestyle,' says Dessie Dolan, one of the many players who thrived under the manager and became one of the best known forwards in the game.

'Everything we wanted was provided. You didn't have to ask a second time. We were well kitted out. The treatment was five star … we began living the dream.'

On Inchydoney beach Páidí would join the lads for a run. Half way down the beach he would rip off his shirt and shorts, discard his shoes and charge off into the water. Dessie Dolan says, 'He was like a madman … charging 200 yards into the sea. The lads would be looking at him thinking he was wild. And he would come out roaring at us, talking about the healing effects of sea water.

'We would sit and have dinner with him, listening to his stories. We could have listened to him all night. He was so interesting, so intriguing. We heard about teams and people that were heroes to us and Páidí had a different story every evening. We began to understand his character and his good nature.

'He had an aura about him. You were under no illusions about who was boss and you played to his tune. But as he told us about all his adventures and achievements, he also said that we could do those things ourselves. We would never have believed it was possible before but we began to get a bit more belief.

'He would say "What's the difference between maroon and white, and green and gold?" They're only colours. And that meant that when he or Tomas asked us to do things at training, to put ourselves through torture, that we would do it. We did it because we were beginning to believe that he could guide us to the top. He was breaking down the mental barriers that had been in our way.

'Páidí's castaway stories that came off the cuff about football and footballers became memories we would have forever.'

By the time the Championship came around Páidí had the team billeted in the Portmarnock Hotel and Golf Links in north County Dublin. Again, it was luxury to which they were only becoming accustomed. It furthered that feeling that they were special.

In the build up to the opening round of the Championship he brought the squad to Rosses' Point in Sligo. Páidí loved the smells and sounds of the sea.

They inspired him.

There was eloquence in his talks, to the squad and individually. He was conditioning the players, physically and mentally. 'It was totally new to us,' Dolan says. 'We began to believe him and believe in him.'

At home in Dingle Páidí approached the jeweler, Brian de Staic to design a small badge that would bear the inscription in Irish 'Bualadh dair le dornaibh'.

'It essentially means,' explains Tomas O Flatharta, 'that hitting a Westmeath man is like hitting an oak tree.' He presented one to every member of the panel and he repeated its message every session.

The players learned the mantra: practice the basics; conservative defending, the bigger the prize the closer you stay to your man; move the ball with pace;

pride in where you come from; steely, steely tough.

'If you get hit you do not go down,' he would shout. 'And if for some reason you do go down make sure that you get straight back up. Never let an opponent know he has hurt you.' It was the same message he had repeatedly delivered in Kerry. Later that summer a speech on that subject would be memorably captured in the documentary 'Marooned'.

Content that the players were absorbing his message he began to examine the individuals. Gary Connaughton, the goalkeeper, had been playing soccer with Athlone Town for a number of seasons. Once a trialist with Newcastle United, Connaughton had been a member of the Ireland team which was successful at the European Under 19 Championships in 1998. Páidí made him his number one.

No more messing with that other game.

One evening, sat with O Flatharta talking about some of the players. They came to Michael Ennis. He had been full-forward on the Under-21 team in 1999 and was playing wing-forward for them. They recognised his talent but they were not happy that they were getting the best from the player. They had substituted him a number of times.

Páidí dipped into his well of experience. 'Do you remember Tomas what I did with Gearoid Casey in '84,' he asked. Casey was a very talented footballer from Lispole who was lining out at half-forward for West Kerry. Páidí switched him to wing back and Casey was a key member of the county Championship winning team.

'We'll do that with this lad.'

Michael Ennis became a defender and would play on both wings and as a corner-back in the 2004 Championship.

Denis Glennon was just a teenager, raw and inexperienced. Páidí liked the way the kid approached his football, his attitude and the fact that he had so much skill. There were concerns that he was too young. 'If he's good enough … he's old enough,' said the man who himself was just a teenager when he first played for Kerry.

As May 23 loomed, the date of the opening game in the Leinster Championship against Offaly, the players noticed Páidí 's excitement growing. He was more animated at training, constantly talking, cajoling, demanding and encouraging.

Páidí was preparing to go home; his second home.

Croke Park.

—⁓—

The Garda outriders, sirens blaring, cleared the traffic through Fairview on Dublin's Northside as they escorted the Westmeath team bus towards the stadium, gleaming in its makeover.

It was May 23 and Páidí was coming back.

Tomas O Flatharta sat at the front of the bus with Páidí. His friend was like a kid going to Croke Park for the first time, straining to catch a glimpse of the stand for the first time, pointing to knots of supporters drifting towards Clonliffe Road or standing outside various hostelries gaining sustenance for the day.

They waved their flags as the bus went by. Páidí waved back.

'How are you feeling Tomas,' he asked. 'Are you nervous?'

'Nah ... I'm alright,' came the reply.

'Jesus Christ, do you ever get fucking excited about anything,' came an exasperated retort.

And as the players and their management disembarked within the stadium Páidí turned to his aide and whispered, 'You know ... I love this place. I have always loved it. I'm happy every time I come here, even if I am only here to pick up a ticket.'

Páidí also felt the pressure that day. After the drama of his appointment, the almost soap opera-like fascination with Westmeath because of his position as manager, the time had come to deliver. There had been a lot of talk about two-year plans but he knew, deep down, that all plans would be revised if Westmeath did not beat Offaly.

They hadn't done it for 55 years in the Championship. He forcefully reminded the players of that. 'You have the chance to create a bit of history. Don't waste it. Remember the 55 years of hurt everytime you're going for that ball. Let no Offaly man stand in your way today.

'Be the boss.'

They led by four points at half time, 0-7 to 0-3, having played with the wind advantage. Rory O'Connell was sent off 11 minutes after the restart after an off-the-ball incident. Páidí didn't panic.

No one did. They kept to the script – steely tough, close marking, pride. At the end there was just a point between them.

Westmeath 0-11, Offaly 0-10.

In the *Irish Independent* Martin Breheny wrote, *Who knows where Páidí Ó Sé's Championship voyage will end with Westmeath but it has started in a pleasant, fertile land which the county hasn't visited in 55 years.*

Westmeath may have enjoyed more dramatic Championship victories but since this was their first win over Offaly since 1949, it left them with the warmest of glows as they left Croke Park yesterday evening. Behind them stood a tale of resolute defiance that ensured they weren't going to script another hard luck story, while ahead of them lay the exciting challenge of a Leinster quarter-final with Dublin on Sunday week.

Páidí had no difficulty talking about the Dubs.

'The Dubs are among the counties who are thinking of the fourth Sunday in September. That's the level we have to move up to.

'But sure isn't it great to be going into a quarter final with Dublin. As a new management we had to try out lots of players and put our own shape on things. We have made progress but there is still a long way to go.'

—ɯ—

The Dubs.
June 6.
Half time.
Dublin 0-9, Westmeath 0-6.

In the dressing room on the Cusack Stand side of the ground Páidí grabs one of the dozens of towels soaking in ice.

He looks around for a player; grabs one.

Russell Casey.

Starts towelling.

Hands are working furiously.

'Fucking outstanding. You're having a blinder. Just keep it going. One more half ... just one more...'

Tomas interrupts.

'What ... what?' Páidí growls.

'Russell's not playing.'

'Oh.' Sheepishly Páidí moves on.

For two weeks Páidí had been talking non-stop about the Dubs.

'Imagine what they're saying up there,' he would tell his players. 'Laughing at us. Boggers ... still living in caves, they think. No respect for us atall.

'Smart men ... the Dubs. Know it all.

'What are ye going to do about it?"

They went back to Croker without Rory O'Connell who was suspended; Martin Flanagan was still injured. Those would have been mortal blows in the past. Páidí would not let them dwell on it.

'Deal with it,' he said

Now the players were feeling the heat of battle. This was new territory. In with the big boys. 60,000 people in Croke Park. Alan Brogan and Jason Sherlock were tormenting them.

Superstars.

Six points scored between them in 16 minutes.

'Closer ... stay closer,' roared Páidí from the sideline.

He paced up and down the sideline, face lined in thought. He hopped and skipped, watched every ball kicked. He looked like a bundle of nervous energy. But when he came back to his selectors on the sideline they were struck by just how calm he was. He listened to their views, made a few comments of his own. Their fears abated.

Páidí had relaxed them!

Changes were needed. There was no rushing around or scrambling. Instructions were quiet and measured. David Kilmartin was summoned to replace James Davitt. John Keane was switched to police Brogan. Damien Healy went back to mark Sherlock. The defensive unit became tighter.

A couple of minutes before half time the three selectors and the manager stood together again. Gary Dolan and David O'Shaughnessy were playing well at midfield but the Dublin pairing of Ciaran Whelan and Darren Homan were physically very powerful and were wearing them down. Westmeath needed to do something to help their players.

Páidí looked to his substitutes; his eyes fastened on the frame that carries David Mitchell. Big man. Strong in training all the time. Good full-back.

'I know what we'll do,' said Páidí . 'Get Mitchell down here.'

Tomas, Paddy and Jack were surprised. Mitchell had never played around the middle of the field before. But they quickly realised what Páidí was thinking. In the heat of battle he was the calmest man in Croke Park.

His advice to the player was simple – don't be afraid to throw your weight around. At the break there was no panic. Páidí 's gaffe with the towel actually lightened the mood.

At the start of the second half Mitchell had become a nuisance to Dublin. Ciaran Whelan didn't appreciate the newcomer's presence and dumped him. The referee, Michael Collins from Cork, waved a yellow card. *An offence for which he should have been sent off,* wrote Colm Keys in the *Independent.*

Mitchell was furious. He jumped up and shook off the effects of the blow. The free was taken. Mitchell got possession and booted the ball straight over the bar. 'None of us had seen that before,' jokes Denis Coyne.

'But it was a rallying cry. David was inspired.'

There were heroics all over the field. Dolan was outstanding. *It was Dessie Dolan who turned the screw,'* wrote Colm Keys *'with his ability to repeatedly win ball ahead of Barry Cahill and use it intelligently. Everything Westmeath did had its source in Dolan's creativity.*

Gary Connaughton made a match-winning save from Sherlock when the teams were level towards the end of normal time, 0-12 each. Joe Fallon, introduced in injury time, scored a point and then Paul Conway added another of real quality, fetching the ball high within a thicket of players, turning and calmly sidefooting the ball over the bar.

Westmeath 0-14, Dublin 0-12.

As the Dublin players and their manager, Tommy Lyons, left the field under a barrage of abuse from angry supporters, Páidí was met by a Dublin fan.

'Jaysus Páidí ... why did you come back to haunt us?'

Yes, Páidí loved the Dubs.

'He really enjoyed that battle,' reveals O Flatharta. 'The players fought the way he wanted them to fight; he had preached to them about belief, about confidence and about pride in their jersey and their place. They displayed all of that against Dublin. Alan Brogan and Jason Sherlock started brilliantly.

'It could have broken our team. It would have in the past.

'But that day they stood up.

'He made good calls himself that day. He was brought to Westmeath for his experience and his knowledge. We saw both of those attributes at their very best against Dublin. He won the battle on the sideline. He never talked about that but we knew he was pleased.'

Amidst the celebrations Páidí was already planning, thinking about Wexford in the Leinster semi-final. Wexford, a county with pedigree. 'He was always looking for an angle,' explains Tomas O Flatharta. 'For the Wexford game he talked about their proud history. Most people wouldn't have known that history. Páidí did. They won four All-Irelands in a row between 1914 and 1918.'

The players were becoming accustomed to a new lifestyle. Normal life was put on hold. 'The whole place was gripped by football fever,' says Denis Coyne. 'People talked about nothing else. Everyone was in good form. It was amazing for us to see the effect success could have on a community. It had happened to a certain extent with the minor and Under-21 successes. But this was at a different level. It seemed to matter more.'

Three weeks later they were back in Croke Park. After 25 minutes they led Wexford by 0-9 to 0-1. Westmeath folk had never witnessed anything like it. Páidí preached caution at the break. That was wise.

With fifteen minutes still to be played the scoreboard read, Westmeath 0-12, Wexford 0-10. Then Dolan and Shane Colleary scored a goal each. Westmeath had reached the Leinster final for the first time in 55 years.

In the *Westmeath Examiner*, staff writer John Fitzsimons reflected the views of a mesmerised people. *It is simply amazing what a transformation we have witnessed in Westmeath's footballing fortunes in the past six months. A near disastrous League campaign did not bode well for the more important summer series but Páidí and his backroom team have certainly turned things around and now the sky is the limit.*

There is no doubt that the side, liberally sprinkled with quality footballers, is playing with renewed confidence and on Sunday they matched that prerequisite with equal quantities of passion, commitment and sheer determination.

Páidí himself reacted quietly. He told reporters, 'In the past our forward line has been described as a bit of a one-man band but today we showed that is far from being the case. All of the forward line really played well. We know we will have to show improvement all over the field against Laois.'

Laois and Micko.

—ᴍ—

Tomas was driving Páidí around Dublin a couple of weeks before the Leinster final. The banker was full of chat, discussing strategies and tactics, the stuff that would usually have Páidí on fire.

Páidí wasn't saying a word.

He was brooding.

'Something wrong?' a frustrated O Flatharta asked.

'Got a phone call this morning. Some PR lad. Bank of Ireland ... want myself and Dwyer to have a press conference. Dangerous ... not sure I want to do it.

'You wouldn't know what he'd get up to.

'Set me up somehow.'

'You'll have to do it,' advised O Flatharta. 'It would be far worse if you don't turn up. They'd say you're running scared or something.'

Back at home, Maire noticed his black mood.

He explained his dilemma.

'You'll just have to prepare for it like you prepare for a game,' she told him. 'What do you think Mick will do?'

Páidí knew exactly what Mick would do.

He would tell everyone how great Páidí was; what a great football team Westmeath were. He would build them up … the Real Madrid, All Blacks and New England Patriots of Gaelic football.

Well, Páidí could play that game too.

'I wouldn't be here only for this man,' was Páidí 's opening line when the two men sat together at the bank headquarters on Baggott Street in Dublin on the Tuesday before the final. 'He gave me the road, my P45, back in 1988 and I didn't speak to him for three years. But he is the best man in the business for management.

'Normally I'd be uptight before games like these but with this man involved I'm more comfortable and looking forward to a great occasion.'

Micko did not disappoint.

'I said it at the time people were questioning Páidí 's commitment to Westmeath that he would come with the cuckoo. And he has done. He's been a fresh face with a fresh approach to the players.

'Páidí likes to enjoy life and he does it over the winter. That's our structure in Kerry. That's the way it has always been. But I knew he would come good and by God he has revitalised them.'

When the sparring was over they went for lunch. The one subject they did not discuss was football.

—◦◦◦—

Dessie Dolan is unequivocal to this day in his belief. 'Páidí Ó Sé's greatest achievement in football management was winning a Leinster title with Westmeath.'

Almost a decade on he speaks with deep passion about what the people of Westmeath have dubbed 'Redemption Day' – Saturday, July 24, when they won the Leinster senior football Championship for the first time.

'People might find it strange that I would regard it as Páidí 's greatest triumph after everything he did in Kerry,' Dolan continues, ' … but you have to understand where we were coming from. Luke (Dempsey) had done fantastic work … but without Páidí I don't believe we would have been able to make the breakthrough.

'He was consumed with winning.

'His belief was unbreakable.

'He was constantly working on our heads, the mental side of the game. Remember we had never won anything. And he convinced us that we could win a Leinster Championship. His speeches at training and in the dressing room before a game would have the hair standing on the back of your neck. He changed the way we thought about ourselves and about others.

'There were times you would be mad with him; he could be frustrating. But he had the ability to connect with the players; he could communicate the message to us in his unique way. And he loved Croke Park.

'It was his theatre. We bought into that as well.'

In the documentary 'Marooned' which captures the eventful summer of 2004 there is a scene that articulates better than anything the Páidí effect on Westmeath.

The squad stand in an oval shape on the side of a field. The youthful faces are serious; some of them look concerned. The manager is standing in a small space amongst them, constantly moving and gesticulating with his hands

'We're going well lads … but lads, bring the bit of fucking devilment into ye're play the next day … the devilment, the tightness … the … the rough and tumble stuff out in the middle of the field … the fucking breaking ball.

'A grain of rice is going to tip the scale.

'Just remember that lads … a grain of rice to tip the scale … but you will have to get steely tough upstairs and you must be willing to fucking break your gut.'

He then turned towards Alan Mangan.

'You were fucked over the line twice … fucked over the line like you catch a fucking loaf of bread and fucked you over the line with a shoulder. And what that does is it lifts the opposition.

'We don't want to see no Westmeath man fucked about.

'Is that clear now Alan … no more.

'We'll have to crash into these fellas and test out their pulse because I'm telling ye lads these fellas will play good football if they're allowed.

'Give me one fucking guarantee each and every one of you … that you're going to be tighter, that ye're going to be more disciplined … that ye're going to be more tigerish and that ye're going to take the game to these fellas … that these fellas will get such a fucking shellshock next Saturday evening … that we'll put them back on their fucking arses for fucking ten years.

'Alright lads.'

Mangan was Westmeath's top scorer in the replay, kicking four points from play. His contribution drew warm praise in the newspapers.

The *Independent* reported, *Mangan, taken off six days earlier after an ineffective 45 minutes, re-invented himself to such a degree that he scored four points and always looked like causing trouble for Laois.*

In the replay the Westmeath players were more disciplined, were tigerish and they did win the breaking ball. The led by 0-7 to 0-5 at half time; they exploded into action at the start of the second half and added five points in 15 minutes.

They didn't score for the last 20 minutes but they didn't need to. They had done enough. Champions for the first time in their history.

0-12 to 0-10.

Westmeath will never feel the same about itself again, Martin Breheny wrote in the *Independent. A liberating force swept into Croke Park on Saturday evening, ripped off the shackles of history and presented the county with a whole new identity.*

This morning, Westmeath people at home and abroad, will go about their daily business with a swaggering confidence they never experienced before. But, of course, Westmeath were never Leinster senior football champions before.

Even in print it almost looks unrecognisable but then Westmeath people will need time to become accustomed to living in a different sporting world after trading up so spectacularly this summer.'

It was a theme taking up by Seamus O'Faolain when he described his feeling to reporters from the *Westmeath Examiner, It's absolutely the greatest day in the history of Westmeath GAA, there's no doubt about that. It's brilliant to win minors, it's brilliant to win under-21s but the real showcase is the senior and we had to crash that painful barrier of never having won a provincial title and I know it will bring the most wonderful joy and elation to Westmeath people, not just in the county of Westmeath but all over the world.*

Today I've got texts from Latvia, from France, from Spain and more places I haven't even checked yet – all very, very proud Westmeath people. We will walk tall and we will take our place in the Kingdom of Gaeldom in Leinster by finally smashing that barrier.

The newspaper's chief sports writer, John Fitzsimons recorded his views.

To the delight of a heaving, swaying army of followers who transformed the rich green sward of Croke Park into a maroon meadow, David O Shaughnessy became the first ever Westmeath captain to pick up Leinster's premier footballing trophy on the steps of the Hogan Stand.

Around him, grown men and women, frustrated by past failures, fought to stem the swell that threatened to expose their emotions. On the field, sweet tears of joy stained many a cheek as proud parents and devoted supporters saluted the finest group of young footballers to emerge from the Lake County.

A team imbued with honest endeavour, a concentrated mind and a work ethic hitherto unknown in Westmeath were sampling the rich desserts their commitment deserved. And there amongst them was a cute Kerry man, Páidí Ó Sé, who ultimately provided the impetus for this side to stride to glory.

Dessie Dolan says simply, 'We all have treasured memories. We are grateful and we are fortunate that we got to spend some time with him. We cannot measure the lift he gave us and the enjoyment he gave us.

'Some man.'

—⁂—

In the days after the Leinster final replay of 2004 Seamus O'Faolain kept replaying images in his mind of the game and the celebrations. He had often wondered what it would feel like to see a Westmeath football team with a Leinster senior title and the reality had lived up to expectations.

As he pulled into the Maxol Service Station on the Dublin Bridge in

Mullingar he reflected on the 10 months that had passed since he had first taken the fateful phone call from Denis Coyne. He recalled his own caution about an approach to Páidí Ó Sé, who was still at the time hanging on to his position as Kerry football manager.

Páidí had come amongst them and weaved his magic.

Seamus was about to find out just how much.

He filled his car with petrol, replaced the cap and took his wallet from his jacket pocket. 'Put that away,' came a shout from a few yards away. 'I'm not taking any money from you today.'

It was the proprietor, Millie Walsh, a lifelong Westmeath football supporter. And sufferer.

'When I was a young lad,' Millie told Seamus, ' … my father brought me on the annual outing every year. We mightn't have been able to afford a train ticket but we never missed a game. If, by any chance, they got to the second round, we were there too. A second round was an adventure.

'We never dreamed that one day Westmeath would be Leinster Champions. Well my father lived to see Westmeath win a Leinster title. And that means the world to us. Seamus, yourself and Paddy Collins have dedicated your lives to the GAA in Westmeath. And this is just my little way to say thanks.'

CHAPTER 17

'Small man, get up …
'Jesus Christ do you know what time it is?'

Padraig Og Ó Sé, or 'small man' as he was known to his father, might not
have known what time it was but as soon as he heard Páidí 's voice rousing
him from sleep he knew what day it was – match day.

Páidí was not in the habit of waking his children during their childhoods.
There were times when, because of the hours he worked in the pub across the
road, he would rise after Maire and the kids had left for school.

And if, on occasion, the kids were a little late rising or getting ready Páidí
would be the least ruffled person in the household. One or other might be
charging around the place looking for a book or some item of clothing but
Páidí was an oasis of calm.

That all changed as Padraig entered his mid-teens.

From an early age he had shown an interest in football. Given the
influences around him that was probably inevitable. As he grew it became
obvious that he had talent and that was recognised by the club and by his
school, Pobal Scoil Chorca Dhuibhne.

'He was always more excited about my matches than I was,' Padraig says
with a smile. 'I'd be fairly laidback about them. He was so nervous that he

would make sure I got to bed early the night before and he'd be checking on me to make sure that I went to sleep.

'And in the morning he'd be up before me getting ready.

'If I didn't get up early he would call me and he wouldn't be happy until I was up and dressed and ready to go. I might have been late for school but I was never going to be late for a match.'

Padraig, who had been born on December 16, 1993, cannot remember a time when there wasn't a football around. The two of them were always 'messing about out the back'. The sessions could become competitive when Padraig got older. His father never lost the spirit. 'He enjoyed kicking the ball around the garden as much as I did. It was rare that he couldn't find the time.'

They would frequently be joined by the 'lads', his cousins Fergal, Darragh, Tomas and Marc, and other boys from the locality. Dara O'Cinneide would get a call from time to time to join them when Páidí was doing a bit of coaching with his son.

'After a game we would always talk about how I played. We would look at things I had to work on … my weak foot, passing, positioning, marking. He was always on about close marking. And he would work with me.'

It was never going to be an easy ride for the youngster.

It was tough enough having such a famous father but he had three famous cousins as well. 'I got to hear the usual stuff,' says Padraig with an air of resignation. 'You'll never be as good as your father, stuff like that. It was pressure but over the years I learned how to give the same answers. You get on with it.'

Páidí was conscious of that pressure so he provided support. He was proud of how Padraig coped but he did not display it publicly. His family knew.

'He loved going to games and watching Padraig play,' explains Neasa. 'I think he was re-living his own playing days. He always said he would love to have been 18 again.''

'He would say to me, "I'd love to be in your shoes,"' says Padraig.

Never were the nerves of the father more frayed than the day in early March of 2012 when Chorca Dhuibhne played De La Salle, Macroom, in the

Corn Ui Mhuiri (Munster Senior Colleges 'A') final. The school had lost the final a year previous after Padraig had received a red card.

This time there was no mistake.

They won by eight points.

It was a proud father who headed for home that evening.

The *Irish Examiner* reporter picked Padraig out for praise. *With Pádraig Ó Sé orchestrating play from his centre-back berth, feeding his attack with assured passes, Pobalscoil Chorca Dhuibhne were in a strong position,* it wrote.

They lost the All-Ireland semi-final to St Michael's of Enniskillen. Páidí blamed Micheal O'Muircheartaigh. 'Whenever I sit with you at a match ... we lose,' complained Páidí.

Páidí would never wait until Padraig got home to discuss a game. 'I always knew that about an hour after a game my phone would ring. He would have been thinking about it ... about things I had done or things I hadn't done. And we would chat away. He would always have a few words of praise but he would tell you if you had gone badly.

'All through this year I would automatically take the phone out to be ready for the call. It's a habit I'll find hard to get rid of.'

—m—

During his time as Westmeath manager Páidí once provided a description of himself that earned the approval of Maire, the children and others close to him.

'All my family would have the greatest confidence in me to do a job when I am tuned in; at times it's difficult to get me tuned in but when I am I'm extremely good. I can be extremely bad as well ... when I'm not tuned in,' he said.

He tried to stay tuned in after Westmeath won the Leinster Championship in 2004. From the stage in Mullingar town centre he pleaded with the supporters to give the players time and space to prepare for the All-Ireland series.

'Our journey is not over,' he warned them.

But the reality was that the journey was over. He didn't understand until much later the full significance of what had been achieved. He saw it as a provincial success. For Westmeath football, it was much more than that. It was a seismic event from which the county would not recover for some time.

And once Westmeath lost to Derry in the All-Ireland quarter-final a few weeks later Páidí 's concentration began to flag.

'He had achieved in less than a year what he had expected would take at least two years,' says Denis Coyne. 'Maybe he put all his energy into that campaign and he didn't have a lot more to give. But he had given us more than we could ever have expected.'

He wasn't helped by injuries to players like Dessie Dolan during 2005 and when Westmeath lost to Clare in the All Ireland qualifiers in early July Páidí made a very quick decision. 'It has been a very, very enjoyable two years but it is time for me to take a little time out.'

Naturally, there were some who voiced criticism.

Dessie Dolan rejects any of that. 'What he achieved will live with us forever. To win a Leinster Championship ... remember we had to play five games, more than any team in any province – was a spectacular achievement for us and for Páidí.'

Maybe his own journey as a manager should have ended there.

Páidí was a director of Failte Ireland. He had business plans for the Dingle Peninsula that would have absorbed enough of his time. He was writing a column in the *Sunday Independent* where the subjects he covered were wide-ranging.

The children were growing up. The pub was doing extremely well during the holiday periods. The nephews were feeding his passion for Kerry football. He followed their achievements with enormous pride. And still he hankered for more.

Jack O'Connor's term as Kerry manager had come to an end.

Páidí sent out feelers. The negativity received in return surprised him. He still had friends in high places in the GAA in Kerry.

Just not enough of them.

An old friend, Tom Downes from Clare, made contact in late November 2006. Clare were looking for a new manager and a long search had failed to find a suitable or willing candidate.

'Would you be interested,' asked Downes.

'Let's talk.'

A meeting was arranged in Dingle between Páidí and a delegation of Clare officials, including the Clare chairman, Michael McDonagh. Views were shared and the Clare party headed home to report to the Board.

Páidí went home to speak to Maire.

What happened next was inevitable.

The news leaked.

Páidí was in the headlines again.

They travelled to Carlow on February 4, 2007 for the opening game in the National League. The newspapers carried a photograph the following day. It was of an almost empty terrace. The sole occupant was a red terrier who was looking away from the action.

That was the same weekend that 81,678 supporters thronged into Croke Park for the first floodlit game at the revamped stadium.

Clare won their first two League games, against Carlow and Leitrim. It didn't get any better than that. They lost to Waterford in the opening round of the Championship. It was Waterford's first Championship victory in 19 years. At least it meant Páidí would not have to face Kerry in the Munster semi-final.

The played in the Tommy Murphy Cup and beat Tipperary in Ardfinnan. Antrim visited Ennis for the Murphy Cup semi-final staged on Saturday, July 14.

Clare lost by four points. Three days later it was confirmed that Páidí had resigned. It wasn't the big story of the day. Liam Mulvihill's decision to retire as Director General of the GAA swamped all other stories. Even Páidí.

He addressed the issue the following Sunday in his column.

And so it is farewell to my friends in Clare, that county of fine people, with great hearts, and a love of life and sport that is a tonic. If I try to look at it clinically – not easy when there is sadness in my heart – I would say that I just didn't have the time and space to do justice to the potential of Clare football.

When I went to Westmeath I had a ready-made team to work with. They had already won minor and Under-21 All-Irelands. Not so in Clare. A number of players had retired, making it very much a team in transition. I had to find replacements for six or seven players, so there was a big team-building job to be done.

To do that properly would have required my attendance at every senior county Championship match and every Under-21 Championship match in order to identify players with the talent, the promise and the ambition to make it to the senior county team even if they had not, as yet, caught the selectors' attention.

I have no fault to find with the Clare players. In truth, the fault was mine. I simply didn't have the time to do the massive development job that was needed there, not with the resources at my disposal.

I like to bring a sense of freshness with me wherever I go. It wasn't possible in this case so it was with great sadness that I stood down.

Páidí did not express publicly the other great sadness in his life at the time. On June 4 Beatrice passed away.

She would have been 88 two days later. Illness had dogged her final days. He could not find the words to express his desolation. It was one of the rare times in his life when football didn't matter.

—⚏—

Neasa noticed a change in her father during the late summer of 2007. 'I think when he eventually ended his involvement with football he was happy,' she explains. 'He came back home to look after the bar and he enjoyed watching Padraig play.

'People thought he missed the involvement but by that stage I don't think so. He had enough. He was happy to bow out when he did.'

Time that had been devoted to football was now shared by other interests – his family, the pub, his nephews and Kerry, plans for the future and, of course, politics. He also kept aside time for some fun.

The weekend of the All-Ireland football final was special to Páidí. From 1997 on it became even more so. It became a ritual. A room was permanently booked in The Burlington Hotel, Friday to Monday. Various plans were made annually, but not all worked out quite as expected.

There was something special about the 2007 final. Kerry qualified to play Cork. Darragh, Tomas and Marc were playing some of the best football of their lives. Páidí was determined to make it a good weekend. Maire recalls the frenetic activity as Páidí made contact with a variety of friends.

Fergal, his eldest nephew, was summoned. 'We're playing golf in Dublin on Friday. Be here at 11.0. The helicopter will collect us at 12.0.'

'What helicopter?' Fergal demanded to know.

'Just you be here ... don't be late.'

Páidí got the old suit dry-cleaned. He also bought a new one.

He got the golf clubs ready.

'Jesus ... he was a terrible golfer!' says Marc.

Fergal was on time on Friday. The helicopter was not.

Páidí stood at the door of the pub, listening.

The only sound was the wind.

'He's late!' said Páidí .

'Sound," said Fergal. 'I'll have a pint so.'

'No pints!' commanded Páidí . 'We have golf to play.'

Fergal had a pint.

Then a second pint. Páidí looked on with a disapproving glare.

At one o'clock the helicopter still had not come. Páidí paced up and down outside the pub, constantly checking his watch and listening for the telling whoop. By two o'clock he was back at the bar, still waiting.

'Give me a pint so,' he said.

They got stuck in. Two hours and four pints later the air reverberated with noise. Their chariot had arrived.

It landed in a field below the house where Padraig had his football posts erected. A wire mesh had been installed to keep the sheep out. It was now a barrier that would have to be negotiated by the two would-be golfers.

Maire looked on with amusement as her husband headed down the road. Marc watched from his family home. Páidí, bedecked in his dry-cleaned suit and with the golf bag over his shoulder, reached the wire.

It would require a delicate manoeuvre to conquer this Everest. He threw one leg over, not quite elegantly, then the other. As he did so the golf bag toppled.

Páidí grabbed it.

He didn't notice the putter falling out.

From his home Marc started waving. Páidí waved back.

Marc pointed.

'What?' mouthed Páidí .

Marc ran over. When he got close enough for Páidí to hear he shouted, 'You dropped the putter.'

Páidí looked back. 'What do you think I want that for?'

Up, up and away.

Marc retrieved the abandoned implement. No one is quite sure if any golf was played.

CHAPTER 18

The usual suspects had gathered in Paid Quinn's pub in the centre of Ventry village on the night of December 14, 2012. They were playing cards. Someone would go home with a Christmas hamper.

Páidí was late.

His brother Tom was there with Mícheál Ó Sé and Muiris Fenton. Solid men, good friends. 'Where is he?' someone asked.

'Last I heard was Sligo,' said Mícheál. 'But he'll be here.'

And he duly arrived. A little tired but with merriment in his eyes. He was home and that is where he was happiest. A pot of tea was ordered and the entertainment began.

It wasn't a late night.

Páidí was back in Ard an Bhothair to supervise the closing of his own hostelry. Later, at home, he chatted with Maire for a while, reporting on his travels up the west coast and those he had met during the previous few days.

He had visited Limerick, Galway, Mayo and Sligo. In previous months his travels had taken him all over Ireland and abroad, to Spain and the Netherlands. All the time he was meeting with GAA clubs and encouraging their participation in his Comortas Peile.

The February, 2013 edition of the football tournament in his name would be the 24th. What began as a two-team event in 1989 had risen to become a major weekend celebration of football and Irish culture that would involve 48 teams, men and women, from all over Ireland and from Europe.

Over 1,500 people would descend on the Dingle Peninsula on the last weekend of February. The Comortas had become a significant event for the business community in the area, especially those offering accommodation and food, who would have endured a very quiet period without the competition.

Páidí was already working on the 2014 event, which would be the 25th. He was determined that there would be 50 teams competing. He was reaching out to China, to Singapore and Australia. There were no limits, no boundaries.

Without the constraints that playing football and managing teams had made on his time for so much of his life he dedicated himself with typical passion to the Comortas. 'He was constantly on the road,' says Maire. 'Every second of the day he was on the move and he put up a lot of mileage. He had a driver but it was still very tiring.

'He was worried about it.

'He wondered was he taking too much on; was he being too ambitious bringing so many teams together. Páidí was a worrier. He worried about the pub and he worried about the Comortas.

'That's just the way he was.'

He told his friends that night that someone had contacted him about a team coming from Outer Mongolia.

'Them's the boys for Ard an Bhothair,' he laughed.

On the morning of December 15 Páidí carried out a few chores around the pub. He felt the effects of his travels of the previous days. He was tired and decided to head back to the house for a rest.

He slept.

—⚉—

It is late Summer and the sun's rays have the colours dancing through the water as the waves roll gently onto Ventry Beach.

Strollers leave trails in the sand. The sounds are of children laughing and shrieking, dogs yapping and gulls calling.

Of course, there is also a group of youngsters, boys and girls, kicking football.

The roads around Slea Head are busy. Bus drivers edge their way around the sharp bends as their cargo gaze with wonder at their surroundings.

Mount Eagle looms over the scene, resplendent and majestic, protecting the burial ground of Reilig Naomh Caitliona where the citizens of this corner of West Kerry are laid to rest.

It is a stunning vista that has inspired poets, artists, musicians and seanchaí. Páidí lies there now.

They laid him there in great splendour.

Dwyer.

Bomber.

Ogie and Mikey.

Seanie.

Charlie, the Spillanes, Powery, the 'Private'.

Ambrose.

Johnno and Ger.

Jimmy Deenihan.

Paudie Lynch, Ger Lynch, Timmy Dowd.

Everyone came.

The Dubs came en masse and they shed tears, of sorrow and joy.

Billy Morgan and Dinny Allen led his friends from Cork.

Matt Connor and Seamus Darby came from Offaly.

The Westmeath lads came in large numbers to pay homage to the man who had changed their lives immeasurably.

Everyone.

They came from everywhere.

Famous and not famous. Tomas O Flatharta was travelling in South America when he heard the news. He flew home.

Former Taoisigh, Brian Cowen and Bertie Ahern, lifelong friends, attended. Labour's Pat Rabbitte mourned the loss of his great friend. The Haughey family paid their respects. Páidí had not deserted their man in his hour of need.

And there were musicians and singers, dancers and songwriters, journalists and businessmen, lords and ladies and those who never knew the man but were admirers.

Páidí was 57.

Too young to die.

The news spread rapidly throughout the land and then the world. President Higgins paid tribute and sent words of solace to the family. 'Páidí Ó Sé had a reputation that went far beyond his great achievements in sport and far beyond the boundaries of his own beloved country.

'It was a great contribution and I send my sympathies to him and his family and all those related to him.'

Liam O Neill, the President of the GAA spoke for all the association's members. 'There was hardly a person on the island of Ireland, never mind in the GAA, who did not recognise or know of Páidí Ó Sé, such was his contribution to the association and to Irish life over a prolonged period.

'His excellence on the field of play in what was the greatest football team of all time still stands out to those of us who saw it and his passion for the game in no way ended with the completion of his playing days.

'His elevation to management, firstly at Under-21 level but then at senior, saw his reputation further embellished and he is one of the few people to have succeeded in claiming All-Ireland honours both as a manager and a player after a distinguished career that stretched far beyond his native Kerry.

'Páidí's affection for the Irish language and Irish culture in general were other hall marks of a man who was steeped in the area he called home.'

As his friend Mícheál Ó Sé told the thousands who attended Páidí's funeral, 'He will always be our greatest hero of all time. I'm sure the passion, the fire, the animation, the free spirit that once drove this Colossus to become the stuff that dreams are made of, will in due course shine forth in his own family.'

Sometime during the summer of 2013 a visitor from the northern part of the island paid his or her respects, and laid a jersey across Páidí's grave.

Maire, Neasa, Siún and Padraig Og make sure on every visit that it is secure.

It is a Tyrone jersey.

Páidí would love that.

—⟋⟍—

Sean Walsh, chairman of the Kerry County Board for six seasons while Páidí was the senior team manager, and a firm family friend, was invited to deliver the graveside address.

'The Ó Sé family have bestowed a great honour on me by requesting that I speak at Páidí's funeral.

'I am fully aware, as indeed we all are, that we are mourning the loss of an extraordinary individual and that words are not adequate to convey our deep sense of loss; but we feel it in our hearts, in our bones and in our minds.

'From our midst has been taken an icon, a legend in his own lifetime, a man of many talents and many parts, a man we will remember for these talents. But the greatest sense of loss and grief will be felt by his family and our thoughts and prayers are with them, not only at this time, but into the future.

'Páidí Ó Sé, Peileadóir Chiarraí, Captaen Foireann Chiarraí, Bainisteoir Foireann Chiarraí, garda, Fear an Tí anseo i dTigh Pháidí in Árd A'Bhóthair, fear clainne, fear a raibh scéalta iontacha greannúr le h-insint aige. Tá sé deachair dúinn a thuiscint go bhfuil sé imithe uainn.

Is i ngeansaí Chiarraí is mó a bheidh cuimhne againn go deo ar Pháidí Ó Sé. Peileadóir den chéad scoth a bhain cliú agus cáil amach dó féin is cuma pé áit sa pháirc ina raibh sé ag imirt. Ocht mbonn uile Éireann sinsear buaite aige comh maith leis na gradaim go léir eile a bhuaidh sé san Sraith Náisiúnta, Corn An Bhóthair Iarainn agus i gCraobh Na Mumhan, agus anseo i gCiarraí i gCroabh an Chontae.

'Bhí sé mar cheannaire den chéad scoth againn i bpáirc na h-imeartha agus go h-áirithe in 1985 mar chaptaen na fóirne. Chruthaigh sé ceannaireacht fíor iontach ní h-amháin ar an bpáirc imeartha mar imreoir ach chomh maith mar bhainisteoir na fóirne laistigh agus lasmuigh den pháirc.

'Ní dhéanfaidh éinne dearmad go deo ar an óráid a thug sé as Gaeilge tar éis dó an Chorn Sam a ghlachadh i ndiaidh an Chluiche Cheannais i bPáirc An Chróchaigh in 1985. Ba chruthú é sin ar an gcaighdéan ard a bhí aige féin. Bhí sé fíor lámhach lena chuid ama agus é ag bualadh le daoine a tháinig anseo chun chainte leis. Táimid uilig bródúil as an méid a rinne sé ar son Cumann Lúthchleas Gael agus do Chíarraí i gcoitine.

'Páidí was truly in every sense of the word a Kerry great on the field, and off the field he was always so entertaining to listen to.

'He will be sadly missed by all.

'Today we lay to rest the unconquerable Páidí Ó Sé, a friend to millions, a loving husband to Máire, a loving father to his children Neasa, Siún and Padraig Óg, and the proudest uncle in the world to Feargal, Darragh, Tomás and Marc and ever present friend and brother to Tom.

'His memory will be lovingly and proudly remembered by all who knew him.

'Today the GAA mourns the passing of one its greatest ambassadors. Few have earned the affection of so many sports people not alone for their sporting achievements and for their infectious, warm and charismatic personalities off the field as Páidí Ó Sé.

'Páidí had many friends not alone from the sporting world but from every walk of life. He was as comfortable and happy sitting with the locals in Foxy John's as he was in Government buildings with the Taoiseach of the day.

'It was highly appropriate that leading the many tributes paid to Páidí since his untimely death last Saturday was one from Uachtarán Na hÉireann, Michael D. Higgins. Appropriate because Páidí throughout his life embodied everything of what it meant to be Irish. A fíor Gael, he was passionate about everything Irish.

'Coming from An Ghaeltacht his love of our native language was nurtured from the cradle and it was in his own native language that he articulated his great joy of being a an All-Ireland winning captain in his speech on the steps of the Hogan Stand in 1985. When speaking in his native tongue it was always spoken with such colour and beauty that it would bring on tears of joy and often laughter.

'He loved our Gaelic culture, music, song, dance and literature and his passion for politics was widely known.

'But it was in our games that his passion truly blossomed from a very young age. And when his playing days and his times in management were over he never lost that passion and kept it alive in his weekly column in the *Sunday Independent*.

'He contributed to many TV and radio programmes and documentaries about Gaelic games and at the time of his death was busy organising his annual football tournament which in 2013 would be his own personal contribution to The Gathering where he planned to invite teams from overseas. As a director of Fáilte Ireland he was passionate about the importance of promoting tourism particularly to his beloved Chorcha Dhuibhne and Kerry.

'Everybody here today will recall their own personal memories and if all those memories were collected and put together it would indeed be filled with many stories of his illustrious years as a player and team manager, it would be funny because Páidí had the charm and roguery to be a great storyteller who would have an audience in the palm of his hand as he told some wonderful stories of his own exploits and those of others.

'Stories, that he embellished so well with his unique gift to entertain that his listeners would always have a good laugh, often at his own expense.

'As a player and manager his achievements are huge ...

As a footballer...

Schools titles

4 O'Sullivan Cup (Kerry Colleges): 1971, 1972, 1973, 1974.

2 Munster Colleges A with St. Brendan's Killarney: 1972, 1973.

1 Munster Colleges B with St. Micheal's Listowel: 1974.

3 Munster Under-21 Championship: 1973, 1975, 1976.

3 All Ireland Under-21 Championship: 1973, 1975, 1976.

8 All Ireland Senior Championship: 1975, 1978, 1979, 1980, 1981, 1984, 1985, 1986.

11 Munster Senior Championship: 1975, 1976,1977, 1978,1979, 1980,1981,1982, 1984, 1985, 1986.

4 National League: 1974, 1977, 1982, 1984.

4 Railway Cup: 1976, 1978, 1981, 1982.

5 All Stars: 1981, 1982, 1983, 1984, 1985.

2 County Senior Championship: 1984, 1985.

As a manager ...

2 All Ireland Senior Championship: 1997, 2000.

6 Munster Senior Championship: 1996, 1997, 1998, 2000, 2001, 2003.

1 All Ireland Under-21 Championship: 1995.

2 Munster Under-21 Championship: 1993, 1995.

1 National League: 1997.

1 Leinster Senior Championship: 2004.

3 County Senior Championship: 1984, 1985 (Player/Manager), 1990.

'Árd A Bhóthair was a very special place to Páidí.

'Here he grew from boy to man in a close knit and happy family environment that made a deep imprint on his future life. Here his early passion for football was nurtured and encouraged by his parents and older brothers.

'In this happy household Beatrice reigned as mother and queen, and woe betide any misguided interloper that interfered with one of her brood. This loving caring and wise matriarch was considered by the youthful Páidí as having opinions that were far superior to any verdict of the Supreme Court and he left nobody in any doubt about it.

'And it is true that while Páidí made many long journeys the length and breadth of this country his heart remained firmly planted in the soil of Árd a Bhóthair. Agus táim cinnte gurb'é anseo i measc a mhuintir féin in Árd a Bhóthair i nGaeltacht Chorcha Dhuibhne i gCiarraí Thiar go mbeidh an bhrón is mó, tuisc nach bhfuil an ard rí ann a thuilleadh.

'It would be fair to say that in the game of backs and forwards played high in the sky last night, that John Egan would have found a lot less room in the forwards now that Páidí has joined Tim Kennelly in the back line, and I have no doubt that the after party is still ongoing.

'It is true to say that here in Kerry football defines us as a people. We are proud of our 36 All-Ireland titles and the players and mentors who achieved that distinguished roll of honour. For generations, our players and teams have been immortalised in song, in story and in poetry.

'Good poetry has that special ingredient that will evoke the deepest emotion of the human heart, indeed, is the spirit that remains unmoved in the presence of such genius – because genius is what it is. Liam MacGabhann, a native of Valentia, was one who had it in rich abundance. His *Blind man at Croke Park* captures brilliantly the spiritual essence of Kerry's football pride exuded by Páidí Ó Sé.

> *Listen, asthore, for those old eyes are sealed*
> *Tell me once more when the Kerrymen take the field*
> *Tell an old man who is feeble, grey and old*
> *Do they walk proudly still wearing the Green and Gold?*

'When Sigerson Clifford wrote, *I Am Of Kerry* you would think that he wrote the last verse with Páidí in mind:

> *Twas thus I lived, skin to skin with the earth*
> *Elbowed by the hills, drenched by the billows,*
> *Watching the black geese making black wedges,*
> *By Skelligs far west and Annascaul of the willows.*
> *Their voices came on every little wind,*
> *Whispering across the half door of the mind,*
> *For always I am Kerry.*

'Árd A Bhóthair was his birthplace, the place where he and Máire raised their family and ran their business. It was his homeland physically and spiritually, the place he never left and, today, as we bid our sad farewells that the man, who achieved stardom and rubbed shoulders with the great, was in essence the boy from Árd A Bhóthair, full of boyish mischief with a great sense of fun and enjoyment, and without a touch of malice in his generous spirit.

'May the Ventry sod rest lightly on this noble warrior and may the angels bear him gently to God's happy playing field.

'Go dtuga Dia suaimhneas síorraí dá anam Uasal.'

—❦—

The Kerryman newspaper paid its own tribute in a special supplement celebrating Páidí's life and reminiscing. It's editorial was devoted to a man described in the headline as *A beacon of Kerry pride*.

It read, *Our Páidí – son, brother, player, uncle, manager, publican, rogue, Kerry man, West Kerry man, Ventry man agus Laochra Gael.*

The true essence of Páidí Ó Sé was that he meant so much to so many in many, many different ways. He made his name on the GAA fields of Kerry and in Croke Park but his story transcended his heroic deeds with the pigskin.

He was the rogue with the smile who rubbed shoulders with many leaders of this country: Charles J Haughey, Bertie Ahern and Brian Cowen - All Fianna Fáil, all friends. Páidí liked their company and, no doubt, they loved his. The fact that he could defend them - when needed - as if defending a Kerry goal in an All-Ireland final would have copperfastened that friendship.

In short, he was a man that you would want in your corner.

He was the player who could play anywhere, and usually did. His claim to fame: conceding just one point from play in All-Ireland finals, sums him up.

"Amhuintir Ciarraí agus a chairde go léir."

Páidí Ó Sé's now iconic speech after the 1985 All-Ireland win over Dublin still fills Kerry hearts with pride. Here was the man from Ard A Bhóthair bursting with passion on the steps of the Hogan: his life's dream now a reality. The pride was etched on the face of our warrior in green and gold.

He was the manager who, in 1997, retrieved the glory that had eluded the county for 11 long years. He loved his players and they repaid him on the field of play. For many, some of the best Gaelic football played on this island was in 2002. The All-Ireland wasn't won by Kerry that year but the football will be long remembered. That was Páidí's team, Páidí's football.

Above all though he was a son of An Gaeltacht. His grá for his homeland propelled him on and off the field. With the fame he garnered on the field he set about the task of getting as many people as possible to visit his home place.

Of course, the fact he had opened Tigh Pháidí Uí Shé was a bonus for him. But he did all he could to promote Ceann Trá, Corca Dhuibhne and West Kerry. He did it to a fault but needn't apologise for it. He had fought for his home all his life, why should he change.

Our Páidí is in that great stadium above us now. He's taking a pass from Tim Kennelly and setting up John Egan for a goal worthy of the Gods.

Ar Dheis Dé go raibh a anam dílis.

—⚭—

Every day there is a new story.

The night a call was received at William Street Garda Station in Limerick. A concerned citizen had reported seeing a group of young men rolling a barrel of beer down the street, purloined from some nearby establishment.

'That's student country,' said the Garda at the desk. He sent two young recruits to check it out. Garda Páidí got as far as the door of the flat where the revelry had begun. He heard voices.

Dubs, a Galway midfielder, a couple of Kerrymen.

He ran before they saw him.

Many more stories cannot be committed to print.

Neasa, Siún and Padraig helped run the Comortas in February, 2013. It was a huge success. The 25th event will be held in 2014.

They will have 50 teams.

It is what he wanted.

They have set up Fundúireacht Páidí Ó Sé, a charitable foundation to provide services in Kerry and nationally. The first event was a charity cycle from Croke Park to Ventry. Funds raised will provide a cardiac CT scanner for Kerry General Hospital. There is also a commitment to the Mater Foundation and its research into heart disease.

During the summer of 2013 the visitors came, many of them regulars and many who wanted to pay homage. Maire, the girls and Padraig greeted them.

'It is amazing,' says Neasa, ' … the feeling people have for him. They have asked so many questions, have shown such interest.

'I think I only now realise what it was like for him over all those years. He loved dealing with the people, chatting to them and telling stories. He was so good at it.'

Mícheál Ó Sé sums it up as we leave Tigh Páidí Ó Sé after another evening of conviviality.

'You still expect him to appear, chewing a biro … and hopping some ball.

'He was a right rogue.'